D1060317

Law and Economy

LAW, STATE AND SOCIETY SERIES

---

1. Marx and Engels on Law *by* M. Cain and A. Hunt
2. Reading Ideologies: an investigation into the Marxist theory of ideology and law *by* C. Sumner
3. Pashukanis: selected writings on marxism and law *by* P. Beirne and R. Sharlet
4. Law and State in Papua New Guinea *by* P. Fitzpatrick
5. Law, Society and Political Action: towards a strategy under late capitalism *by* T. Mathiesen
6. Housing Action in an Industrial Suburb *by* A. Stewart
7. The Police: autonomy and consent *by* M. Brogden
8. Justice and Politics in People's China: legal order or continuing revolution? *by* J. Brady
9. Law and Economy: the legal regulation of corporate capital *by* K. Jones

Forthcoming Titles

The Limits of the Legal Process: a study of landlords, law and crime *by* D. Nelken

Law and Economy

The Legal Regulation of Corporate Capital

KELVIN JONES

La Trobe University, Victoria, Australia

1982

ACADEMIC PRESS

A Subsidiary of Harcourt Brace Jovanovich, Publishers

London · New York

Paris · San Diego · San Francisco · São Paulo

Sydney · Tokyo · Toronto

ACADEMIC PRESS INC. (LONDON) LTD.
24/28 Oval Road
London NW1

United States Edition published by
ACADEMIC PRESS INC.
111 Fifth Avenue
New York, New York 10003

British Library Cataloguing in Publication Data

Jones, Kelvin
Law and economy. — (Law, state and society series)
1. Conflict of Law — Antitrust law
I. Title II. Series
342.3′72 K7582.M6

ISBN 0-12-390040-9

LCCN 82-72322

Phototypeset by
Dobbie Typesetting Service, Plymouth, Devon

Printed in Great Britain by
St. Edmundsbury Press, Bury St. Edmunds, Suffolk

Preface

The use of law to regulate economic affairs depends upon a definite conception of how law and economy are interrelated. It implies a basic faith in the capacity of law to intervene in economic affairs to effect a specific objective and it assumes, also, that law and economy are sovereign domains. Without this belief legal regulation would be reduced to the status of a King Canute, making fine gestures but bearing little relevance to the conduct of economic activity. Some would argue that this is the inevitable fate of all forms of legal regulation of the economy. This sort of perspective may even be correct, although where held with any degree of seriousness it is invariably for the wrong reason.

The fact of the relationship of law to the economy is quite basic to the pursuit of economic objectives by legal means, although it is seldom acknowledged with any degree of precision or attention to consequence. Of course the law and economy relationship has had much coverage—principally within Marxism and right-wing conservatism—but it is rarely in terms which link the discussion to a specific example of legal regulation or which address the basic presupposition of the law/economy relationship. In this context the book aims to discuss both the relationship between law and economy and to offer an analysis of anti-trust legislation as an example of a prototypical form of legal regulation. The focus is upon the general and the particular and aims to display the manner in which they are in fact interdependent.

The objection may be made that there are perhaps rather too many texts on anti-trust legislation. The topic has generated an enduring fascination for academics ever since senator Sherman successfully articulated proposals for the 1890 Sherman Act. So the question becomes why add yet another to the near infinite catalogue of texts which address the issue? If this book were merely an addition then it could be judged against the backcloth of a cumulative tradition and criticized for its superfluity. This book, however, makes no claim to belong to any such tradition. In one sense it could even be said that it is not about anti-trust legislation *per se*. Its purpose is to unveil the prinicples of legal regulation together with the mechanisms which are conventionally used toward that end. Anti-trust legislation facilitates this process by providing what is possibly a unique legislative attempt to control monopoly. Therefore, it is of interest only insofar as it provides an example of the more general issue of the feasibility of legal regulation. But the question remains, how does this differ from other accounts?

Anti-trust legislation is normally regarded from two, essentially conflicting, standpoints. First of all, it is examined as a purely technical response to the problem of monopoly. Anti-trust legislation is subjected to a rigorous process of legal scholarship whereby the origins of certain regulatory concepts are traced to common law antecedents (Thorelli, 1954). Also, the precise germination of special interpretations is located within judicial rulings sanctioned by historically determinate supreme court ratifications. This exercise, whilst valid, is basically an exercise internal to legal history. A number of studies widen their scope to include an analysis of corporate structure or economic performance but the level of analysis remains purely technical. For example, there is a current preoccupation with the so-called economic impact of price regulation on performance, output and so on. But the basic issue of whether or not law in general, and the specific articles of anti-trust legislation in particular, can regulate monopoly is seldom asked. Even where the issue is addressed it is from a perspective which seems to argue for greater legal control or enforcement in apparent disregard of what will be argued is the quite limited potential of law in this respect. There are, however, a few exceptions to this general trend which require special attention. These will be dealt with separately.

On the other hand anti-trust legislation is often regarded in terms of its fundamental irrelevance to the basic issues of industrial concentration and corporate ownership. For example, Pearce (1976), Kolko (1963) and Weinstein (1968), each advance substantially similar explanations of anti-trust legislation and its fundamental irrelevance. They are joined in this by a number of pessimists of a liberal or conservative persuasion who believe that the means for effective control of monopoly are incompatible with the freedom they associate with private enterprise. Accordingly, anti-trust legislation is inherently and necessarily inadequate. For whatever reason, then, anti-trust legislation is irrelevant to the problem of monopoly or, worse still, actually enables the process of concentration (Arnold, 1937) or else constitutes an ideological screen or an imaginary social order (Pearce, 1976) behind which concentration and centralization goes on apace.

What these, admittedly diverse, proponents of the weakness of anti-trust legislation fail to consider is the reason for such evident failure or, where reasons are adduced, they concern the co-optation of the regulatory machinery by the very monopolies which are supposedly regulated. In other variations the role of co-opter is undertaken by the ruling class allies or representatives of big business.

Irrespective of which agency predominates it will be argued here that such explanations are necessarily inadequate as forms of social explanation and that they lack the specificity required for an accurate account of the actual failure of anti-trust legislation. It will be argued that anti-trust legislation is unable to affect the process of monopolization even in a fantasy of regulatory potency, and even if it is administered impartially and with critical vigour. It is this factor which requires proper explanation.

The object of the book is to examine the possibility of the legal regulation of monopoly in general, paying particular attention to the example of anti-trust legislation in the United States. It is not intended as a general survey of all the ways and all the geographical contexts in which law is involved in economic affairs. It attempts, instead, to address the way in which the issues of concentration, centralization and monopoly signalled a major transformation in the form of ownership, the ramifications of which were riven deep in American culture. It seeks to deal with the involvement of law in the process of organizational change or adjustment by locating both the general and the specific reasons for the impotence of law in this respect.

Compared with the more conventional accounts or dismissals of anti-trust legislation, this analysis starts off from a rather different perspective. After examining some of the ways in which corporate behaviour is criminalized the argument commences upon what is, after all, the essential element of anti-trust legislation, namely, the very issue of the legal regulation of economic affairs.[1] The mere existence of anti-trust legislation implies that law and economy are interrelated in a manner which enables the relationship of regulation to be valid. By way of an analysis of some of the major proponents of the law/economy relationship it is argued that the regulatory relation invariably rests upon a definite conception of the legal and the economic as separate instances of sociality. Not only is this portrait of social relations basically inadequate but, more especially, it will be argued that this inadequacy contains within it the very seeds of the failure of anti-trust legislation and possibly legal regulation in general. Accordingly, the principle of legal regulation is criticized on the basis of its prior assumption of a particular division of social relations into legal and economic realms and the consequences that this division heralds for the prospect of a truly viable form of regulation.

If the idea of a relationship between law and economy is inappropriate to the question of legal and economic relations then it becomes apparent that an alternative means of regarding the issue is required. This alternative is formulated on the basis of a sociological typology of ownership. For this sort of perspective there is no reason why the law of property must be viewed as something which engages (or is engaged in) a separate form of social action. On the contrary, a general typology of ownership formulated within the auspices of sociological theory should be capable of addressing so-called legal and economic relations from a standpoint which does not split sociality into legal and economic instances or orders. For example, the elaboration of a general typology of ownership precludes the rather artificial distinction between ownership and control characteristic of most discussions of the corporation and the law. Instead ownership is seen in quite general terms as something which comprises three distinct relationships—title, control and possession. These are defined in some detail for each type of ownership. Thus a given form of ownership is constituted, first of all, by a definite arrangement of these relations and, secondly, by the character of the relations *per se*.

As a statement concerning the proper conduct of sociological enquiry the idea that law and economy cannot be represented consistently as separate instances may be wholly unexceptional. But when anti-trust legislation is seen to be bound up with the development of a type of corporate ownership which was, in its initial stages, anathema to the pioneers of American industry, agriculture and labour then its importance becomes all the more pointed. For anti-trust legislation was seen to be an attempt to use the law to redress the balance which had been dangerously upset by the incursion of the large corporation. The use of the law as a separate agency of review and regulation was to have ramifications upon the effectivity of regulating corporations in this way. Perhaps more importantly monopoly is established by foreclosing alternative forms of independent ownership. This may be achieved directly through the monopolization of trade or covertly through conspiracy in restraint of trade. Either way, the law is used to get to grips with a particular type of corporate ownership insofar as it precludes other forms of ownership and, moreover, it is used in ways which are quite specific. Therefore, the typology is necessary for an appropriate demonstration of the differences involved between *laissez-faire* and corporate ownership. It establishes the parameters of the analysis by defining the central contenders as forms of ownership.

Of course, monopoly and the corporate form of ownership are far from being identical, but there is very persuasive evidence that it was the way in which ownership was transformed from a bourgeois to a corporate type which was at the back of the issue of monopolization and the trusts. Accordingly, it was the impersonal control of the market by distant corporations which elicited the wrath of the various real politico-social groupings which constituted the backbone of the anti-trust movement. The manner in which ownership was held in the form of the trust was correctly identified with the growth of monopoly. Whilst it is quite conceivable that a system of *laissez-faire* capitalism could comprise a number of corporations, the very nature of corporate relations of ownership is such that they generate monopolistic forms and practices by precluding large areas of endeavour from alternative forms of ownership. Accordingly, the essence of the trust question, and monopoly in general, is inevitably bound up with a discussion of the corporate form of ownership. It is no accident that the form of legislation is styled in the negative as *anti*-trust legislation for this does indeed suggest the very real measure of opposition which characterized the issue in its formative stages.

We have seen how the existence of anti-trust legislation relies upon a particular conception of how law and economy must interrelate in order for legal regulation to be viable and this conception generates a vital weakness in any such regulatory device. Taken together with the way in which law conceives of the corporate form of ownership this reduces still further the possibility of effective regulation. For example, it is argued that within the legal system in question anti-trust legislation depends upon an implicit conception of ownership which highlights the centrality of private property. The fact that the legal concept of private property is riven through with an implicit 'philosophical anthropology', which ultimately relies upon individual or collective subjects as owners, means that the concept of the corporate form of ownership is inadequately drawn. This is not to say that the category of the subject is basic to all law, merely that it occupies a central place in the legal analysis of corporate forms of ownership. There is no reason why the subject must be the atom of juridic theory (as in Pashukanis, 1978) since we are concerned only with the conception of ownership and private property unfolded within a particular sort of legal system. It will be argued that the corporate form of ownership depends upon the radical denial of any form of essential subject, collective subjects or even aggregates of human attributes. Thus for law to address the corporation as if it can be comprehended via a theory of (human) subjectivity is to constrict the potential of the regulatory relationship in a way which renders anti-trust legislation relatively impotent.

The particular centrality of the subject and private property to the legal system in question is far from being a general pervasion of all law irrespective of the content of any given Act. On the contrary, it is the basic structure and content of anti-trust legislation which is responsible for the characterization of the corporation in terms of subjective attributes. For example, the concepts of conspiracy in restraint of trade, monopolization and intent are basic to anti-trust legislation and they each imply certain attributes of (human) subjectivity. Therefore, the manner in which anti-trust legislation addresses the corporation, as well as the fact that regulation is seen as an essentially legal process, place certain constraints on the viability of anti-trust legislation. Of course this does not mean that law has no effect whatsoever or that a system of law which is capable of regulating economic affairs cannot be constructed. Still less does it assume that law has a necessary, unalterable and inadequate structure. All that is argued is that this particular system of law, and especially anti-trust legislation and the law of property, is constrained in a way which prevents it from restructuring the relations of corporate ownership.

The argument against using law to regulate monopoly is twofold. In the first place, the conceptual structure of law in general, and the articles of anti-trust legislation in particular, impose severe constraints upon the entirely laudable objective of controlling monopoly. Law is ill-equipped to tackle the complexity of corporate interrelationships. Secondly, irrespective of the concepts available to it, the use of law *per se* further restricts the possibility of controlling monopoly. Even if law were supplied with concepts which respected the complexity of corporate interrelationships then the very fact that law is seen as a separate agency of review would limit the potentiality of legal regulation. Whereas the former is argued in the strong sense of the word the latter is perhaps more agnostic concerning the possibility of effective regulation.

Finally, it will be argued that because it is due to specific constraints the failure of anti-trust legislation does not depend upon the existence of a conspiracy between big business and government. On the contrary, the anti-monopoly movement was an authentic political movement subject to definite organizational contingencies which do not collapse into the overall movement of history or the class struggle. Therefore, the anti-monopoly movement will be analysed according to its radical independence which, at least for a time, challenged the very basis of the corporate form of ownership.

At this point it is perhaps as well to issue a number of disclaimers. First of all, it should be reiterated that anyone who expects to find here a detailed examination of anti-trust legislation in action should look elsewhere. This is relatively easy since there are any number of texts which attempt exactly that.[2] The intention here is to concentrate on the way in which the concepts and the various controversies of anti-trust legislation depend upon a distinct vision of what the corporation is like. This vision reproduces the corporation in a fashion which is wholly inadequate to the further regulation of corporate conduct. And this goes a long way toward accounting for the relative failure of anti-trust legislation irrespective of how and whether such legislation is enforced or interpreted. Secondly, there will be further disappointment if the book is viewed as a historical study of the Granger, Populist or Progressive movements. The purpose of the final chapter is to demonstrate that the anti-monopoly movement cannot be written off as an irrelevant adjunct to a real conspiracy between big business and the state and that the movement had an authentic organizational structure of its own. In this sense the argument is no more than a suggestion that there are alternative ways of looking at the issue. In short the chapter is not concerned to describe the 'emergence' of anti-trust legislation in any great detail nor should the thesis be viewed as an historical account of agrarian society or the roots of 'American individualism'. There are volumes which claim this as an objective but this is not one of them.

Finally, the demonstration of a typology of ownership is intended merely to facilitate the description of, and the contrast between, two definite types of ownership. It is not intended as a general survey of several modes of production or types of society. Accordingly, feudal and soviet relations of ownership are included only inasmuch as they demonstrate the potential versatility of the typology in question.

July, 1982

Kelvin Jones
Australia

Notes

1. The concept of 'criminalization' is relevant because the Sherman Act is a criminal statute with criminal sanctions over and above the realm of civil remedy normally associated with 'regulation'. Chapter One attempts to assess the various ways in which Criminology has handled 'corporate' crime etc.
2. For example, Thorelli, 1954; Neale, 1966; Miller, 1962; Kronstein, Miller, Schwartz, 1958.

For M.J.

Acknowledgements

A book is a social product and so it is tempting to spread the responsibility for its limitations. I shall resist the temptation, however, and would like to express my thanks to the following persons. Their responsibility is limited to whatever there is of merit in the book and does not extend to its shortcomings: Ian Taylor, Paul Hirst and Neil McCormick, together with friends and colleagues in Sheffield and Edinburgh, Zenon Bankowski for editing and Mrs. E. Wood for typing the manuscript.

I would especially like to thank Peter Young for his invaluable support throughout and, finally, Mandy Jones.

People of the same trade seldom meet together, even for merriment and diversion, but the conversation ends in a conspiracy against the public, or in some contrivance to raise prices. It is impossible, indeed, to prevent such meetings, by any law which either could be executed, or would be consistent with liberty and justice. But though the law cannot hinder people of the same trade from sometimes assembling together, it ought to do nothing to facilitate such assemblies, much less to render them necessary.

Adam Smith, *The Wealth of Nations* (1884) Vol. I, p.54.

Contents

1 *Organizational Crime and Criminology*

Any discussion of the limits encountered in attempting to regulate large corporations would have to extend beyond the mere technical appraisal or cavalier dismissal of anti-trust legislation described in the introduction. It would have to extend beyond those specific confines to address the problem of the relative immunity afforded to certain social groups or organizations in lieu of formal legal sanction. There is indeed a substantial body of literature which addresses just such a problem. For the most part, it derives from sociological and criminological attempts to deploy the concepts of power, prestige, class and the state as explanations of the a-criminalization of white collar crime, corporate crime and so on. These explanations tend to suggest predominantly external reasons for the effective de-criminalization of certain types of socioeconomic and extra-legal activity. For example, it is often argued that the power of big business and its control or influence on the state prevents the proper and effective implementation of the law in certain areas which directly affect the interests of the ruling class. Over and against this type of explanation it will be argued that whatever defects there are in the legal regulation of corporate relations they are not due primarily to the discriminate implementation of law but inhere in the nature of law *per se* or, more accurately, in the manner in which law construes certain types of socioeconomic relations.

Certain sorts of criminological accounts have fallen prey to the appeal of these concepts in an apparently unending quest for explanatory force. Increasingly they have referenced and come to rely upon the concepts of power, state, capital, class and, lately, totality as the intellectual crutch with which to sustain what, arguably, remains an inherently weak form of social analysis. It is necessary, then to ask whether these concepts are entirely adequate, whether they are used in an appropriate manner and what effect, if any, their incorporation has on the overall structure of criminology as a discipline. These issues are fundamental both to the proper location of the corporate violation of anti-monopoly law within sociological analysis and to the construction of what can be described as a fully social theory of crime and law (Taylor *et al.*, 1973).

The area of criminology conventionally described by an abiding interest in white collar crime signalled a major contribution by the exemplary manner in which the concept of social structure achieved an unequivocal place on the criminological agenda. Newman makes the following observations: "The most important theoretical implication of white-collar crime is that it presents a problem almost exclusively sociological . . . To comprehend it adequately a fundamental knowledge of class structure, values, roles and statuses, and the many other essentially social process and concepts, is needed" (Newman, 1958, p. 60). He goes on to say that ". . . the concept of white collar crime has forced the theoretician into an analysis of highly complex and very abstract relationships within our social system" (Newman, 1958, p. 63). Finally, and perhaps most pertinent of all, he argues that "whether he likes it or not the criminologist finds himself involved in an analysis of prestige, power, and differential privilege" (Newman, 1958, p. 56). This call for a wider criminological horizon echoes quite generally amongst those concerned with crimes of the powerful. After all, Sutherland (1949) was at great pains to emphasize the general nature of his theory of crime and law and again the superabundance of structural terms attests quite convincingly to the general persuasion as to their relevance.

Attention to white collar crime was supposed to break with the conventional criminological agenda by ushering in theories of crime and law which were truly general in scope. In addition criminology was clearly seen to feed off and to replenish more general sociological debates. Notwithstanding this clear articulation of general sociological relevance, there is an equally transparent failure to measure up to the more stringent requirements set by the overall tenor of the enterprise. A brief examination of the sorts of explanation commonly adduced for the a-criminalization of organizational crime reveals a host of inherent ambiguities which go a long way towards accounting for the relative failure of what remains a laudable attempt.

The most common explanation for the relative immunity of white collar criminals is to be found in the class bias of the court and the prevailing influence of the powerful in moulding the criminal law according to their own interests. For example, Kolko asserts that the involvement of big business in the drafting of railroad legislation was a major factor leading to the attenuation of law in this respect (Kolko, 1963). Likewise Sutherland argues that: "White collar criminals are relatively immune because of the class bias of the courts and the power of their class to influence the implementation and administration of the law" (Sutherland, 1940, p. 44). Such immunity is both an analogue of respect and prestige but also derives from the cultural homogeneity of legislators, judges and administrators and their congruence with businessmen. Conspiracy of this order, albeit latent, reaches its apotheosis in the assertion that certain presidential regimes, for example, McKinley, Harding, Hoover and Coolidge, were friendly to business and, therefore, their administrations correlated with a low incidence of criminal prosecution of business activity. As a corollary, the climate of trust busting is associated with an identifiable hostility toward big business on behalf of particular administrations. The example of Theodore Roosevelt is often used in this respect, although its use is particularly galling given its largely undeserved character (Hofstadter, 1955). One thing these interpretations share is an equal commitment to the idea that public policy is but an outward manifestation of the self-conscious attitude of a political regime or a homogenous elite. What is more, self-consciously formulated attitudes are seen as an index of real regulation and successful criminalization of corporate activity: an assumption which is arguable to say the least.

There are more sensitive and indeed opposite explanations to be found and Newman is a prime example of an important, but nevertheless incipient, tendency:

> The diffuse nature of the perpetrator (the corporate body), as well as the diffuse nature of the victim (the public), does not fit many white collar cases to the normal criminal format. Then, too, the virtual absence of intent, of *mens rea*, on the part of the violators makes criminal sanction seem inappropriate. (Newman, 1958, p. 54)

Even here the fact that Newman finds it necessary to preface such a revealing remark by the more conventional "The relatively infrequent use of criminal sanctions is undoubtedly a reflection of many factors including the high social status of many violators and the lack of consensus about the criminal nature of their behaviour" (Newman, 1958, p. 54)—would seem to suggest a sense of paralysis in the analysis of 'organizational crime'. A form of paralysis which structures explanations around a series of highly ambiguous and wholly inadequate concepts and which has, as its underlying cause, the entirely inappropriate relationship of sociology to criminology: sociology is seen as a resource made available to criminology in the interstices of explanatory seizure.

Other sorts of explanations may be characterized by the idea that government was impotent in the face of a business plutocracy which would simply take over at the slightest hint of government moves against its interests (Sumner, 1963), or the somewhat simple assertion that 'corporations are powerful social forces', as if that explained anything at all! (Geis and Meier, 1977). Further, the essentially Weberian argument that formal and complex rational law often favours corporate bureaucracies is given new form in the assumption that specialist corporate lawyers invariably run rings around government prosecutors (Braithwaite, 1979), and the idea that foreclosing loopholes is self-defeating given the fact that complexity favours corporate organizations (Pepinsky, 1976). Yet again the idea that the a-criminalization of organizational crime is to be found in the location of the relevant statutes in civil rather than criminal codes (Geis and Meier, 1977), is perhaps slightly disingenuous given the number of activities which are in principle able to be made criminal, by for example, the Sherman Act provisions. Furthermore, Taft's (1956) argument that the social system compels the business institution to be exploitative and at times even criminal, and Quinney's (1963) assertion that deviant behaviour is a reflection of social structure appear to say a lot without explaining anything at all, evincing a conception of social structure which at once explains everything and nothing: criminal totalities merely replace identifiably human authors of criminal action.

Others have attempted to salvage the essential ambiguity of the concept of white collar crime rather than explain its causal antecedents. Of these undoubtedly the most important is Aubert who argues that the controversial nature of white collar crimes

> . . . is exactly what makes them so interesting from a sociological point of view and what gives us a clue to important norm conflicts, clashing group interests, and maybe incipient social change. One main benefit to be derived from the study of white collar crimes springs from the opportunity which the ambivalence in the citizen, in the businessman and among lawyers, judges and even criminologists offers as a barometer of structural conflicts and change potential in the larger social system of which they and the white collar crimes are parts". (Aubert, 1952)

More recently, Carson (1980) has attempted to recover the ambiguity of white collar crime by arguing that its ambiguity can become institutionalized in the space between the movement of the 'totality' and the historically specific organizational forms of, for example, the factory, which collide at various points with the seemingly inexorable logic of the totality.

One thing these various attempts seem to imply is that sociological theory is at its most incisive at the margins of legitimacy and illegitimacy and that further, the contradictions inherent in the concept of white collar crime offer a unique insight into social structure or the workings of the totality. A peculiar form of sociology indeed where relevance is confined to the margin and importance reigns supreme only when the mask slips: a kind of sociology of error or a sociology limited to the measure of ambiguity rather than regularity. Furthermore, the way in which the concept of a totality insinuates itself into the explanatory framework is perhaps one more example of the way in which the repertoires of criminology, whilst exhausted in the face of complexity, are replenished through a parasitic relationship to sociology, Marxism and political economy.

Still others have sought to question the elasticity of the concept 'crime' and, therefore, the very basis of the field of organizational crime. Thus the classic 'debate' between Sutherland and Tappan takes place against a backcloth of the essentially positivist concern for the differentiation of criminal and non-criminal action (Sutherland, 1949; Tappan, 1947). They both share a deep-seated concern for the criterion of criminality and hence for the basis for specifying a violation of the criminal law. Accordingly, they penetrate to the heart of the issue of the a-criminalization of the crimes of the powerful. Whilst Sutherland argues that white collar crimes are real crimes and that the prevalent use of administrative agency merely parallels the bureaucratic response to juvenile delinquency. Tappan argues that real crime should be restricted to the statutory definition of crime and the actual processing of criminals through the criminal justice system. Otherwise, as he puts it, "the rebel may enjoy a veritable orgy of delight in damming as criminal most anyone he pleases" (1947, p. 98). Tappan's position would indeed find limited support amongst those disaffected by the characterization of Standard Oil or General Motors as criminal organizations, and those not convinced by the efficacy of reversing the arsenal of criminal sanction. For example, Clark highlights the absurdity involved in such a reversal:

> Presidents, congressmen and corporation bosses on long-term prison sentences for tax frauds, illegal profiteering, and war-mongering, while petty thieves freely wander the streets attending occasional and voluntary, therapy classes. (1978, p. 53)

Pepinsky (1976) makes a similar point in arguing that the 'debate' between Sutherland and Tappan hinges upon the definition of relevant social injury rather than the existence of social injury *per se.* Therefore, Pepinsky attempts to extend Sutherland's classification of white collar crime as real crime; a definition which he argues is gripped by a particular form of socioeconomic bias and hence partial definition of social injury. Pepinsky's definition of white collar crime would include the concept of exploitation based on a definition of private property as a superior right. Exploitation is the infringement of a superior right, these rights are enshrined as property rights which in turn provide the basis for a definition of white collar crime. This approach echoes that of Macpherson (1975) who also attempts to extend the concept of private property to encompass a whole series of basic rights the violation of which is a crime. Ultimately, however, the definition of white collar crime as exploitation is gripped by an inherent circularity in that exploitation implies the priority of certain (proprietal) rights over other (proprietal) rights and hence the problem of relative social injury. If a selection of relevant social injury is to be avoided then an absolute concept of social injury and an absolute definition of (proprietal) rights is required. Apart from the advocates of transcendental and absolute justice such a concept would not find any particular favour.

These are the general sorts of explanations and issues which tend to characterize criminological attention to 'organizational crime'. I would like to concentrate in more detail on a specific attempt to break with the conventional criminological approach to this area, one which has as its dominant motif the idea of a Marxist analysis of organizational crime. It can be argued that in seeking to extend the frontiers of criminology in this way, through an articulation of Marxist concepts, the inherent contradictions of the field, evident in themselves, become all the more sharply revealed. The criticism is offered not as a negative assertion of the irrelevance of the field of organizational crime—whether for Marxism, criminology or sociology—but rather as a prologue to what is perceived as a more acceptable programme of research, oriented toward the specific problem of the corporate violation of anti-monopoly law.

Beyond 'Organizational' Crime and Criminology

The most recent, and arguably the most developed, exponent of organizational crime is Frank Pearce who, in *Crimes of the Powerful* (1976) and *Crime, Corporations and the American Social Order* (1973) presents a fully developed combination of criminology and political economy. For the most part Pearce is concerned with three major themes. First of all, that the American economy has not been based on free enterprise since the late nineteenth century. As such he is presenting an internal critique of legitimation ideologies based on the persistence of free enterprise, that is, based on an imaginary social order. Secondly, he deals with the criminality of big business in the sense of its direct involvement in criminal acts, for example, Standard Oil in its formative years. Thirdly, he examines the ability of big business to enact legislation in its favour; to skew enforcement procedures to its advantage; to refocus anti-trust law from monopoly practices onto unionization and, finally, to encourage the growth of racketeering within, or in opposition to, the labour unions. In this sense his work provides an opportunity to examine both the possibility and the consequences of the combination of criminology and political economy.

Two main questions must be borne in mind with regard to such an enterprise. First of all, is it possible to constitute criminology in order that it can address the powerful, and what consequences follow for criminology in general? Secondly, does Pearce reformulate criminology so that it can achieve this objective? These two general questions locate Pearce's work in relation to the criminology of the powerful. More specifically Pearce's work will be situated in relation to two criteria:

1. Its internal consistency or accuracy.
2. Its more general theoretical validity.

These twin criteria, it will be argued, provide the grounds for a continuous critique of *Crimes of the Powerful* through an examination of its handling of the specific areas of capital, the state, history and empirical evidence. They also serve to demonstrate the exact range of inconsistencies and problems generated by the arbitrary conjunction of two areas—political economy and crime. The critique is extended by the attempt to offer a concrete alternative account of anti-trust legislation together with a basis for the proper conceptualization of crime and law within political economy.

Crimes of the Powerful is committed to an instrumentalist conception of the state with all the consequences for theoretical and political practice entailed in that position. It will be argued that *Crimes of the Powerful* is internally inconsistent in its application of this position because it depends upon the concept of state autonomy and also relies upon highly selected empirical evidence. Moreover, the two series of problems—internal inconsistency (conceptual and empirical) and the theoretical failings of the instrumentalist/idealist couple itself—stem directly from the contradictory relationship established between political economy and criminology.

It is almost possible to detect the presence of big business on every page of *Crimes of the Powerful*, a shadowy presence that somehow functions as the ultimate, if not the proximate, explanation of events. For example, big business was supposedly in control of the major political parties, the federal legislature, the federal agencies, and so on. Implicit in this omnipotence is the idea that the state apparatus was in some way controlled by big business. The state is reified as something to be captured, as a powerful instrument to be used by big business. It follows that it is quite clearly established as a thing rather than as an autonomous subject. This commitment to an instrumentalist conception of the state in fact invokes the more general alternative of viewing the state either as a thing or as a subject—the instrumentalist/idealist couple. Pearce's choice of an instrumentalist conception, however, does not do justice to the complexity of the empirical evidence adduced in its favour, nor is it anything like a consistent resolution. As Poulantzas demonstrates, it is the instrumentalist/idealist couple itself, independent of any commitment to one side or the other, which entails a conception of the state as an entity possessing its own power. The hegemonic fraction of capital is then free either to absorb the state's power, through fusion with it, or be resisted by the state's power involving the independence of, or arbitration by, the state. Whether the state is seen as an active subject or as an instrument, it is endowed with the power to achieve its own, or someone else's, ends. It is this conception of state power which is itself contestible. That Pearce advocates the fusion thesis is central to the question of consistency and application, but it is not pertinent to the question of adequacy. In this last sense what is important is the overall location of *Crimes of the Powerful* within the idealist/instrumentalist couple itself, a couple which generates the conception of the state as guardian of its own power. It can be argued, following Poulantzas, that

> The state does not have its own 'power', but it forms the contradictory locus of condensation for the balance of forces that divides even the dominant class itself, and particularly its hegemonic fraction—monopoly capital. (1975, p. 158-9) [1]

The thesis of state power is far from settled for political economy and the fact that Pearce treats it as if it were, is of crucial importance to the conditions under which criminology and political economy can or cannot be conjoined. Further, *Crimes of the Powerful* is inconsistent in its formulation of a theoretical position, inconsistent in the application of that position to a series of data, and appears to be unaware of the problems generated by the formulation of the position in that way. These systematic silences and anomalies, it is argued, betray a somewhat contradictory relationship between political economy and criminology.

Attendant on the failure to adequately derive a concept of the state is the lack of any explicit division within capital itself. Capital is simply left as an unfractured whole and its conditions of existence conceived as a unity. For *Crimes of the Powerful* there is only big business, the rest is reduced to nothing. As will be seen there is an implicit demonstration of the empirical consequences of different fractions of capital, of a clash of political interests relating to diverse conditions of existence. But these remain outside the theoretical display since they are not part of Pearce's central concern, namely the demonstration of the total dominance of big business. There is a contradiction, therefore, between the concept of capital used and the range of empirical evidence which implies a rather different concept. Accordingly, the theoretical analysis appears to be at variance with the supporting empirical display, with the result that two series of inconsistencies intersect to generate still further problems.

In addition to the problem of the state and the unitary concept of capital, the ahistorical approach of *Crimes of the Powerful* creates serious difficulties. For example, there is little attempt made to confront the differential relationship between the conditions of existence of various capital fractions and the forms in which they are secured through time. The differential mobilization of state and federal levels in relation to the historical displacement of the conditions of existence of non-monopoly capital by those of monopoly capital is given short shrift. This particular silence requires that all class interests be subordinated to those of big business at all periods under consideration. The dynamic element in the development of the monopoly capital form is thereby ignored. Furthermore, because Pearce is committed to an instrumentalist view of the state and its relationship with big business, this presupposes a prior separation of big business from the state. Whilst this separation is necessary for Pearce, it is nowhere demonstrated in the analysis. The omission is two-tiered, for there is also no indication of any prior instrumental relationship between the state and, for example, entrepreneurial capital; big business is simply projected backwards in time as if it had always controlled the state. Therefore, the specific analysis of the historical derivation of the state is both inadequate and inconsistent in relation to the concept of state power which supposedly sustains the work.

The range and treatment of sources by *Crimes of the Powerful* suggests two criticisms. Firstly, the inadequacy of the concept of merger and, secondly, that the empirical evidence is at variance with the argument. For example, when he states that mergers were largely completed by the beginning of the twentieth century Pearce ignores two basic factors:

1. The fact that there were three merger booms; 1898-1902; 1925-9; 1955-69, corresponding to three definite moments within the formation of monopoly capital, namely: (a) the phase of relative transition from relations of production characterized predominantly by non-monopoly capital to relations of production characterized by the pre-eminence of monopoly capital. (b) The phase of consolidation of the conditions of existence of monopoly capital. (c) The phase representing the partial re-integration of economic ownership and possession signalling a new conjuncture of increased political conflict.[2] In short mergers were not "completed" by the beginning of the twentieth century and, more importantly, mergers occurred after they had supposedly finished. These mergers had a very precise theoretical significance; they were far from small scale and negligible as Pearce seems to suggest.
2. The crucial distinction between economic ownership—(the ability to assign the means of production and to allocate resources and profits to this or that use), and economic possession (the direction and relative control of a certain Labour process), is lost to Pearce. In effect the distinction indicates that possession is not a necessary pre-condition for control, for example subcontracting, oligopoly, minority shareholder control and price leadership all represent effective forms of economic control of the market. So that to argue the completion of mergers is to say very little. Not only is this very dissociation of economic ownership from economic possession a consequence of the relative transition from competitive to monopoly capitalism, it denotes a particular phase of monopoly capitals formation, but it also means that the process of concentration and centralization of capital are effected under forms that are often hidden by legal ownership.[3]

To place such store by the concept of merger in the light of the above considerations is to reveal a theoretical deficiency associated with a poorly specified empirical content, in that mergers were not completed anyway. Where he does raise the problem of other means of control he does so in terms of the subordination of all else to big business. The process fulfills a different function within Pearce's theoretical framework since it serves to establish the absolute domination of big business rather than its conditions of existence and mode of operation in the market. Although monopoly capital did, in effect, control large sections of industrial production and distribution through merger and economic possession, there were still significant sectors that were not controlled by monopoly capital.

Anti-trust Legislation

The problems which the state, capital, history and empirical material raise for a criminology of the powerful have been discussed separately. It is enlightening to consider to what extent they intersect in relation to the specific area of anti-trust legislation. In the process it is possible to trace the existence of continuities that are not accidental but rather reveal a more fundamental problem—namely the conflation of cause and effect.

In an analysis of anti-trust legislation it is expedient to draw a distinction between the anti-trust movement and the effectiveness of anti-trust enterprise. Pearce concentrates on the function and effect of anti-trust legislation and thereby ignores or minimizes the importance of the anti-trust movement. Two statements serve as an occasion for analysis: (1) that "The attitude of the large corporations to the anti-trust laws developed from hostility in the late nineteenth century to an active involvement in their administration by 1914" (1976, p. 85); and (2) that "The corporations became aware of their precarious position in relation to the federal government and at the same time were recognizing their vulnerability to prosecution by socialist state legislatures" (1976, p. 88). Consequently they agitated for a "transfer of these powers to the federal level where they would be able to effectively control the implementation of Federal regulation of their activity" (1976, p. 86). Several points of interest arise internally from these statements.

Firstly, the large corporations' hostility to anti-trust legislation implies a certain degree of effectiveness in such legislation, an element of threat to the corporations. There existed, therefore, a period in time when anti-trust legislation or enterprise was not enacted by, nor under the control of, big business and, as a result, was in a position to challenge its conditions of existence. Anti-trust legislation and, more especially, the anti-trust movement cannot, therefore, be reduced to its control by big business since its prior independence is at least implied if not argued by Pearce. Yet Pearce explicitly argues the opposite, namely anti-trust law is reducible to its functionality for big business.

Secondly, vulnerability to prosecution by state legislatures indicates the existence of significant interests opposed to the mergers and, in addition, suggests that since enforcement of anti-trust legislation could be controlled more effectively at federal than at state level, the federal/state split is an index of the division within the power bloc and an admission of the effectivity of political conflict.

Thirdly, the overall emphasis which Pearce places on the appropriation or control of anti-trust by big business explains away the possibility that anti-trust legislation may be the product of political class struggle. The importance of class struggle is simply ignored in favour of the overwhelming, all-pervasive dominance of big business. Origins are collapsed into ends.

From these critical comments and sources of inconsistency, however, it is possible to detect the existence of an anti-monopoly alliance comprising socialist, populist and entrepreneurial groups which later made up the anti-trust movement. As Hofstadter notes "often a common hostility to big business was the one link that bound together a variety of interest groups that diverged on other issues" (Hofstadter, 1955). This political alliance, once established, could be said to function, at least for a time, in opposition to the conditions of existence of monopoly capital, an opposition that was located in many significant respects in the split between federal and local state reaction. For example, the *laissez-faire* policy of federal government, its non-intervention, aided—or at least did not prove an obstacle to—monopoly capital, especially where interstate monopolies were concerned. This, coupled with the more interventionist stance of local state policy towards monopoly capital's conditions of existence—albeit an ineffective intervention since state boundaries did not constitute an obstacle to monopoly capital in its corporation form—firmly establishes the basis for a division along federal/state lines. Although Pearce makes nothing of this, preferring instead to rely on the domination of the federal government by big business as the explanation of any division.

This is just one example of how *Crimes of the Powerful* may allow an alternative interpretation at variance with the basic project. There are many other alternatives which derive as much from internal theoretical inconsistencies as from the particular choice of evidence. For example, in apparent contradiction of the earlier fusion thesis—which relates the state directly to big business—Pearce seizes upon the state's short term autonomy *vis-à-vis* a section of the ruling class in the interests of the whole ruling class. In one sense this is merely a change in terms since the alternative which allows the state to have its own power is retained. The state's relative autonomy of big business means that big business was simply restrained in order that the wider capitalist interest and the system of hegemony *vis-à-vis* the dominated classes was not challenged. By whom or by which class or combination of classes or fractions and indeed by what process? Pearce cannot answer these questions because his conception does not contain any extended analysis of the power bloc he has in mind.

There are then at least five components to Pearce's analysis of anti-trust:

1. Mergers were effectively complete before the advent of anti-trust legislation which was thereby rendered ineffective: anti-trust legislation was too little, too late.
2. Mergers made a dramatic impact upon the public which made it necessary to assuage radical socialist and populist demands. These demands

are not theorized at the political level but are merely referenced by Pearce.

3. Anti-trust legislation was a genuine endeavour but the entire apparatus of control was appropriated or emasculated by big business.
4. Mergers involved only one section of the ruling class, big business, and the whole ruling class made its presence felt in opposition to it in the general interest of long-term survival.
5. Big business was actively involved in the advocacy of anti-trust legislation with the result that anti-trust legislation becomes a front behind which the market is ordered and structured in the interests of big business.

These five components are positions made explicit at various points in *Crimes of the Powerful.* They represent the more or less *ad hoc* importation of an eclectic series of explanations or accounts borrowed in the main from what has been called 'revisionist' history (Kolko, 1963; Weibe, 1967; Weinstein, 1968; Appleman Williams, 1961). In themselves these accounts are not necessarily contradictory and thus Pearce is able to maintain their mutual articulation without too much trouble. What is important is that these various components, taken together with the positions which are either implicit or logically entailed in Pearce's work, reveal the fundamental absence of any critical comment on the concepts and theoretical systems introduced willy nilly into the area. The absence of a coherent framework introduces a whole range of inconsistencies and contradictions which serve only to cloud a criminology of the powerful. That such inconsistencies are registered at an overtly concrete level is evidenced by the apparent need to buttress *Crimes of the Powerful* with an eclectic reading of revisionist history. The inadequacy of the concepts results in a retreat into a form of history which, far from producing a solution, simply re-inforces the inconsistencies already there.

The historical sources for *Crimes of the Powerful* are supplied by revisionism in general and the work of Kolko in particular. Accordingly, anti-trust legislation is seen as part of a conscious strategy advocated by big business and engineered by a powerful elite with a view to the rational stabilization of an increasingly competitive market. As a result big business controlled itself through the agency of a unified elite rather than being controlled by anti-trust enterprise. This formulation offers a voluntaristic conception of big business which views it in terms of a series of interlocking elites. This results in a reified political strategy of conspiracy being arbitrarily coupled with an abstract economic need or necessity. Furthermore, the perception of an increasingly competitive market, which supposedly contains within itself the need to be rationally organized, is based upon a series of misconceptions; of the conditions of existence of monopoly capital, of its eventual compatibility with elements of competition and of the increasing anarchy of monopoly capital production (Lenin, 1971).

We now arrive at the more general theoretical implication of *Crimes of the*

Powerful in that anti-trust legislation is seen as a product of the whole ruling class in the interest of the long-term survival of the capitalist system as a whole. This position assumes an internal discipline within the power bloc together with the historical subservience of big business to the general capitalist interest. It is a characteristic of this position that it takes two general forms involving either the relative autonomy of state power in relation to its function of organizing factor of or for the ruling class or the pre-given internal consensus of the ruling class and its simple translation into state power through fusion with it. As a result anti-trust can be viewed as an anticipation of harsher measures, as a reaction to the reform movement or, finally, as the self-organizing principle of the capitalist system.

It is inherent in the method of *Crimes of the Powerful* that the inconsistencies generated within the concept of state power—the failure to produce a consistent resolution of the concept in terms of either instrumentalism, idealism or even relative autonomy—force Pearce to attempt to bury those inconsistencies in the apparent anarchy of empirical history. The decision to engage revisionist history (in the form of Kolko) leads inexorably to the demonstration of the relative autonomy of the capitalist class as a whole *vis-à-vis* big business in particular. This relative autonomy occurs within and on the basis of the more general fusion of the capitalist class and state power. This formulation is upheld notwithstanding the persistent reduction of state power to big business alone. Whilst being consistent in the adherence to state power as a concept, the internal variations within that concept develop severe contradictions which are only compounded by the retreat into historical empiricism.

The preceding analysis has shown that *Crimes of the Powerful* is incapable of handling the concepts of big business, power and the state. The fact that Pearce is aware of the problems is clear. For example he states that: ". . . the ultimate implication of this mode of analysis is the dissolution of criminology as a separate discipline" (1976, p. 80), and that ". . . in analysing 'crimes of corporations' we are ultimately led to ask fundamental questions about the nature of America and the worlds 'free enterprise system'" (1976, p. 105). That neither the conditions nor the consequences of the dissolution of criminology are specified and that *Crimes of the Powerful* fails to ask fundamental questions of the free enterprise system, let alone provide a framework for an answer, is perhaps a function of the relative incompatibility of criminology and political economy. Moreover, by implying the end of criminology the question of the proper formulation of the powerful is redundant, whilst the conditions under which crime and law can become central to Marxism are assumed to be covered by an eclectic combination of concepts. *Crimes of the Powerful* is left in a theoretical vacuum since it belongs neither to criminology nor to political economy. Once the question is posed in these terms, as a relation between criminology and Marxism, then the solution is quite clear. If a criminology of the powerful were at all adequate to its object then quite simply it would cease to be criminology.

The problems of *Crimes of the Powerful* are conceptual and logical. They can, in the end, be reduced to two, firstly, the imperfect and *ad hoc* translation of political economy's concepts into criminology and secondly, the failure to address the contest within political economy concerning the nature of the state, capital and interrelation, or even separate existence of the political and economic levels. This last carries the assumption that such debates either do not exist or can effectively be ignored for the purposes of a Marxist criminology. The position argued here is that not only can those debates not be ignored but that such ignorance obscures the conditions under which crime and law can become central to political economy—namely by theorizing law and crime in terms of their centrality or otherwise to the reproduction of the conditions of existence of determinate relations of production.

It will be readily apparent that the purpose of this introductory chapter is to reject those forms of analysis which deploy the concept of power or the powerful as an ultimate source of coherence between otherwise disparate phenomena, or else which view the concept as a supplementary explanation of residual anomalies (Cain and Hunt, 1979). More especially the concept of power is often conceived in behavioural terms as the hydraulic fluid responsible for the transmission of the desires of business to the organs of state reception and response. Power, therefore, attains an almost mystical or transcendental form at once ubiquitous and invisible and hence perhaps uniquely suited to a discipline which is apparently unable to theorize its object correctly. Power becomes a quality which you either have or have not, an enabling facility which, necessarily, implies a series of instrumentalities to which it may be applied, for example, law, state, and police. Over and against this, I have argued that law and state cannot be conceived of as instrumentalities and that, used in this way, the concept of power is both unnecessary and ultimately meaningless. Alternatively, an analysis of organizational crime can proceed through a discussion of social relations, forms of organization and so forth, without reference to the transcendental ramifications of the concept of power and the consequent heralding of asymmetrical power relations as an explanation of, for example, ambiguity.

Power implies an agency, its source is normally supplied by various forms of state, which either give form to inchoate power or which constitutes the nub of that power—constructing the powerful through the existence of a privileged relationship with state: the powerful are those who have access to state power. The state, therefore, is an important lynchpin which can condense competing claims, focus class conflict by presenting itself as the object of struggle, or else articulate the various instances of the totality according to some ultimate determinative principle (Cutler *et al.*, 1977/8). In conceiving of the state in these specific, albeit discrete, ways it is implicitly assumed that the state acts toward the general orchestration of society, as a means for imposing, constructing, or representing uniformity. The very concept of the state insofar as it applies to discrete operations necessarily implies a form of unity, even if it be a contradictory unity, otherwise the concept of state apparatus would have no meaning whatsoever. Thus social relations are assumed to be stamped throughout according to some determinative principle, the definitive condensation of class struggle or interests, or a material reflex of an ideal state. I will argue against this notion of uniformity, against the idea that law and state, necessarily, represent the interests of capital or the powerful and that relatively autonomous components of social structure ultimately cohere with such interests or conditions. The notion that the fabric of society is woven around a principal design, whether loosely sketched or rigidly marked, is a form of essentialism.

After paying due respect to the particular, it is often assumed that the ultimate explanation of a phenomenon is to be found in the eventual convergence of social relations around a principle of capital reproduction, the realization of an ideal force, the definitive resolution of competing interests, or the totality. In this respect the area of organizational crime is no exception, abounding as it is with absent causes. Although by itself the concept of the state explains nothing and can add nothing. For radical criminologists to act as if the simple introduction of the state as an additional weapon in the criminological armoury immediately rectifies the failings of more traditional white collar criminology is the measure of their overwhelming failure to address organizational crime in any but a token manner. To be sure the state may be defined in a variety of different ways. For example, the state is defined by Nicos Poulantzas as follows, "The state . . . forms the contradictory locus of condensation for the balance of forces that divides even the dominant class itself" (Poulantzas, 1975, p. 158-9). The commitment to a 'structuralist' architecture, notwithstanding, and given the problems involved in rendering a theory of political action within an essentially Althusserian concept of the totality, there is a sense in which Poulantzas is perhaps hinting at a more radical concept of state. A conception which dissolves the state as an entity and as the realization of an ideal force, so much is quite clear in his work, but, further, one which attempts to roll back the state to a point where it becomes nothing other than a site for the intersection of political (class) forces. Quite simply the state does not exist: it is merely a bourgeois distraction which encourages social democratic politics. This also provides a clue to the sustained dialogue between Poulantzas and Miliband and, in particular, the issue of whether the 'family' is part and parcel of a state apparatus.[4] It can be argued that the proper focus is on forms of organization, social relations and what Paul Hirst (1979) would describe as political practices and criteria of decision making. Far from halting analysis by describing an operation under the auspices of a state apparatus and thereby implying a source of ultimate conformity, the state, this procedure has the merit of analysing concrete forms of political process rather than suspending analytical endeavour by the invocation, even incantation, of state.

The utilization of the concept of power often implies that it is the source of a fundamental cleavage between the power-full and the impotent. This implicit concept of class assumes that the powerful form an elite unified by their conscious reflection that they are powerful and united in defence of that power and, consequently, in defence of the structure which sustains them in power. In the absence of an overt conspiracy the mere possession of power is apparently sufficient to generate a congruence of interests and their subsequent and simultaneous transmission to organs of state. Power, therefore, structures the scenario, possibly under the direction of an absent economic actor, through the mediation of powerful actors who implicitly or explicitly support these underlying structures of power and implement their requirements. Conscious conspiracy or structural congruence tend to exhaust the repertoires of power available to criminologists in their quest for an analysis of organizational crime, and it is precisely this exhaustion which is characteristic of their relative failure.

Finally, the absent economic actor who stalks the wings in anticipation is assumed to be a uniform, regular character, able in one way or another, to achieve the realization of 'his' requirements. It will be quite clear that to talk in terms of a unified font of all power—capitalism, monopoly capital, big business, an ideal spiritual force, or an international Jewish conspiracy—is to devalue the very real struggles and conflicts which shape law and state. Workers against the monolith becomes a slogan which effectively cripples all political action and all forms of concrete analysis.

I have argued that each of these concepts—state, power, capital, class and totality—is gripped by inherent contradictions which raise severe problems for sociological analysis. That criminology tends to use these concepts at random, especially since they are at best equivocal conceptual explanations, is the primary obstacle to a proper analysis of organizational crime. More specifically I have argued that the problems with *Crimes of the Powerful* are instances of the inherent limitation of a criminological approach to organizational crime in general and thus are not specific to a particular text, but refer centrally to a particular enterprise. These problems denote the limits of a Marxist criminology and in particular the problems attendant upon a conjunction of criminology and Marxism. As an alternative I would venture to suggest that the problems of the legal regulation of corporations are more complex in that they cannot be reduced to the capitulation of law enforcement agencies and the genuflection of state in the face of almighty corporate power. One thing 'white collar' criminology does not seem to consider in any great detail is the possibility that corporate activity cannot be regulated by classifying it as real crime and utilizing the machinery of law, that criminalization may not be a viable means of controlling corporate crime.[5] It is this possibility which the text seeks to take up and explore.

Notes

1. For Poulantzas it is the "complex contradictory unity in dominance" of the several dominant fractions that explains ". . . how the concept of hegemony can be applied to one class or fraction within the 'power' bloc. This hegemonic class or fraction is in fact the dominant element of the contradictory unity of politically 'dominant' classes or fractions, forming part of the 'power' bloc" (Poulantzas, 1973, p. 237). Whilst having no explicit concept or theory of the power bloc, and hence no conception of the hegemonic class of fraction, it is quite clear that the position occupied by the hegemonic class or fraction in relation to the state would, for Pearce, be occupied by "big business". See Poulantzas (1973).
2. Beman, L. (1973) "What We Learned from the Great Merger Frenzy", *Fortune*, April 1973, pp. 70-150.
   The three merger booms may be described as follows:
   (i) The first merger movement was, conventionally, caused by the business failures of the 1890s together with the proliferation of railways, telegraph and telephone leading to the establishment of the first truly national markets. The dominant types of monopoly organization were trusts, mergers and combinations which in many industries embraced all existing capacity, that is more than 90%. Pearce is quite correct in stating that the basic corporations were established prior to merger mania.
   (ii) The second movement was governed largely by the parallel responses of separate organizations. The 1929 peak extended the domain of big business to new industries and created numerous vertically integrated enterprises, that is the consolidation of monopoly capital. The conventional cause was the shift to autos and trucks with the consequent enlargement of markets and the destruction of local monopolies.
   (iii) The third movement was more of an extended trend starting in the 1950s and peaking in 1968. The process produced the giant conglomerate form signalling in part the re-integration of economic ownership and possession with the co-incident elevation of the problem of the multi-national companies to the political agenda. Of course effective control still extended beyond possession.
3. The centralization of capital is defined by growth through merger and combination, whilst the concentration of capital is defined by the growth of separate companies.
4. See Poulantzas, N. (1976). The capitalist state *New Left Review* **95**. Miliband, R. (1973). Poulantzas and the capitalist state *NLR* **82**. Also Poulantzas, N. (1969). *NLR* **58**, and Miliband, R. (1970). *NLR* **59**.
5. It is quite true that Cressey hints at such an outcome arguing that the criminal law cannot effectively be used to attack organizations, although his solution — the creation of an offence of 'organized crime' and his explanation; that corruption causes organized crime — tend to thwart any radical potential and belie the original promise (Cressey, 1972, p. 82).

2 *Law, Economy and Sociological Analysis*

Anti-trust legislation is an attempt to restructure economic relations by legal means and, as such, it is an excellent example of the law intervening in the conduct and organization of economic affairs. It might be expected, therefore, that the issue of how and in what manner legal and economic relations are interdependent would be central to any discussion of anti-trust legislation. Indeed, its very existence presupposes a definite form of the interrelationship of law and economy; a form which allows law to intervene in economic relations. Even though the law/economy relation is a necessary support of the possibility of legal regulation, it is seldom acknowledged in quite those terms. For the most part law seems to be considered as an instrument for effecting change within the economy —as in anti-trust legislation—or as a reflex of certain types of economic or capitalist relations, as in certain Marxist accounts. What these admittedly diverse perspectives share in common is the idea that law and economy exist as separate spheres of sociality capable of being interrelated in definite ways. It is this conception which may be challenged, not only because it involves intractable problems of priority and so on, but also because it imposes definite limits upon the efficacy of legal regulation. Simply by casting law as a separate agency of review and regulation it is put at a considerable disadvantage *vis-à-vis* the relations of corporate ownership which it ostensibly controls.

To be fair there is a considerable literature which argues the sceptical view, but where the relative disadvantage of law in respect of large corporations is recognized it is often assumed to derive from the fact that the law lags behind economic developments and, therefore, needs to be buttressed with increased refinement and further institutionalization. I have no wish to deride these entirely laudable objectives but they do seem to depend upon a conception of the law/economy relationship which is at best questionable. For example, the prior question of whether or not it is appropriate to view legal and economic relations in such a way that one is in advance of the other, which is thereby rendered obsolete, or whether it is proper to regard law as capable of keeping up with economic changes, is normally absent from any such discussion?

As an alternative to those conceptions which pose law and economy as separate realms capable of being interrelated in definite and general ways, it is argued here that so-called legal and economic relations are nothing more than social relations subject to quite specific and local connections. Not only is this a more appropriate way to regard the law/economy relation but also, it provides a more secure basis for the analysis of the concept of legal regulation and the possibility of effective control. Furthermore, it is sustained by a sociological tradition which would regard it as quite natural to view law as a social relation rather than in terms of its social effects. Hence the work of Parsons and Weber, whilst ultimately generating problems reminiscent of certain Marxist accounts of the law/economy relation, does in fact suggest an alternative manner of regarding the law/economy or law/society nexus. This alternative is by no means their exclusive preserve since it resonates quite deeply within sociology in general. For example, Durkheim and Gurvitch each address law as a fundamental item of sociological enquiry and as a basic constituent of sociality. It may not always be possible to agree with the conclusions reached, but the fact that they put the issue in this particular fashion suggests more appropriate analysis of the relationship between law and economy. In any case it certainly does not give rise to the same sort of problems encountered below.

What then do we mean by the relationship between law and economy? The idea that law and economy exhibit a general interrelationship is perhaps a commonplace. Whether it is the relatively simple assertion that company law provides the framework for capital organization or the somewhat stronger claim that legal relations reflect economic reality, the idea that law and economy are related in some way remains paramount. Consequently, the only task would seem to be to establish specific points of convergence. Indeed this is the standard brief of much 'socio-legal' research. Against this, however, it is arguable that the very idea of a relationship between law and economy entails a particular conception of the nature of the legal and the economic as separate orders. This sort of conception is both inadequate, as far as it goes, and, moreover, heralds a portrait of the social formation which is at best unacceptable and at worst plagued with contradictions. I would question, therefore, both the manner in which the issue of the law/economy relation is traditionally posed together with the very idea of a relation between separate instances of the social formation.

To this end the present chapter is concerned to outline the terms in which the law/economy relation is conventionally established; to demonstrate the concepts generated in pursuit of a law/economy relationship and to argue the particular consequences of these respective positions. The critical thrust of these remarks is sustained in turn by a demonstration of the pertinent features of what is, arguably, a more appropriate analysis of legal and economic relations. This alternative formulation emerges more clearly in the context of an examination of corporate relations of production, private property and forms of ownership undertaken in subsequent chapters. The demonstration of this alternative, however, is essential for the proper conceptualization of the historical relevance and effectivity of anti-trust legislation together with the proper assessment of the more contemporary influence of legal controls on corporate forms of business activity. For example, it will be argued that the very separation of law from economy, achieved via the constitutional doctrine of the separation of powers, is directly responsible for the limited impact of anti-trust legislation.

What then is wrong with the conventional portrait of the law/economy relationship? The problem is easily stated. In order to describe a relationship between the structure of legal relations, on the one hand, and the relations or forces of production, on the other, it is necessary to effect what Cutler *et al.* (1977, p. 135) would call a prior distribution of social space into economic and legal realms. It is arguable that not only is this distinction untenable in itself but also that it generates a series of quite specific problems which will be set out in due course. In apparent disregard of these twin problems the particular distribution of social space in mind constitutes the under-acknowledged starting point for the perspectives described below. More importantly perhaps, this division of social space appears to operate as a given beyond analysis which is unavailable for examination by the positions which, nevertheless, claim it. Therefore, the prior distribution of social space into distinct legal and economic instances, first of all, is not normally justified by the perspectives which rely upon it and, secondly, constitutes an obstacle to the proper assessment of legal/social relations. Accordingly, the refusal to either remove or justify the prior separation of legal and economic instances means that the conditions of the relation, together with the status of that which is related, cannot be adequately assessed.

In general the analysis of the relation between law and economy takes one of two forms. Either is law seen as absolutely autonomous of economic affairs with the result that it is viewed solely as a logico-deductive system which is both consistent and self-sufficient, evolving on the basis of the self-realization of an eternal legal essence. For example, legal positivism achieves just such a cleavage between law and economy. Or else law is reduced to the economy in one of two ways. Firstly, in terms of the functionality or co-optability of law for the economic substratum which leaves law as a positive, although empty, framework which is then subject to various purposes or uses through time. For example, it will be argued that the work of Karl Renner (1949) evinces this general tendency as do certain of the propositions within the work of Max Weber (1968). This particular perspective displays a basic instrumentalism with regard to the external relationship established between law and economy. In effect the law is there to be used at will by successive economic substrata irrespective of the relations constitutive of each. Secondly, on the basis of the parallel development of juridic and economic thought, Pashukanis (1978) argues that juridic categories are reflections of objective social relationships and that the form of law is basically the form of commodity exchange. For Pashukanis, the form of law thus expresses the form of commodity exchange or production by virtue of an essential parallelism between the analysis of law and the analysis of value. The reduction of law to economy is accomplished in both cases; for Renner, through a form of instrumentalism and, for Pashukanis, through a sophisticated, albeit ultimately more compelling, variety of economism.

A rather different, although contiguous, procedure can be seen in the work of Althusser and Balibar (1970) and Poulantzas (1973). This is not to suggest that all three can be reduced to a common or essential problematic, indeed there are quite substantial differences between them, but merely to point out some of the similarities in their respective treatment of the law/economy relation. Althusser, and to a certain extent Poulantzas, do not directly analyse the relationship between law and economy but instead, along with Balibar, assign each their respective locations within the totality. The conditions of the combination or, more generally, the relation which holds between law and economy, therefore, is reduced to an effect of the specific combination of the invariant elements of production. In the last instance this sort of position can, with some justification, be described as a more elaborate version of economism. For example, this perspective quite clearly depends upon a definite conception of the totality as an expressive force which underlies and ensures the ultimate coherence of relatively autonomous (regional) instances.

The distribution of social space into an economic and a distinctly legal realm, so vehemently affirmed in the positivist insistence on abstracting the logical structure of legal systems as a separate object of analysis, is shared also by economistic and instrumentalist positions on law and economy. Therefore, the prior separation of law and non-law and law from economy are effectively parallel positions. This follows for the simple reason that the two cannot be distinguished by this criterion alone. This particular distribution of social space is found again in the work of Cutler *et al.* (1977), who also manage to achieve a somewhat similar separation between, in this case, the relations of production and the provision of their (legal) conditions of existence.

The analysis of law and economy does not only surface specifically in those works which take the idea of a relation between law and economy seriously. The relation is often subsumed under more general considerations which take the law/society nexus as their point of departure. A common theme persists in these positions: a theme which is reflected particularly in the work of Alice Tay (1978). The theme in question stresses the intactness of the concept of juridic property whilst noting the proliferation of different types of property. This proliferation does not affect the abstract concept of private property but merely induces specific regulations for, or against, distinct types of property (Tay, 1978). Further examples can be found in the development and extension of various satellite institutions in order to square jural and economic reality (Berle and Means, 1967) or more consequentially, the mutual transformation of deeper legal realities and social relations in the context of abstract juridic stasis (Gurvitch, 1947). In almost all these formulations law appears as an abstract positive residue whilst its institutions, functions, manifest variations or its relation with forms of sociality are granted at least a measure of autonomy.

From the standpoint of an examination of the relation between law and economy these approaches mark a considerable distance from the work of Pashukanis and Balibar. Whereas Pashukanis sees that the essence of law is inextricably bound up with its form, a form which in relations of commodity production is stamped throughout with notions of equivalence derived precisely from those same relations, the above theorists, with the partial exception of Gurvitch, each seem to insulate the realm of law from its concrete social functions. There is also a considerable difference between Balibar's position on law as an instance of the social formation ultimately determined by the relations of possession of and separation from the means of production and a position which holds that law is distinct with regard to its juridic and its functional/institutional aspects. The particular problems involved in the former do not provide grounds for the acceptance of the latter. Pashukanis' economism is matched by the basic instrumentalism with respect to law of, for instance, Renner, Tay and to a much lesser extent, Gurvitch, but it is not transcended by it.

These are the general boundaries of the law/economy relationship. It is necessary, however, to provide a more detailed description of each perspective. Whilst paying due regard to the specific problems encountered by each respective position, the critique will be sustained by the argument that these specific problems are but instances of a more basic fault. This fault, it will be argued, is the prior separation of law and economy as distinct orders of sociality.

The choice of specific advocates of the law/economy relation is evidently selective in as much as there is a preponderance of avowedly Marxist accounts. Whilst this may be viewed in terms of overepresentation, it can be justified on the grounds that, by and large, it has been Marxist accounts which have addressed the issue with more sustained attention than any other. Where the influence of Marx is not readily discernible it stems, nevertheless, from an implicit dialogue or from confronting the issue of the economic and the non-economic (Parsons, 1956) or the relation of law and capitalism (Weber, 1968).

Pashukanis

For Pashukanis "the primary basis of law is rooted in commodity relations", both in that the form of law and the form of value share a common conceptual structure and in the sense that law is necessary for commodity production as a condition of existence of exchange. As Arthur notes, "For production to be carried on as production of commodities, suitable ways of conceiving social relations and the relations of men to their products have to be found and are found in the form of law" (Arthur, 1976/7, p. 35). The suitability of law for this particular function lies in the supposed centrality of the concept of equivalence in law. Equivalence is fundamental to the law and refers to the ideal that all men exist as private and abstract social beings endowed with the capacity to have and acquire equal rights and equal obligations. As Pashukanis notes "every sort of juridic relationship is a relationship between subjects. A subject is the atom of juridic theory: the simplest element, incapable of being resolved further" (Pashukanis, 1951, p. 160). In order for commodities to exchange it is necessary that agents "don the mask of owners" and enter into relation with other 'owners' and other commodities.

Pashukanis sees a clear conceptual parallel between the derivation of value in Marx's *Das Kapital* and the derivation of the form of law in that the category of the 'subject of rights' is an abstraction from acts of exchange in the market. This conceptual parallel between law and value is supplemented by the 'necessity' of law as a condition of existence of commodity production in general and as a condition of existence of capitalist relations of production in particular. It is not clear, however, whether law stands in a relation of expression to relations of production, in which case formal juridical relations of property are considered as economic relations. For example, Pashukanis asks the question "where shall we search for the unique social relationship whose inevitable reflection is the form of law?" (1951, p. 138) and states that the required relationship is that of the possessors of commodities. Elsewhere he remarks that "a juridic relationship between subjects is merely the other side of the relationship between the products of labour which have become goods (commodities)" (1951, p. 140). Pashukanis also makes the point that property relationships, ". . . are the very same relationships of production expressed in juridic language" (1951, p. 145). The essential economism entailed in seeing property relationships as relations of production has been noted by Poulantzas when he points out that ". . . this renders the cardinal distinction between real appropriation (that is, economic property) and formal juridical property . . . theoretically impossible" (Poulantzas, 1973, p. 72, note 20).

The inability to draw this distinction between economic and juridic ownership results in very real difficulties when Pashukanis attempts to theorize the corporate enterprise in terms of a 'lapse' of private property and the partial suppression of commodity exchange between formerly separate units of the corporate enterprise. Moreover, if law is a condition of existence of relations of production then such a radical separation subverts the essential equivalence between commodity and legal relations established above. To be sure Pashukanis is ambiguous on this point, at one stage he consistently denies that law can function as a condition of existence of relations of production. He states that law can assure or guarantee relations of production or exchange but it cannot generate such relations and, in the absence of relations of commodity production, the corresponding juridic relationship is inconceivable. Although at another point he argues that the existence of man as a subject of rights is a condition of exchange according to the law of value and consequently views law as a condition of existence of relations of exchange.

This dual determination of law, once by its function and once by its reflexive expression of commodity relations, points up another, perhaps more basic, weakness within the work of Pashukanis. The existence of two strands to the analysis of law (the form of law as the form of commodity production and law as a condition of existence of commodity production) is compounded by the fact that they are contradictory and, as a result of their combination, inherently unstable. If law does reduce to commodity production, through the nominal equivalence of their respective forms, then commodity production establishes its own conditions of existence through the dominance of its 'form'. As a consequence law cannot at the same time be a condition of existence of commodity production since the form of commodity production is a condition of existence of (bourgeois) law. If the concept of conditions of existence is rejected then the economism of the residue is evident. For example, Hirst makes the point that "Possessive right, the essence of the legal form, is a derivative of commodity relations between economic subjects. One reductionism, of law to class oppression, is rejected in the interests of another, of legal form to commodity form" (Hirst, 1979, p. 110). Otherwise Pashukanis must posit an immutable essence underlying the variability of all phenomena; a position which underlines the incipient idealism of Pashukanis's work. Finally, for legal relations to be seen as economic relations, and for property relations to be seen as relations of production expressed in juridic language, there must be some specification or assumption of two separate instances—law and economy. This must follow if one instance can be expressed in the language of the other and if one can be seen as the other. A prior separation exists both ways. Moreover, for Pashukanis, to cite the equivalence of method as between the derivation of value and the derivation of law is to imply that political economy, for example, is applied to distinct domains and, therefore, to distinct instances, law and economy. If, on the other hand, law is seen as a condition of existence then the separation between law and economy is evident yet again, as are the consequences attendant upon that separation.

Poulantzas

For Poulantzas, "The relation, between legal contract and exchange is a relation of structures" and the limits of intervention of one regional structure on the other are ultimately set by the conditions under which the direct producer is separated from the means of production (Poulantzas, 1973, p. 89). The relation is not based on any measure of equivalence between contract and exchange, nor is legal contract an expression, or a condition of existence, of an economic relation. Instead the separation of the direct producer from the means of production has two series of effects. First of all, at the economic level this separation results in the concentration of capital and the socialization of the labour process. Secondly, at the juridico-political level this separation, "sets up agents of production . . . as political and juridical 'individuals-subjects', deprived of their economic determination" (Poulantzas, 1973, p. 128). The relation between the economic and the juridico-political level is not an expressive relationship but depends instead upon the specific combination of invariant elements of production in a determinate mode of production and upon the particular social formation under consideration. The juridico-political level comprises two component realities and two relatively autonomous levels—the juridical structures (law) and the political structures (the state) (Poulantzas, 1973, p. 42, note 8). This subdivision of the juridico-political level does not alter the relationship of effectivity between the relations of production and law, although it does pose a relative dislocation between law and state, each conceived as separate, though related, instances of the social formation.

Although the juridical structure is determined in the last instance by the structure of the labour process, the juridical structure has reciprocal effects on the (economic) class struggle. This primary effect of the juridical structure consists precisely in concealing the fact that the relations between agents of production are specifically class relations. As Poulantzas notes,

> This means that agents of production actually appear as 'individuals' only in those superstructural relations which are juridical relations. It is on these juridical relations, and not on relations of production in the strict sense, that the labour contract and the formal ownership of the means of production depend. (Poulantzas, 1973, p. 128)

The implications of this are clear; individuals are not constituted as subjects for the relations of (commodity) production nor is the 'individual-subject' the unique expression of the form of (commodity) production. Poulantzas is quite clear on this; agents of production only exist as 'individuals-subjects' in the field of juridical relations at the level of juridical structure, agents of production do not exist as individual-subjects in the production process. This isolation of individual-subjects has an effect on socioeconomic relations; namely, it results in the "... ideological conception of the capitalist relations of production which conceives them as commercial encounters between individuals/agents of production on the market" (Poulantzas, 1973, p. 130). It results in the (ideological) concept of (free) competition. The effect of the juridical structure is restricted to the field of socioeconomic relations and, therefore, it does not alter the structure of the capitalist relations of production. In the juridic sense, private property belongs to the level of juridical relations, its effect is that of an ideological concept which has no substantive basis in the relations of production but is designed to conceal these by representing them to agents of production as relations between individuals-subjects. The ultimate convergence of law and economy is not secured by any simple correspondence or expression but is orchestrated by the requirements of the totality. Poulantzas thus separates the juridic and economic levels and any relation between the two is consequently external, being secured by the mode of production in question. Determination in the last instance by the character of the labour process ensures the unity, albeit contradictory, of the economic and juridic instances within a totality ultimately structured by the relation between the direct producer and the means of production which, in turn, is ultimately dependent on the mode of possession of, or separation from, the means of production. Poulantzas, therefore, avoids the vulgarities of economism and instrumentalism although only at the expense of a formal structural-functional architecture effected on the basis of structural causation and the implicit notion of an expressive totality. Instead of law reflecting economic reality or being a condition of economic production it is but an instance of the totality. Furthermore, the fact that the totality of the social formation is ultimately structured according to a single determinative principle, namely, the character of the labour process, means that legal relations necessarily cohere with economic relations. The correspondence is an effect of the structure; it emanates from the totality.[1] Therefore, legal relations are assigned a particular function which consists of the portrayal of an imaginary social order where commercial encounters are meetings between individual human subjects. Two very important consequences follow from this. First of all, law and economy are assigned distinct places within the social structure. Secondly, each is an effect of the structure (structural causation). The picture is complicated, further, by the ultimate determination of the whole by the economic. To be sure, this is no simple economism, but it does have the effect of drawing a purely arbitrary distinction between law and economy.

In his last book, *State, Power, Socialism*, Poulantzas attempts to jettison some of the more unacceptable implications of his earlier work. This reformulation starts by attempting to take seriously the profound interconnection of state and social relations. Or in other words, "... the necessity of relating the state institutional structure to the capitalist relations of production and social division of labour" (Poulantzas, 1978, p. 123). Thus the state is both rooted in the field of social relations and at the same time has a vital role in their constitution and reproduction. This is not the entire story, however, for the state also exhibits a peculiar material framework irreducible to the structure of social relations but none the less co-extensive with them. The state, therefore, is poised rather precariously on the edge of the field of social relations of which the state is both member and alien, part and non-part. The picture is further compounded when the original definition of the state as the mere locus for the condensation of a balance of forces is re-affirmed. All this is maintained within a general adherence to an implicit conception of the totality and a vision of ideology as the cement of the social formation.

No doubt there are a number of telling ambiguities in what Stuart Hall (1980) in his postscript to Poulantzas, calls an unfinished and unsettled work. Nevertheless, there are certain observations on the nature of law which are richly suggestive. For example, Poulantzas demonstrates the inherence of law in the social order . . .

> Law is always present from the beginning in the social order: it does not arrive post festum to put order into a pre-existing state of nature. For as the codification of both prohibitions and positive injunctions law is a constitutive element of the politico-social field. (Poulantzas, 1978, p. 83)

Likewise the fact that ". . . the capitalist separation of state and economy was never anything other than the specifically capitalist form of the state's presence in the relations of production" (Poulantzas, 1978, p. 167) appears to allow for a rather different conception of the interconnectedness of state, and economy and, by implication, law. This allowance is indeed taken up in what Poulantzas terms ". . . the very delimitation of the respective spaces of the state and the economy" (Poulantzas, 1978, p. 166). Furthermore, Poulantzas argues quite explicitly that the roots of the specific features of capitalist law ". . . have to be sought in the social division of labour and the relations of production" (Poulantzas, 1978, p. 86) which evidences a clear break with those who base the ". . . specificity of the capitalist juridical system in the sphere of circulation of capital and commodity-exchange" (Poulantzas, 1978, p. 86). Finally, Poulantzas does indeed go some way toward specifying exactly how law is rooted in the relations of production:

> The axiomatic system of capitalist law constitutes the framework wherein agents who are totally dispossessed of their means of production are given formal cohesion . . . The formal and abstract character of law is inextricably bound up with the real fracturing of the social body in the social division of labour—that is to say, with the individualisation of agents that takes place in the capitalist labour process. (Poulantzas, 1978, p. 86)

Therefore, over and against those who, like Pashukanis, seek to derive state and law from commodity-exchange and relations of circulation, Poulantzas tries instead to find law and state from within the relations of production. That this position is plagued with internal difficulties stems, in the main, from the retention of the concept of a totality and the positioning of the state as the central organizing instance. The state is at once historically determinate as well as representing nothing other than the essential moment of class struggle.

Balibar

An adequate discussion of Balibar's work on law is exceedingly complicated. It is not just that he appears to change his mind in midstream—effectively re-evaluating his earlier work—but the earlier work itself is complex and even contradictory. Thus, on the one hand Balibar may be grouped alongside Poulantzas as a more or less orthodox exponent of the Althusserian perspective. On the other hand there is a marked re-emergence of a somewhat older and rather crude version of law and class politics in *On the Dictatorship of the Proletariat.* In between these two polarized positions there are a number of more specific indications on legal and economic relations, some of which evidence great potential, others of which merely reiterate more familiar positions.

The starting point for Balibar and for that matter Althusser and Poulantzas, is the definition of a mode of production as a system of forms representing one state of the variation of a set of invariant elements. These elements are:

1. The labourer (labour power).
2. The means of production (which comprise the object of labour and means of labour).
3. The agent of appropriation of surplus labour.

These three elements are subject to two relations or connexions between them. The relations, or connexions, refer to the articulation of the three elements and not to the elements themselves. The two relations or connexions are:

1. The relation of real appropriation; "the real material appropriation of the means of production by the producer in the labour process"; the appropriation of nature by man. For example, in the individual appropriation of natural objects the labourer controls himself. This relation, then, is the connexion between the direct producer and the appropriate means of immediate production, between labour power and the relevant means of production. Balibar says of this relation "Nowhere does the Capitalist intervene as owner; only the labourer, means of labour and the object of labour" (Althusser and Balibar, 1970, p. 213). (Althusser diverges slightly since he characterizes this relation of real appropriation as the productive forces understood as relations rather than as things or "technological imperatives". Accordingly, despite the 'technicist' overtones this should not be confused

with the idea that the dislocation between the forces and relations of production constitutes the motor of history. This conception is generally induced by arguing the irrepressible expansionism of the forces of production which thus burst asunder the corresponding relations of production thereby calling for and in effect generating new relations of production.)[2]

2. The relation of (economic) property. This connexion . . . "describes one of the presuppositions of capitalist production: Capital is the owner of all the means of production and of labour, and therefore it is the owner of the entire product" (Balibar, 1970, p. 213). In effect, this relationship defines the mode of appropriation of surplus labour and the form of its (social) distribution. Althusser would characterize this property relation as the "relations of production".

For Balibar, this . . . "property relation is itself specified according to several complex forms, notably the duality of 'possession' (use, enjoyment) and 'property' (property strictly speaking)" (Althusser and Balibar, 1970, p. 213). Accordingly, the juridic concept of property does not enter at all as a connexion between the invariant elements but is instead specified by the juridic instance, the ultimate foundation, of which is located within the specific manner in which these two connexions combine the elements of production. Strictly speaking then, juridic property belongs to, or rather is a level within, the superstructure. Its role appears to be the ideological interpretation, specification or expression of the property relation and, therefore, it does not intervene either directly between the elements or as a relation of those elements to each other. Therefore, the division between economic and juridic structures is effected as a division between material or economic reality and legal ideology. Accordingly, it is the homology or non-homology of these two relations—real appropriation and the property relation—which constitutes the determination by the economic in the last instance. In the last instance the combination of forces and relations of production, or the relation between the two connexions, determines each level, including the juridic, within a mode of production.

This, broadly speaking and with certain minor modifications is the position shared by Balibar, Althusser and Poulantzas. Balibar, however, has developed the relation between law and economy considerably further than the other two. Whilst he never escapes the problems of an ultimate economism and the prior separation of law and economy as instances, he does at least offer a framework which enables a proper theorization of the divorce between ownership and control. Although in the end it can be argued that the tensions introduced by two or more competing conceptions of the law/economy relation are inescapable and degenerate into serious contradictions. Nevertheless, it is important to examine Balibar's work mainly for the way in which he poses the problem and for the issues raised as a result of posing the problem in that particular way.

For Balibar, the starting point of a more complex analysis of the relationship between the labour process and the legal structure, is the prior "... question of distinguishing sharply between the connexion that we have called 'property' and the law of property" (Althusser and Balibar, 1970, p. 227). 'Property' logically preceeds the law of property and therefore, cannot be dependent on the law of property for its existence. This is in stark contrast to the sort of position put forward by Hans Kelsen (1955) who argues that such priority is a logical impossibility. More important, however, is the fact that on this basis law cannot be a condition of existence of the property relation and consequently cannot function as a condition of existence of relations of production. It is necessary for Balibar to draw the distinction between property and the law of property, in order for him to theorize the relationship between the economic and juridic instances in terms of the articulation of regional structures each with its own relative autonomy. This follows because it is the relation between the property connexion and the relation of real appropriation which defines the determinism of the economic in the last instance. Property, understood as one of the basic connexions, is a determinant of juridic property understood as a juridic instance. Balibar is quite insistent that the concept of articulation precludes the simple duplication of one regional structure by another. For example, the relation between law and economy is not one of duplication but of the articulation of two heterogeneous instances. Indeed, Balibar makes the point that the "... very concept of expression is difficult ... once it no longer means duplication but rather the articulation of two heterogeneous instances" (Althusser and Balibar, 1970, p. 229). Moreover, "... since contradictions are induced within the law itself by its non-correspondence with the relations of production, law must be distinct and second in order of analysis to the relations of production" (Althusser and Balibar, 1970, p. 228).

Balibar clearly establishes several points in this and in following passages. To some extent they remain contradictory but, nevertheless, go some way toward establishing a more appropriate analysis of ownership.

First of all, law is part of, or belongs, to the superstructure, not in the crude sense of being a mirror image or duplicate of the economic base, but as a regional instance replete with its own relative autonomy. It has often been argued that relative autonomy is an inadequate concept with which to grasp the law/economy relation and that the concept of relative autonomy contains an inherent reductionism by which it slides inexorably into economism. For example, Hindess (1978) and Hirst (1977) argue that in the absence of any attempt to specify the conditions and the mechanisms of relative autonomy this conclusion is unavoidable. Further, relative autonomy requires a guiding instance which is capable of ensuring that autonomous levels are only relatively autonomous. Something is required which will produce some sort of overall coherence.

Secondly, law is secondary to relations of production and, therefore, can be theorized on the basis of its non-correspondence with the relations of production. There are obvious conceptual parallels between the technicist conception of the economic forces in terms of their correspondence or non-correspondence with relations of production. For this position law is effectively exhausted by the question of its correspondence or non-correspondence with the economic. No other relation is conceivable between these two (separate) levels: either law is an adequate expression or duplicate of the economy or it is not. If law does not correspond then it is because the economy has transformed itself and will eventually manage to secure a new correspondence in law.

Thirdly, it is quite clear that neither law's functionality for, nor its analytic subservience to, relations of production can guarantee the generation of law. For example, Balibar argues that

> What we can see from the reproduction of economic relations is the necessary function of the law with respect to the system of economic relations itself, and the structural conditions to which it is therefore subordinate; but not the generation of the instance of the law itself in the social formation. (Althusser and Balibar, 1970, p. 229)[3]

Balibar does not assume that because law may be functional for production relations that this, necessarily, explains its genesis. Balibar's precise meaning is demonstrated by the fact that he reserves, or restricts, the functionality of law to the re-production of economic relations thereby excluding law from holding as a prior condition of those relations as such.[4] Nevertheless, this does not prevent Balibar from arguing at the same time that

> . . . the whole of the economic structure of the capitalist mode of production from the immediate process of production to circulation and the distribution of the social product, presupposes the existence of a legal system; the basic elements of which are the law of property and the law of contract. (Althusser and Balibar, 1970, p. 230)

The legal system apparently functions as a condition of existence of the capitalist mode of production. It is difficult to envisage, however, quite how the formulation of the mode of production as a coherent totality structured in the last resort by the combination of the property connexion and the relation of real appropriation can avoid becoming any more than tautological with regard to the reproduction of the relations of production. Quite simply, as a level within the mode of production, law is a pre-condition of reproduction. Insofar as law is construed as a condition of existence of relations of production and consequently of the mode of production then law is external to the mode of production as well as being a level within it. Moreover, law is effectively a condition of itself—self-determined and self-secure. There is of course a solution to this evident contradiction, but it is a solution which is entirely circular namely, the capitalist mode of production contains an economic and a legal structure each level, as members of the same mode of production, presupposes the other. Therefore, the concept of a totality, again ensures the coincidence and ultimate coherence of the dual determinants of law.

Fourthly, Balibar points out that the peculiarity of the (capitalist) legal system

> . . . is its abstract universalistic character; by which . . . this system simply distributes the concrete beings which can support its functions into two categories within each of which there is no pertinent distinction from the legal point of view: the category of human persons and the category of things. The property relation is established exclusively between human persons and things (or between what are reputed to be persons and what are reputed to be things); the contract relation is established exclusively between persons. (Althusser and Balibar, 1970, p. 230)

Furthermore, Balibar goes on to argue that . . . "this universality of the legal system reflects, in the strict sense, another universality which is part of the economic structure: the universality of commodity exchange" (Althusser and Balibar, 1970, p. 230). Accordingly, the necessary presence of universal categories (for example 'commodity') ensures the correspondence of law and economy. There are evident similarities between this sort of perspective and that of Pashukanis. Balibar himself, however, voices doubts over the very concept of expression. For example, he argues that the Hegelian concept of Civil society

> . . . includes both the economic system of the division of labour and exchange, and the sphere of private law. There is, therefore, an immediate identity of appropriation in the economic sense and legal property and, in consequence, if the second can be designated as an expression of the first, it is a necessarily adequate expression or duplication. (Althusser and Balibar, 1970, p. 227)

As we have seen already, for Balibar these two aspects are sharply distinct which would seem to rule out any concept of duplication or correspondence.

Finally, "whereas the 'law of property' is characterized as universalistic, introducing no differences between the things possessed and their uses, the only property which is significant from the point of view of the structure of the production process is the ownership of the means of production" (Althusser and Balibar, 1970, p. 231). A dislocation obtains between the law of property and economic ownership or the distribution of the means of production. The law of property can then be seen as a generalized extension of the ownership of the means of production. Similarly, the labour contract is an extension of wage labour, an extension of a social relation of production. Contract and property are two separate forms in law but they define a single connexion within the economic structure . . . "the ownership of the means of production and productive wage labour define a single connexion, a single relation of production"

(Balibar, 1970, p. 232). A similar conclusion is reached by Renner (1949) who argues that one economic process corresponds to a whole group of legal categories—although the substitution of process for relations and categories for forms betrays a far greater distance between the two than is first assumed. The important point is that both view law as a separate level: either as a collection of forms effectively exhausted by two fundamental categories (Balibar) or as a collection of categories. Where they differ is that Balibar sees in these forms the generalized extension of a relation of production, an ideological specification or derivation, whereas Renner sees legal categories in their functional subservience to one economic process. Whilst the elements—economic and juridic instances—are substantially similar, the relation between them, together with the specific determinants of each—legal logic or labour process—are substantially dissimilar. Nevertheless, the concept of law as a generalized extension of relations of production cannot adequately grasp the law/economy connection. At most the concept simply resonates the general economic determinism of the last instance. It most assuredly does not develop any new relation between the legal and economic instances although it does supply a variation in the imagery.

Taken as a whole there is a distinct difference in Balibar's work between the analysis of the legal system, or the legal structure, as a 'functional' level within the capitalist mode of production and the more concrete analysis of the relationship between property and the law of property outlined above. As a functional level law is structured by the mode of production which is in turn determined by the labour process; a kind of remote or mediated economism. Quite clearly, this position is rendered ambiguous if serious attention is paid to the additional specification of law as a condition of existence of relations of production. The central importance of law as a level within the mode of production provides the main thrust in Balibar's work on the general location of law with respect to economy. Insofar as he makes the specific relation between the labour process and the law of property the focus of his work, however, then the connexion between law and economy is far more complex since the relation is founded internally within the relations of production. This connexion does seem to replicate the economist overtones of Pashukanis but, at the same time, it generates a whole series of internal dislocations between possession, on the one side, and the law of property, on the other. As a result a tension is induced between law as an ideological or functional level within the mode of production and the foundation of law in the relations of production—that is, law is considered only in relation to its position within the social relations of production. In this sense juridical property is but one moment in the possession of or separation from the means of production; it is not a separate level, merely a distinct kind of relation of possession of or separation from the means of production. This marks a radical departure from the sort of perspective which sustains the conception of law as a superstructural item within an expressive totality.

In his later work on the dictatorship of the proletariat Balibar (1977) poses the problem of law and economy in somewhat sharper terms. Balibar suggests that a consistent anti-instrumentalism requires that law cannot be the basis of the dictatorship of the bourgeoisie. Law cannot be its own source nor can it be locked in mutual relation, and hence circularity, with democracy—democracy guarantees law which in turn guarantees democracy. In short, law must either reduce to class power, or the mode of production, or else it ends up confirming the bourgeois fiction that the law is the law namely, law is its own source subject to no conditions of existence. In this he seems to forget the more sensitive outline of the relation between property and the law of property developed in his earlier work and remembers the dominant conception of law as an instance of the mode of production. The consequences of a full blown extension of what remains only a suggestion in Balibar's work will be examined later. Suffice it to say that in this suggestion one finds both the differences between Balibar and the earlier work of Poulantzas and a more productive aspect of the law/economy relation.

At bottom, Balibar argues that law belongs to the superstructure. Therefore, he is at one with Poulantzas and Althusser since they each state that law and economy are two separate instances ultimately structured in their relative autonomy by the nature of the labour process specific to a determinate mode of production. This general thrust can be neither denied nor ignored. Contained within this general thrust, or perhaps in spite of it, there are a number of more complex, sensitive and contradictory indications on law and economy. In the last resort, these indications vanish in the wake of the reassertion of the dominant position on law as an instance of a determinate mode of production. Sadly Balibar's subsequent work confirms the hegemonic thrust of such a position.

Renner

Karl Renner (1949) is concerned primarily with the impact of economic forces and social changes on the functions of the legal institutions of private law. For him, there is an obvious and prior separation between the economic and social realms on one side and legal institutions on the other. Therefore, any relation is theorized in functional terms on the basis of the correspondence or non-correspondence between the economic substratum and the legal system. The fundamental problem of functionality is posed in terms of the adaptation of relatively immutable legal frameworks to successive (economic) relations of production—pre-capitalist, capitalist and post-capitalist or corporatist relations of production. The central theme is that law as such is static and only its functions change. Renner embraces both instrumentalism and legal positivism and he does so on the fundamental premise that law, as law, is quite separate and self-contained, it provides its own conditions of existence. Law is its own source. To be sure, Renner does attempt to introduce a dialectic between function and law although this attempt is evidently difficult given the starting point and the instrumentalist and positivist problematic in which he is situated.

Renner's main concern is with the functional development of private property as the legal framework of capitalist relations of production. Since law is indifferent to its function and since law is effectively its own source, Renner does not so much produce a sociology of law as an analysis of its social functions. Law, as the law, is sufficient unto itself and, therefore, does not constitute an object of sociology. As a positive system it is given and only its functionality constitutes a legitimate object of analysis with the result that the determinants, or the conditions of existence, of law are outside the scope of Renner's analysis.

The cornerstone of Renner's work is his analysis of property. This analysis hinges upon two further concepts; juridic individualism and economic function. Whereas juridic individualism characterizes the law of property, economic function refers to the power of command over large aggregates of labour power which defines its social utility. Renner distinguishes between the social or collective function of law and its individualistic form. Notwithstanding the general separation of legal and economic orders, Renner appears to assume that the law of property and property are co-extensive. This apparent failure to register the internal dislocation within property, between its so called juridic and economic aspects, stems from Renner's insistence that property is unified by its legal essence on one side and that its functions are reified on the other. Property and the law of property are seen as identical and in their identity they are counterposed to its social utility. Accordingly, Renner is unable to see the relative dissolution of the property form as directly bound up with the predominance of the corporate organization of relations of production. Instead, on one side, he sees the corporate economy and, on the other, private individualistic law. It follows from this alleged co-existence that a functional relation holds between the two. Renner is thereby restricted to analysing the conditions of that functional relation, seeing the development of legal institutions as the locus of that functionality. For Renner, the development of the complementary institutions of contract, loan and lease ensures that the relation between the law of property, which is static, and the relations of production, which are variable, is in fact functional. The re-activation or re-ordering of legal institutions in accordance with specifically capitalist property relations consitutes the mechanism whereby the untransformed norm is functionally transformed. The conditions of this re-ordering, however, are not theorized by Renner and can be explained only through a relation of functional necessity. Since he concerns himself with positive law only to the extent that it generates institutions which are open to scientific observation and analysis then Renner can, with justification, be located within the confines of another positivism, positivism as understood in sociology. This sort of analysis has the somewhat dubious merit of appearing to genuflect before the alter of legal absolutism at the same time as it denotes a residue of concrete institutions amenable to empirical analysis.

Essentially, Renner overemphasizes the importance of juridic property for economic property with the result that he concludes that in the end only individuals can work, command and possess things. This represents the direct extension of juridic categories to economic relations with the result that relations of production are seen exclusively as relations between persons and things. Consequently any analysis of the relations of corporate organization in their own right is denied to Renner. As Balibar notes, from the standpoint of production it is the ownership or distribution of the means of production which is important, not the juridic form of private individualistic property relations. For Balibar the juridic form provides the ideological 'wrapper' of relations of production but not their conditions of existence. The fact that possession and economic ownership of the means of production can be lodged at respective levels of the corporate structure, thereby registering the separation of the components of private property from each other, indicates that the form of individualistic property, in the juridic sense, is irrelevant from the standpoint of production. Gurvitch (1947) makes the point that Renner fails to take notice of the existence of deeper levels of law which vary in "direct and immediate functional relation with the totality of social life" and that the transformation of the structures of jural institutions can occur independently and in opposition to abstract propositions of law. To some extent this criticism is misplaced since this is perhaps Renner's point. It remains true that Renner draws the distinction between law and function externally and that Gurvitch sees the distinction as an internal expression of frameworks, systems and kinds of law each corresponding to, and being formed by, respectively collective groups, inclusive societies, and forms of sociality. At bottom, however, they are perhaps echoing each other but using competing concepts and different lines of demarcation between law and non-law based on diverse levels of abstraction or generalization.

Renner, therefore, effects a prior separation between law and economy, sees law in an instrumentalist sense as something to be used by the economic relations of production and views the conditions of that utility as framed by the necessary functionality of law for production. All this takes place within a positivist insistence on the role of institutions and a positivist insistence on the origin and the self-sufficiency of law as a system. In concrete terms he is unable to distinguish between property and the law of property and his analysis of the corporation is incomplete by virtue of the failure to view it as a distinct organizational form. This last point derives from the over extension of the legal categories—person and thing—to relations of production. Thus legal categories remain intact and the relations of production are distended in order to enter a functional correspondence between law and economy. This particular portrait of law is extremely important when it comes to assessing the form and impact of anti-trust legislation since it imputes a basic capability to law. It will be argued that it is a fundamental mistake to attribute this capacity to law.

Cutler, Hindess, Hirst and Hussain

An underlying continuity with Renner can be traced in the work of Cutler, Hindess, Hirst and Hussain. For Renner, law does not cause economic development although it may, none the less, be a condition. For example, law makes the transformation of property into capital possible but it is not itself the agency of transformation. The cause is external to law. Likewise law confers the power to act upon the owner but it does not determine his action. Cutler *et al.* (1977) appear to argue a somewhat similar position by stating that law is a condition of existence of determinate relations of production. For them and for Renner, the law/economy relation is not posed as the determination of one by the other, as a unilateral determination of law by the economy or vice versa. On the contrary political process is the key to the law/economy relation. For Renner, it takes the form of a functional or institutional mediation or connexion between law and economy and, for Cutler *et al.*, it takes the form of conditions of existence and the political and social practices which meet those conditions. In the last resort Cutler *et al.* also have no choice but to rely upon some sort of functional explanation of the relationship between law and economy.

Compared with their radical separation of law and economy the notion of conditions of existence does not, of itself, entail a break with other theories of law and economy. To some extent, Pashukanis 'anticipated' this idea in the use, albeit ambiguous, of the notion of law as a condition of existence of relations of production. This similarity with aspects of Pashukanis and Renner is echoed in the collective adherence to a quite general separation of law and economy as distinct realms.

The relationship between law and economy can best be summarized by the following representation of their position: "Capitalist forms of possession are . . . dependent on definite legal and political conditions of existence" (Cutler *et al.*, 1977, p.246). The statement contains two important implications: firstly the phrase "capitalist forms of possession" refers to a specific form of social possession entailed in capitalist relations of production. Therefore, some " . . . definite social form of possession of the means and conditions of production" is necessary for production to take place at all (Cutler *et al.*, 1977, p. 220). Possession, in some form or another, is a precondition of all production, it is a universal requirement. The form of their argument is that if there is production then possession must have already been secured. Secondly, forms of possession are firmly separated from their legal conditions of existence. Production and law are two distinct realms and possession is divided according to its juridic and economic aspects (Cutler *et al.*, 1977, p. 244). Forms of possession refers to the mode of exclusive possession of the means of production and the ability to set production in motion. The legal conditions of an exclusive possession are many and varied. No one legal form corresponds to a particular mode of exclusive possession, no one legal system is entrenched in and secured by a particular mode of production. There is no reason why law cannot be equally functional for diverse relations of production. For example, the individualistic form of juridic property can function equally well as a condition of entrepreneurial relations of production and as a condition of corporate relations of production—providing that the corporation is viewed as an economic agent in its own right. Law, despite its position as a condition of determinate relations of production and despite the apparent specificity of law *vis-à-vis* these relations, appears to reduce to an empty instrumentality, a form with no content. The functional circle would seem to be closed.

Cutler *et al.* appear to embrace a functional explanation of the relation between law and economy by virtue of the manner of their rejection of determination in the last instance by the 'economic'. They reject all forms of final determination by the economic irrespective of whether the economic is conceived as forces or relations of production. They argue as follows

> To say that capitalist relations of production presuppose a legal system with definite forms of property and contract is merely to specify some abstract and general conditions which a legal system must meet if it is to be compatible with capitalist production . . . But the concept of determinate relations of production does not tell us in what precise form those effects will be secured nor does it tell us the precise character of the relations which secure them. (Cutler *et al.*, 1977, p. 209)

The effects pre-supposed in specifying determinate relations of production are defined as the conditions of existence of those relations. Since capitalist relations of production require means of production and labour power to take the commodity form, a legal system is required in order to define and sanction property in the form of commodities and to specify and guarantee contracts of sale and purchase (Cutler *et al.*, 1977, p. 208). The nub of their argument is that if there are capitalist relations of production then a legal system of a specific character must emerge to service or facilitate them. There can be no general and concrete relation between law and economy on the condition that the connexion can only be specified either as an abstract functionality or as empirically diverse. Any other connexion would depend upon the economy effectively specifying and securing its own conditions of existence and its own specifically legal forms. This argument follows whether the mechanism which relates law to economy is viewed in terms of the correspondence or non-correspondence of forces or relations of production leading to the necessary establishment or re-establishment of an equilibrium or whether the economy delimits the form, or the structural features, of law and indicates only a residual role for the exercise of relative autonomy. Even though both conceptions presuppose the distribution of social space between legal and economic realms, the economic and legal can have no separate existence in either. They can have no separate existence because the forces or relations of production effectively predetermine the corresponding legal forms or content and thus create their own conditions of existence and, therefore, themselves. Far from providing a way out of this impasse the concept of relative autonomy only compounds the problems it supposedly solves —not least among them being that autonomy, in being qualified, is emasculated.

Strictly speaking, for Cutler *et al.* there is a further distinction between ". . . conditions of existence and the social relations and practices which provide them" (Cutler *et al.*, 1977, p. 219). Whereas conditions of existence can be inferred from the concept of determinate relations of production, the means and the form in which these conditions are provided cannot. On one side, there are relations of production which specify their conditions of existence in purely abstract quasi-functional terms and, on the other, there are the means of rendering those abstract functional conditions a specific form. In "precapitalist modes of production" Hindess and Hirst (1975) were able to argue that the economic is determinant ". . . in the sense that the conditions of existence of the dominant relations of production assign to each of the (structural) levels a certain form of effectivity and mode of intervention with respect to the other levels" (Hindess and Hirst, 1975, p. 13). This position is now explicitly rejected. In the earlier work the task of providing conditions of existence was assigned to structural levels within the mode of production. These conditions were secured by rational extension from the concept of the mode of production or relations of production whilst a measure of regional autonomy was retained with respect to the empirical means by which those conditions were eventually secured, and with regard to their final form.

The difference between a relation whereby the conditions of existence are secured through being assigned to specific levels within a structured totality and no relation at all, the difference between a previous and a current position, is at first sight considerable. Apart from rejecting the concept of a mode of production as a structured totality determined by the economic in the last instance, Cutler *et al.* also remove the idea that law and economy are in any general and necessary relation from their present position. In the abstract sense there is a quasi-functional relation between law and economy which derives from the logical necessity of law for economy. They argue that if determinate relations of production obtain, therefore, so must a law of contract and a law of property. This is a logical analysis couched in functional terms and demonstrated entirely within discourse. At the same time, however, the legal institutions of property and contract in their empirical diversity fulfill those abstract functions—not by any necessity, rational projection or extension but by a process subject to specific conjunctural determinants. The analysis ends there. Some attempt at introducing political process, pragmatic considerations or emergent studies in legal development may be made but the end result is the same. Cutler *et al.* have produced the most radical form of the separation between the specific empirical form of legal institutions and the logical-functional complex of relations of production and their conditions of existence. The attempted rejection of all epistemology, and hence all modes of representation or correlation between discourse and reality, paradoxically, has ended up by reproducing discourse on one side—relations of production and the conditions of existence which can be inferred from them—and, on the other, the empirical diversity in which the law of contract/property is realised in specific conjunctures. Therefore, Cutler *et al.* appear to produce what amounts to the same combination of rationalist and empiricist conceptions for which they berate classical Marxism (Cutler *et al.*, 1977, p. 220).[5]

Throughout this critical exegesis of various exponents of the law/economy relationship it has been argued that its inadequate specification stems directly from the failure to pose the initial problem in the proper manner. For example, the concept of a relation between law and economy is inappropriate to a consideration of the ownership of/separation from the means of reproduction of material existence. If this argument is sustained then the twin problems of economism and instrumentalism are each the result of conceiving the economic and the legal as separate realms so that the one can then be reduced to the other—as in economism—or used by the other—as in instrumentalism. Alternatively, if the two instances are not assumed to be distinct concepts ultimately referring to different ontological objects and if the relations of ownership of or separation from the means of re-production of material existence are sharply focused then it is possible to avoid both economism and instrumentalism and, it is argued, the pitfalls of positivism and functionalism.

To develop this further, there is a profound difference between the reduction of a legal instance, as an instance, to the economic instance and the radical dissolution of instances, economic and juridic, as such. Consequently, all that is left is the mode of possession of, and separation from the means of production. In other words the social relations of reproduction of material existence in their entire complexity. This would seem to avoid the reliance on structural determination, or co-ordination, of instances of the mode of production and the ultimate drift into economism; it avoids the economism of, for example, Pashukanis;

and it avoids the positivism and instrumentalism of, for example, Renner. It also avoids the functional hybrid proposed by Cutler *et al.* But does it reduce the specificity involved in the analysis of law/economy with the result that the concepts involved are inadequate to law and economy? Or, on the other hand, does this formulation drift into a more profound economism reminiscent of certain aspects of Pashukanis? The idea that there is a 'juridic' aspect of relations of production does not necessarily connote an abstract connexion between a juridic instance, superstructure, or form and an economic process. On the contrary the alternative position merely depends upon a developed concept of the relations of production and in particular the regulation of ownership. A truly sociological approach would endeavour to address the relations of production as social relations and not in terms of two separate forms of discourse: a political economy of economic processes and a jurisprudential analysis of law.[6] Nor does sociology apply, in positivist fashion, to a pre-existent jural reality. Whether or not this procedure induces a lack of specificity and whether any loss in specificity is crucial will be seen in the context of the analysis of property outlined below. As for the second question it is difficult to envisage how this position can be construed as economism because in the absence of separate instances the concept of reduction, so crucial to economism, is also absent.

Law and Sociology

To deny the necessity of baptizing instances of sociality as legal and economic orders is no mere idiosyncracy for, in certain respects, this sort of solution has a very real sociological pedigree. From within sociology the most interesting proponents of an alternative solution are, respectively, Parsons and Weber. Whilst not directly concerned with law, the remarks of Parsons on the economy are especially pertinent. As Savage says of Parsons: "Parsonian theory has elaborated what is undoubtedly the most rigorous and systematic analysis of the economic/non-economic relation that has been produced from within sociology" (Savage, 1977, p. 1). Accordingly, Parsons is interesting at this juncture mainly for the way in which he approaches the essential problem of the relationship of economic to non-economic phenomena. Without dwelling too much upon whether or not he is successful in this venture (and on balance there are serious problems with his work) it is sufficient to note here that Parsons quite clearly rejects the reduction of non-economic factors to economic phenomena. Instead he poses the universality of a theory of human action as the basis for any integration of sociology and economics. Thus economic theory is but a special case of the general theory of the social system and the so called economic sphere but a sub-system of the general social system. The economic and the non-economic are conceived in terms of their specific forms of organization centred around different functional items differentiated by the division of labour along functional lines. The economic is both autonomous and functionally interdependent, manifesting both the properties of a sub-system and those attached to it as a component of the larger social system. Whilst Parsons and Smelser (1956) clearly pose the problem in a radically different way—and given that the origins and the content of the arguments are quite different—the formal similarity of *Economy and Society* with the Althusserian notion of the totality and the structural articulation of relatively autonomous instances or levels should not be ignored. Likewise the notion of conditions of existence is not altogether different from that of functional prerequisites.

Parsons, however, does attempt to produce a genuinely social analysis of law and economy. There are no prior grounds within Parsonian discourse for distinguishing between the two except insofar as they are but two special cases of the larger social system. Accordingly, the relation between economics and sociology and thus between economics and law should be regarded as a relation integral to sociology rather than as one forged between separate disciplines. This much is quite clear in *Economy and Society*. It is in this sense, and perhaps in this sense alone, that Parsons' work illuminates the issue of the law/economy relation.

Weber, on the other hand, poses an elusive, even coy, relationship between law and economy. For Weber (1968) the relation of law to economy is to be found in principle in the normative orientation of persons engaged in social action. Thus the relation of law and economy resides in the recognition of legal norms by persons engaged in economic action together with their particular orientation toward those legal norms. Accordingly, the ideal of legal order and the actuality of economic conduct is spanned by the is/ought distinction. Law and economy are related through the role of law as an actual determinant of human (economic) action. The role of law is here quite clearly counterposed to its more abstract location as an ideal juristic system. What is important for the law/economy relationship is the orientation of persons engaged in (economic) action toward legal norms, whether that orientation is obedient or defiant and so on. Therefore, the relationship is contingent upon the subjectively held motives for compliance or deviance and the law/economy relation is but a special example of social action in general. This is indeed the important point for it emerges that there is no reason why the relationship should be abstracted from its social context, no reason why law and economy should be regarded as separate orders which are externally related. Instead, the relation is seen as a basic constituent of social action. Of course the role of law is here separated from the juristic structure of law and to that extent is reminiscent of Renner's work. Likewise the theory of social action is subject to quite specific criticisms. But we are primarily interested in the way in which the problem is posed rather than in the particular solution.

More specifically, law is not represented in any simple way as a condition of existence of exchange or the production of commodities. Instead, economic activity can, in principle and in practice, proceed without reference to any external instance which guarantees contracts or proprietal rights. Rather economic activity can proceed in relation to its own consensus, egoistic interests or expediential rationality. Weber gives the example of the stock exchange and certain cartel agreements. For these law may prescribe a certain durability for existing economic relations and indicate a certainty that promises will be kept but it is not a necessary prerequisite. Although Weber also argues that law can elicit certain types of economic relations and that the development of a complex economic system is unthinkable without law. But in this sense the development of law is heralded as a special case of the development of bureaucratic rationality which evidently would embrace corporate organization.

This particular way of regarding law is not restricted to Parsons and Weber. Durkheim was also at great pains to stress the centrality of law for his sociology. Law was an integral part of sociological endeavour rather than a discrete logical system which has social effects or which engages in social action. Therefore, whatever reservations one may have concerning Durkheim's sociology, it is clear that he did not separate law from other social processes in the quite arbitrary way we have come to expect from socio-legal research. Much the same can be said of Gurvitch who refused to separate out law from deeper levels of sociality. Each of these sociologists suggests a way of addressing law which is not subject to the sorts of problems encountered above. Their value at this point consists in the manner in which they pose the existence of legal relations as social relations rather than in their substantive work on law.

Property

The discussion has tended to concentrate on the general interrelation of economic and legal relations. There is, however, a pertinent relationship between property and the law of property. Amongst other things, this relation involves the issue of how the corporate form of ownership can be said to emerge within the legal framework of private property. This relation directly concerns the possibility of regulating monopoly by legal means because the form of ownership and the structure of law are central aspects of anti-trust legislation. What then do we mean by private property?

> Private property, by its very nature, secures the owner special rights over and against all non-owners. It is essentially a negative notion, an assertion, backed by the full co-ercive force of society, that one man may exclude others from using or benefiting from whatever it is he owns if he so desires. It assumes the possibility—no, the inevitability—of a clash between what he wants to do with his objects and what others want to do with them. (Ollman, 1977, p. 26)

Private property, then, is a fundamental constituent of social life and, like monopoly, it is a form of exclusive ownership. The similarity soon breaks down, however, owing to the fact that each depends upon a completely different type of ownership. In order to demonstrate this difference it is necessary to put forward a typology which respects the basic distinction between private and corporate ownership and that between free-competition and monopoly. For example, instead of arguing that private property is an entirely abstract concept which is hopelessly overwhelmed by the reality of the modern corporation or, conversely, which is fundamentally transformed by nineteenth and twentieth century developments leading to the giant conglomerate form of business, it is necessary to understand the meaning of ownership in each case. Drawing on the argument put forward in this chapter, it is suggested that ownership requires a rather different examination, one which does not create an artificial distinction between legal concepts and economic functions or between legal and economic ownership. On the contrary, it is argued that the proper procedure is by means of a demonstration of a sociological typology of ownership which address' ownership as a fundamental aspect of social structure rather than as an epiphenomenon or condition of real control. Such a typology has the additional advantage of enabling the conceptualization of the basic elements of anti-trust legislation in a form commensurate with the basic parameters of the anti-monopoly movement namely, in terms of the contest between entrepreneurial and corporate forms of social organization.

We have seen how the typology may be of use in analysing anti-trust law and indeed the typology will be given greater attention in Chapter four. There are, however, two more immediate tasks. First of all, it is necessary to theorize the relation of ownership of, and separation from, the means of production in the context of the relative separation of the components of property into title, possession and control characteristic of the corporation. Secondly, it is necessary to record the effects, or the conditions, of this separation on the structure of juridic property. In short, what is the effect of the corporation upon the relationship between law and economy? It will be argued that this relation should be founded internally on the basis of the ownership of the means of production rather than externally as the abstract interaction of two autonomous instances.

The fundamental issue for a sociological analysis of property is the distribution and organization of the means of re-production of material existence. It is the social relations of production—the separation from or possession of the means of production—which must be grasped in detail if the analysis is to be at all adequate to an account of ownership. This approach does not rely upon pre-existing economic and legal levels which can be brought into a relationship. Instead property is best conceived in terms of its distinctly social aspects.

The starting point is the double separation of workers from the means of production and of enterprises from each other. The manner in which the separations occur is basic to any analysis of the concepts of possession, control and title. These concepts are in turn essential for the adequate specification of corporate relations of production, on the one hand, and the various limits inscribed on the effectivity, object, and purpose of anti-trust legislation, on the other. Each separation from the means of production implies a corresponding detention of the means of production or the general relation of ownership or separation. Briefly, as a constituent of ownership, possession concerns the day to day relation of management whilst two further relations affect the relative isolation of workers and shareholders from the enterprise. Insofar as private property can be defined in terms which suggest a definite organizational arrangement of the relations of possession, title and control, based on clearly defined powers of disposal secured through the relation of exclusion, then it is perhaps unnecessary to comprehend the relation of the law to property and property as a relation between law and economy. Furthermore, within the corporate form these components are subject to a re-ordering based, not on private property, but on another type of arrangement of these relations to each other. This change in the organization and substance of the relations defines the essential difference between what is understood as entrepreneurial capital and monopoly capital. Effectively, the social relations of ownership are transformed with the result that the concept of legal lag or legal functionality is an inappropriate way in which to regard the role of private property.

As a social relation the concept of property is devoid of meaning apart from its definition as a relation of ownership. In this sense private property constitutes a particular co-incidence of these elements of ownership or the location of possession, control, and title in one individual bearer otherwise known as entrepreneurial capital. Several consequences follow from this analysis:

1. The distinctly legal character of property relations derives from the coincidence of the elements—possession, title, control—in one agent. This defines the specific character, and the ideological appeal, of the property relation. It does not represent the intervention of a distinct juridic level, merely the definite organizational structure of legal relations in the actual organization of production. Thus the necessary presence of so-called legal relations should not be viewed as a one-to-one correspondence of property and the law of property, nor as the dependence of economic relations on legal conditions but rather as an integral appearance. Property should be viewed as a distinct type of organization of the same basic relations, as a way of interrelating social items of production. There are clear parallels between this position and that of Balibar, particularly where Balibar argues that private property is merely a distinct type of relation. It is true that there may be some sort of distinction between production relations and legal relations but there is no reason why this distinction should take the form of ready made instances. Furthermore, from the point of view of the interrelationship of

law and economy, legal and economic relations cannot be crystallized out as separate instances since they form a complex unity. In any case, the consistent interrelationship of law and economy implies the possibility, even the necessity, that their status as instances is dissolved at some stage or another.

2. Since private property is defined as a definite arrangement of the elements of the relation 'possession of or separation from' the means of production, and since property is a social relation, it can have no separate existence apart from those relations, either as a superstructural level or as a separate form. This does not mean that the relation of private property reduces to the elements of control, possession and title viewed as economic relations. It refers to the fact that as a form of organization private property cannot be specified apart from the elements which it brings into relation. But neither does it reduce to them. Thus private property is a form of organization based upon the centrality of the entrepreneurial agent. Whilst the legal doctrine that private property is indifferent to its function is quite correct as far as it goes, it is perhaps irrelevant and even a little misleading when viewed from the perspective of the interrelation of legal and economic relations within a general concept of ownership.
3. The comparative dissolution of property into its separate components is best represented as the establishment of a new articulation of these relations based on their relative separation rather than on their formal unity. It is not the case that the concept of private property capitulates in the face of the emerging corporate economy. Nor does it reach an accommodation with the corporation. Still less does it mutate into a form commensurate with corporate relations. For example, the corporation does not serve to usher in a new concept of property uniquely suited to its requirements. The significant factor is that possession, title and control are re-aligned by the advent of the corporation. Whilst the legal concept of private property and law in general are implicated at certain definite points in the actual existence of the corporation, private property *per se* is entirely inadequate to the comprehensive identification of corporate relations. This last point will be amplified in more detail later.

Conclusion

This chapter suggests that there is no acceptable reason why law and economy should be regarded as separate orders of sociality and that this portrait of society entails problems which are inherently intractable. For example, the issues of legal or economic priority, reductionism, idealism and essentialism each depends upon the fact that law and economy are separate universes. The problem is by no means purely academic for it will become apparent that the separation of law and economy prepares the way for the idea that the legal regulation of economic affairs is a valid exercise. In fact, far from being an abstract or semantic issue it is of direct concern to the analysis of anti-trust legislation.

Over and against the idea that law and economy are separate domains capable of being related in general ways, it is argued that private property does not exist first of all in a legal sense and only then does it entail social and economics effects according to the particular manifestation of the private property form. This sort of perspective, just as much as positions which reduce law to an epiphenomenon of the economy, depends upon a prior allocation of social space into distinct legal and economic orders. As we have seen this particular division heralds a number of problems. It is not so much that economism, idealism and functionalism and so on are wrong as that they represent the inevitable alternatives once the problem is posed in a particular way. On the contrary, it is the prior allocation of social space into legal and economic realms which constitutes the nub of the issue. Until the problem of the relation of law and economy is posed in a different way, not as a relation between separate items of sociality but rather as a complex fundament of ownership, the issue is doomed to reiterate contradictory and essentially circular solutions or alternatives which establish arbitrary priorities.

It is argued here that a sociological analysis of ownership meets certain of these requirements. For example, a sociological analysis is pertinent for at least three reasons:

1. Insofar as private property can be said to have social effects then it is best seen as a social relation. Viewing it in this manner, however, is not simply a matter of arguing that private property is a legal institution which has certain social effects or which provides certain conditions of other social relations. Rather, if private property is a social relation then its sociality stems from being integrated with other social relations. Therefore, private property is an integral aspect of the social relations of production and should be analysed in terms of a determinate interaction of the relations of control, title, and possession. Accordingly, private property is not regarded as a legal concept which has economic effects but as a basic constituent of social relations.
2. A sociological analysis of ownership in its widest sense entails a scope which is denied to law or economics. Hence, the somewhat arbitrary combination of a Marxist theory of law and a Marxist theory of production is avoided as are the pitfalls involved in a sociology of law and a sociology of organizations.
3. Finally, a general typology of ownership accords with the classical relevance of law for sociological consideration. This particular relevance is all too easily shunted off into a subdiscipline namely, the sociology of Law. It is arguable that Marx, Weber, Durkheim, Gurvitch and even Parsons each addressed law as a fundamental article of their sociological endeavour rather than as a discrete side line of empirical research. The manner in which they

pose the relationship between law and economy or, more generally, law and society provides the basis of a more effective alternative.

For all these reasons a sociological analysis of ownership provides a proper foundation for a realistic assessment of the issue of legal regulation in general and the nature of anti-trust legislation and the corporate form of ownership in particular.

Notes

1. For an elaboration of this sort of argument see Cutler *et al.* (1977), especially Chapters eight and nine.
2. For a forceful criticism of this conception of 'production' and 'social' relations see Hindess and Hirst (1975, 1977). Also for a defence of Balibar's contribution in particular see Cohen (1979), which argues for the necessary separation of forces and relations of production.
3. Althusser and Balibar (1970, p. 229). As we shall see there are certain parallels to be drawn between this particular point and the work of Cutler *et al.* (1977) who argue a substantially similar position.
4. See, for example, Hadden (1977). He argues that a *de facto* form of Joint Stock Enterprise existed prior to the relevant 'enabling' codes of company law. Thus the legal form of the joint stock enterprise was only of use in the reproduction of 'corporate' capital.
5. Although it should be added that they refuse to recognize the conventional distinction between discourse and reality on the grounds that it invariably privileges one form of epistemological relation over another, they argue that any such privilege can only be accorded by fiat. Therefore, the distinction between knowledge and being is artificial.
6. Of course it is quite evident that such a jurisprudence and a form of political economy do 'exist'. The point, however, is that as far as the relationship between law and economy is concerned the communion of separate forms of academic discipline must, inevitably, produce purely arbitrary versions of the relationship.

3 *Ownership, the Legal Subject and Corporate Agency*

We have seen how the law/economy relation is at once a necessary support and an important limitation of the legal regulation of economic affairs. Similarly, a theory of ownership is perhaps the obvious starting point for an appraisal of anti-trust legislation. The point may be made quite easily, for in order to regulate the conduct of corporations the law must have some idea of how they operate and more importantly, how they achieve a monopoly or a substantial foreclosure of the competitive instinct. Put simply, the way in which the law perceives and represents the reality of corporate relations is a vital constituent of any form of legal regulation of monopoly. Therefore, not only does anti-trust legislation appear to depend upon the principle of the legal regulation of the economy, but it also contains a definite view of corporate reality. This view is constructed in accordance with the legal form of ownership which is in turn framed with all due regard to the basic concept of private property.

Chapter one suggested that it is possible to control an industry in ways which extend far beyond the sort of control afforded by formal legal ownership. Accordingly, the legal concept of ownership would appear to be a rather limited mechanism for a full scale assault on the sort of control characteristic of monopoly or restrictive practices. This appearance would seem to be confirmed, historically, by the relatively ineffectual role of anti-trust legislation. The question remains, however, whether the inadequate appraisal of corporate relations of production and distribution is inherent in the nature or status of law and indeed whether it is inevitable and necessary? Arguably, it is the status of law, its entirely artificial separation from the economic processes it supposedly regulates, which explains its shortcomings as a viable regulatory agency. But what is it about the nature of law which prevents it from getting to grips with the reality of corporate relations and why is it so constrained? It will be argued that the legal concept of ownership is doubly important in this respect, for not only is it a vital constituent of the legal portrait of corporate relations, but it is also at the very heart of the issue of monpoly. Quite simply, monopoly is a form of ownership; a way of establishing control over an industrial and marketing process.

Ownership is important for a number of reasons and in a variety of ways. The legal theory of ownership is important because it unfolds according to the ever present reference point of private property which is in turn specified on the basis of an implicit philosophical anthropology. For example, the definition of private property as a relation between a person and a thing depends upon the human subject as the only creator or producer of objects which can then be alienated, exchanged and legally owned. This initial dependency follows because we are provided with a subject and object which are already separate and a prior distribution of material reality into persons and things. This separation allows law to account for and to justify their subsequent interrelation. Moreover, it is the unique relation of the subject, man, to the products he creates in his own image which in fact generates the conditions both for the invasion of the material world by the human subject and for the equation of the subject's real essence with the object that he nevertheless creates or produces. In the first case the object which is owned appears to collapse in on the subject, since the product is but the extrapolation of the will of the human subject, whilst in the second the object or product itself becomes the real subject, since it is the effective reincarnation of the human essence. We shall see that the evident tension between these alternative conceptions of ownership is resolved only at the expense of the reification of the private property relation itself, an over-insistence on the sanctity of private property rights as the guarantor of human liberty, and the equation of rights in private property with the human essence. In this last formulation private property rights are nothing more than the essential predicates of the human subject. At once the inescapable fusion of what I shall call philosophical anthropology and private property, forged on the basis of the structure of Subject-Predicate-Object, stands revealed in its fullest exposure. The circle is complete, just as philosophical anthropology is inherent in the notion of private property, so too is private property inherent in the theory of ownership outlined within law.

It is not only the legal concept of ownership which is fundamental for without the more general sociological concept of ownership, and without the concept of discontinuity and the distinct forms of ownership that are demarcated by it, it is impossible to grasp either the basis of the anti-monopoly movement—rooted as it is in a particular concept of (private) ownership—or the object of anti-monopoly hostility namely, the corporate form of ownership. The intimate relation between the form of ownership and the analysis of anti-monopoly law cannot be theorized within a problematic bounded by philosophical anthropology. This would seem to indicate that the construction of a general typology of ownership is logically prior to the very possibility of analysing anti-monopoly law. Therefore, it is possible to proceed to an adequate analysis of anti-monopoly law only by reference to the way in which the various elements of ownership are articulated, one with another.

This chapter will endeavour to examine what is understood by the concept of ownership with a view to establishing why it is that the legal view is dominated by the concept of private property and, therefore, is skewed toward one particular type. It will be suggested that this one-dimensional view of ownership contributes substantially to the basic misunderstanding of corporate relations and that this in turn hampers the effective regulation of monopoly. This involves demonstrating a number of things. First of all, the conditions under which philosophical anthropology is inscribed within the very structure of private property. Secondly, how the legal view of ownership is influenced by the concept of private property. And finally, why this generates problems for the legal regulation of monopoly? It will be argued that the hegemonic influence of philosophical anthropology on the concept of private property and of the idea of private property on ownership leave law relatively powerless in the face of forms of ownership which cannot be expressed via the language of private entrepreneurial property. Accordingly, corporate forms of ownership are outside the remit specified by forms of regulation derived from the legal concept of private property.

Of course, there have been a number of specific legislative attempts to remedy the defects generated by the legal portrait of corporate relations and these will be examined in Chapter five. In the final analysis, however, it will be argued that these attempts not only do not remedy these defects but in some cases reinforce or even exacerbate them. Accordingly, it is the very structure of legal regulation and the concepts available to it which account for the relative failure of anti-trust legislation rather than, for example, the bad faith of legislators or the political dominance of big business.

Philosophical Anthropology

What then is meant by philosophical anthropology? It refers to the reduction of the social world to the activities of an original producer, man. For example, this tendency is realized in the earlier work of Karl Marx by the argument that in the process of production man creates an object in which are fixed his essential attributes. Man is separated from whatever it is which is essential in him through its externalization in what then becomes an alien object. As Rancière (1971) indicates, the general structure of the argument concerns the general form of Subject-Predicate-Object. In effect the essential attributes of the human subject namely, the predicate, become fixed in the object which he creates. Since the object now contains the essence of the subject, this object becomes the real subject. Whereas man starts off by being a subject, the process of production ensures that it is his very subjectivity which is embodied in the object which he creates. Accordingly, subject and object swop places, man becomes a mere object and his product takes up the mantle of subjectivity. The objective world is but an expression of the essence of man. Therefore, philosophical anthropology can be defined as the overlapping of an analysis of the relations of production, ownership and so on, by the anthropological structure of Subject-Predicate-Object.

Whilst a case can be made for the further influence of philosophical anthropology in other spheres, this is not argued here. The role of philosophical anthropology is quite specific and involves no more than a way of characterizing the conception and elaboration of ownership within law understood in its widest sense. It is not a transcendental force which structures law, state and discourse according to its own internal predilections. It is simply a condition of regarding ownership in a particular way, a form of argument. Accordingly, the influence of philosophical anthropology, if influence is the right word, consists in the manner in which complex structures of ownership tend to be seen in terms of legal subjects, whether in terms of determinate human beings or juristic persons. Thus the use of the concept is no more than a convenient way of describing a particular interpretation of ownership.

The object of criticism and indeed the obstacle to any general theory of ownership concerns the philosophical analysis of the position of man in relation to the social or material world. This position reduces the existence of social relations to the expressive or purposive activity of an essential man. It is a humanist ontology which firmly locates man as the axis and the source of all social relations. Whilst it may be true in a generic or original sense that man, in tandem with nature, produces material reality as we know it, at least two reservations may be made. First of all, the argument that in producing objects man is externalizing his essential attributes is based on a false analogy with the production of God by man. Rancière (1971) demonstrates the way in which the young Marx achieves this slide. He argues, that in the production of God by man, there is an actual equivalence between man and his product, man objectifies the predicates which make up his essence. God only equals man's predicates, nothing more. Therefore, God is a transparent object in which man can, first of all, see himself and, secondly, reappropriate that which he alienated, in other words his essential attributes. The absurdity is revealed, however, when it is considered that the worker and his product are supposed to be equivalent, that the product is supposed to represent nothing but man's essential attributes, his essence, and that the worker's product is supposed to be something in which the worker should recognize himself. Put another way, the manifestation of generic life is equated with the means of maintaining individual existence or ". . . the productive activity is identified with the generic activity (the activity of man insofar as he affirms his own essence) and the object produced is identified with the objectification of the generic being of man" (Rancière, 1971, p. 42).

Whereas the attributes of man and God are essentially the same, the attributes of the worker and the product are quite different. To achieve the successful reduction of social relations to the human subject it is necessary to buttress the entire project with an undue and misplaced reliance on an idealistic conception of the relation of man to his product, a reliance which we have seen is based on an essentially false analogy adopted by, amongst others, the young Marx. Secondly, even if an original position is granted to man in the scheme of social evolution it does not follow that one can continue to reduce all material and social life to the activities of an original purposive subject. The principal objection to philosophical anthropology concerns precisely this objective since it is through the persistence of the hegemonic role of the philosophical anthropology of the subject, man, that the specificity of the social relations of production and, in particular, forms of ownership is denied. Accordingly, it is the continual influence of philosophical anthropology, and not its original truth or generic import, which prevents the proper theorization of social relations of production. It is to this aspect of philosophical anthropology that the present critique is addressed.

Perhaps the starting point for a more detailed analysis of the influence of philosophical anthropology on the theory of ownership is to be found in Marx's critique of the Hegelian inversion of the subject and object of private property. Here, as Lucio Colletti notes, "Property ought to be a manifestation, an attribute of man, but becomes the subject; man ought to be the real subject, but becomes the property of private property" (Marx, 1975, p. 37). Without dwelling too much upon whether Marx's extraction of the rational kernel (essence) of Hegel's thought can amount to an inversion of the same, it is sufficient to note the static position of the human subject with respect to the property right. The 'inversion' neither destroys the primacy of the relation between the (human) subject and the property object nor does it, in actual terms, amount to a thorough-going inversion. The human subject and the property object take on aspects of each other—the property object is invested with a will whilst the human subject takes on the character of an object. In the first case, the definition of property by reference to a subject and object and the idea that ownership represents an exclusive relation between the two is the hallmark of what has been termed the anthropological concept of ownership. In the second case, whilst the content of subject and object are reversed, in that the human subject is an attribute of private property, the formal position of subject and object remain intact. The Subject-Predicate-Object structure survives in that the specific components, supports or agents are merely reversed. Both cases meet the criteria laid down for the identification of the influence of philosophical anthropology and, therefore, will be rejected as inadequate to a truly general theory of ownership.

Developing this further, much in the way that Marx does in the *Critique of*

Hegel's Doctrine of the State (Marx, 1975) and *Economic and Philosophical Manuscripts of 1844*, the issue becomes much clearer. For example, in criticizing the position and rationality which Hegel accords primogeniture Marx states that

> Landed property thus anthropomorphises itself in the various generations. One might say that the *estate* always *inherits* the first born of the family as an attribute bound to itself . . . and that this . . . implies that the hereditary landowner is a *serf* attached to the estate and that the *serfs* subject to him are no more than the *practical* consequences of the *theoretical* relationship binding him to the estate. (Marx, 1975, p.175)

At least two consequences follow on directly from this: firstly, the anthropomorphic nature of private landed property established here is the corollary of the subject/object inversion and also connotes the basic idea of a unique property relation between a subject and an object—however that relation is conceived. Secondly, the relegation of the landowner to a mere serf renders the cardinal distinctions between the various forms of separation from, and ownership of, the means of production impossible. The possibility of an accurate specification of the relations of feudal production is thereby diminished. Rather, the primary question is not whether the estate inherits the first born or vice versa, it is not the inversion of subject and object which is at stake, but the whole anthropological structure of Subject-Predicate-Object which precludes the analysis of forms of ownership that do not reduce to subjects and confirms the drift into the anthropological problematic characteristic of the earlier work of Marx. This can be demonstrated since Marx, despite correcting the Hegelian inversion, falls into the same trap:

> The serf is an appurtenance of the land. Similarly the heir through primogeniture, the first born son, belongs to the land. It inherits him . . . But in the system of feudal landownership the lord at least *appears* to be king of the land. In the same way, there is still the appearance of a relationship between owner and land which is based on something more intimate than mere *material* wealth. The land is individualized with its lord, it acquires his status, it is baronial or ducal with him, has his privileges, his jurisdiction, his political position, etc. It appears as the inorganic body of its lord. (Marx, 1975, p. 318)

Either way the idea of a relation between (landed) private property, and its (human) agent is seen as an expression of a will—the estates' will projected anthropomorphically onto the subject or the will of the possessing individual invading the object so possessed. The result, therefore, is the same, namely a relation between subject and object conceived on the basis of an abstract will. To the extent that the Subject-Predicate-Object structure is retained then ownership can be seen only as a particular manifestation of the general separation of man from his essence, as a specific incidence of the general form of abstraction/alienation.

There are perhaps two distinct ways of looking at ownership within the problematic of philosophical anthropology, two ways which, as we have seen, already imply a third in the form of their attempted resolution. First of all, the human subject is tied to tangible objects even whilst dominating them. For example, the landowner is tied to the land through the projection of his will onto it. Secondly, the human subject is tied to the object even whilst being its subject. Here the landowner is the wilful expression of the essence of primogeniture and the owner of private property is the mere reflex of commodity relations or trade in private property. In the last sense the real subject can, without too much trouble, be described as the commodity structure itself with the important consequence that the real subject could be said to inhabit the relations of commodity exchange. This subjective essence can be put forward to account for the ultimate coherence of law and the state within the economy. It becomes the real stalking horse of conformity with the result that this unseen hand effectively ensures that law and the state assume the form of equivalence. Law and state, therefore, become but manifestations of the general separation of the subject from his essence, they are simply indices and, as such, it is perhaps not surprising that they assume the common form of equivalence.

Adherence to a particular version of philosophical anthropology carries quite specific consequences for the reason that its influence is far from uniform. It is quite true, however, that both of the alternatives outlined above do retain the general relation between subject and object. Where they differ is that whereas the second position idealizes private property as an essence which can be brought into relation with itself in its manifest or phenomenal form—the human subject—the first position is simply inadequate since it cannot cope with the complexities of ownership but only with an idealized conception of bourgeois or entrepreneurial property as the reflex of independent subjective wills.

Before embarking on a more detailed analysis of the legal concept of private property it is perhaps as well to record some of the similarities between the anthropological concept of ownership and the law/economy relationship. The exercise is useful because it shows how both ideas appear to depend upon similar sorts of arguments and, moreover, it points to the ways in which they go a long way towards reinforcing each other. For example, the concept of the subject provides law and economy with a unique excuse for cohabitation.

The particular affinity of the law/economy relation and philosophical anthropology may be argued in two ways. First of all, they each depend upon a common heritage in that they both imply the prior distribution of material reality into, in the first case, law and economy, in order to give the relation of law and economy, and, in the second case, persons and things (subject and object), in order to give the relation of private property. The analysis indicates the parallel construction of purely formal continuities. For example, the prior division creates a space for legal intervention. The manner in which they pose the question is similar and creates the necessary conditions for legal intervention to be possible. The second point concerns the form in which the foregoing problem is apparently solved. In accordance with the substantial diversity of options available, the range of solutions is understandably large. For example, certain versions of the law/economy relation would seem to leave the form of law alone. For example, both Renner (1949) and Cutler *et al.* (1977) appear to allow private property to embrace the reality of corporate relations of production on condition that private property is an empty frame waiting to be filled by an orderly sequence of determinate social relations. For Renner the form of law remains untouched and only the content is functionally implicated with the economic substratum. For Cutler *et al.*, the form of law is preserved on the basis of the functional correspondence between law, as a condition of existence of determinate relations of production, and the determinate relations of production themselves. Thus the conception of ownership in terms of property rights can be accommodated within the notion of conditions of existence, since for Cutler *et al.* the relevant issue is whether the concept of property rights can be a condition of existence of determinate relations of production? And for Renner, it is whether the law of property is functional for the economic substratum. But leaving the form of law out of account implies that law and economy are separate and that the inherence of philosophical anthropology in the concept of private property is left unquestioned. The influence of philosophical anthropology is reinforced therefore on the basis of the functional interrelation of law and economy.

Conversely, when the form of law is addressed in its reciprocal interrelation with the economic, then the continuities between this position and philosophical anthropology are of a different, though persistent, kind. For Pashukanis, the form of law is interdependent with the form of commodity exchange. However, the concept of interdependence can only be formulated on the basis that both law and economy are instances of the same division of the (human) subject from his essence. The law/economy relation, therefore, is forged on the basis of their mutual expression of the separation of the subject, man, from his essence and they are related insofar as they are indices of the same essential source. The particular significance of this sort of relation lies in its ability to explain the apparent specificity or autonomy of law as a mere surface phenomena, as a mere variation in the form in which the same underlying structure—the human essence—is manifest. This means that to argue a relation between law and economy is to do no more than imply that the concepts of one can be translated into the other more or less without residue. For example, the question is at first purely conceptual—whether the structure of commodity exchange can be accommodated within legal discourse. The problem is solved on the basis of the translation of the form of argument used in *Das Kapital* to the categories of legal discourse. The difficulties encountered in effecting a perfect translation lead to the specification of legal relations as an independent ontological category necessary for the exchange of commodities, as a condition of existence of determinate relations of commodity production. It is on this point that we can see a reason for the ambiguous formulation of law within the work of Pashukanis as both the form of equivalent exchange and its material condition of existence. Quite simply Pashukanis shifts ground, from the question of formal parallels between forms of discourse to the specification of legal relations as concrete conditions of existence for economic relations. The form in which the solution is posed—the conceptual parallels between forms of discourse—reverts to the simple reiteration of the manner in which the question is posed, the discrete ontological status of law. Pashukanis appears to conflate question and answer for the reason that the manner in which the question is posed renders it unanswerable. Indeed once the problem is posed in this way, as an ontological separation of law and economy, then there is only one consistent solution. That solution is arrived at with reference to the basic parameters of philosophical anthropology. The solution to the problem of the law/economy relation provides the only means whereby the concepts relating to law and those relating to economy can be subsumed within a larger domain. Namely, the category of the subject, a category which ensures that the economic and juridic spheres are part and parcel of the overall affinity of the subjective essence. Law and economy—whether conceived in an epistemological or ontological sense—are but different manifestations of the same subjective essence. Philosophical anthropology thereby provides a solution, but it is a solution obtained at an unacceptable price: the reduction of all forms of ownership to the relation of private property conceived, of course, on the basis of an essential subject. Quite paradoxically, in attempting to transcend the base-superstructure metaphor and to provide a solution to the law and economy relation, Pashukanis ends by embracing the only possible solution once the problem is posed in this particular way, namely, as a relation of law and economy. For Pashukanis the form of law is interdependent with the form of commodity exchange because both are instances of the same division of the human subject from his essence characteristic of philosophical anthropology. The concept of equivalence can then be interpreted as the hidden hand that ultimately induces conformity between the economic and legal spheres, as a common essence which ensures that apparently discrete phenomena are but different manifestiations of the same essential structure.

In both cases the concept of the subject is a necessary support of, and the most consistent solution to, the law/economy relation. In the first, it operates via the concept of private property, to reinforce the separation of law and economy, only to re-emerge as the only basis on which law and economy can be integrated. In the second, it exists from the start as the basis on which law and economy are separated, as forms of subjectivity, and then becomes the condition on which they are re-aligned, through their equivalent status as subjects. Therefore, the view that private property is encapsulated in the unique relation of subject and object and the idea that law and economy are in relation one with the other are co-extensive. Furthermore, to the extent that the relation of Subject-Predicate-Object defines philosophical anthropology, and given that a relation between law and economy entails the possibility of a legal intervention with respect to the economic then philosophical anthropology and juridic interventionism are one of a piece. Finally, it is argued here that, however, the law/economy relation is conceived the category of the subject or enterprise agent ultimately allows for the effective translation of one form of discourse into another. Once the problem is seen in terms of the relation between law and economy then the concept of the subject provides the only basis upon which law and economy can be related consistently.

It is possible to argue two things against the influence of philosophical anthropology. First of all, private property can be described as a complex internally articulated structure of the elements of ownership, in terms of a general outline of a theory of ownership. Secondly, philosophical anthropology prevents the formulation of forms of ownership which bear no relation to human or any other subjects—corporate and ecclesiastical ownership. An example of how philosophical anthropology functions as an obstacle can be seen in the way that the concept of private property is simply extended or expanded to take in the corporation as what amounts to a legal person. Hayek correctly notes this tendency:

> As in the law of property the rules developed for ordinary mobile property were extended uncritically and without appropriate modifications to all sorts of new rights; thus the recognition of corporations as fictitious or legal persons has had the effect that all the rights of a natural person were automatically extended to corporations. (1949, p. 116)

Having noted the tendency, Hayek fails to observe that the transfer of individual rights to the corporation is the logical result of regarding ownership from the perspective of philosophical anthropology. Within a theory of ownership bounded by the concept of private property it is quite natural for the object (the corporation) to assume the essential attributes of the human subject, to become that human subject by acting as the real subject. Hayek's idealism, coupled with his tendency to reify the concept of private property to a level of pristine purity never fully realized in any determinate relations of production, prevents him from recognizing that monopoly may be inherent in any free enterprise based on the sanctity of private property. As such Hayek can say nothing of the corporate form of business organization save that it be excluded from the primarily individual rights of private property. Only two options are available for Hayek on the question of the corporation; either it is ignored or it is somehow forced to respect the restricted logic of private property 'proper'. The trouble with this last position is that in respecting one logic of private property is contravened another, perhaps more fundamental, form of that logic, the logic that affirms the result of free competition and private property as the existence of the monopoly form and corporate ownership. More simply, the trouble with competitions is that somebody may win.

Private Property

The analysis of ownership within the perspective of philosophical anthropology is an example of the more general separation of man from his essence. It follows that the reduction of various forms of ownership to the limiting case of private property is the means whereby the specific separation of subject and essence is manifested as a general separation. It is because of man's relation of himself as a subject to his own product as an external object that things can be owned, products alienated and commodities exchanged. In this way, the theory of ownership is overlapped by the anthropological structure of Subject-Predicate-Object. This overlap results in the derivation of the private property relation from the primary alienation of man's productive capabilities. The separation of man from his product through exchange results in its re-possession by some other (human) subject. Otherwise the private property relation would have neither utility nor meaning. The concept of legal rights implies the prior separation of a (human) subject from his essence because the idea of a right in any particular object requires the notion of a privileged connection between subject and object. Thus the private property relation is derived by analogy with the logic of Subject-Predicate-Object. As we shall see the relation between subject and object ultimately becomes a relation between subjects and the existence of a legal right connotes the essence of proprietorial subjectivity. In this sense legal rights are the guardian of both the real and the human subject with the result that private property is at least on an equal, if not superior, footing with man.

We have seen the more general features of the private property relation. What, however, are the specific examples of philosophical anthropology's incidence on a theory of ownership? The primary influence of philosophical anthropology on ownership is engagingly simple: just as it can be argued that, for Adam Smith, a philosophical anthropology of the subject, man, and the factory stand instead of an economic system, so too, does a philosophical anthropology of the subject, man, stand instead of a general typology of ownership (Tribe, 1978, p.2). This masquerade entails the reduction of all forms of ownership to the essential (human) subject together with a form of essentialism which holds that the essence of man permeates and measures all material reality. It is important to realize the full implications of this essentialism, for in order to successfully achieve the reduction of all social life to the projects of human subjects, it is necessary to establish the requisite connection between social relations, social life and the material world, on the one hand, and the essential human subject, on the other. Reductionism presupposes the efficient translation of concepts specified at one level into concepts specified at another, usually lower, level of existence.

The main assumption of philosophical anthropology is that all social life can be explained with reference to the primacy of the essential (human) subject. Therefore, the human subject is seen as a constitutive essence. The two are co-extensive; just as social life is nothing but the manifestation of the human essence so too does social life reduce to the various attributes of the abstract human subject. Accordingly, the subject is an ideal essence precisely because it can be separated from its original location, man, and transposed into a theory of property rights. Or, to put this slightly differently, the world of social relations becomes intelligible in terms of the centrality of the subject, man, by arguing an equivalence between man the producer and the objects which he produces. This equivalence is provided by the concept of an essence which expresses the attributes of the subject, man, but which at the same time can be alienated in the object that he produces. Thus the position of the human essence in the anthropological scheme provides a mechanism for the reduction of all forms of ownership to the primary relation of the subject and the object of ownership, to the essence of man as producer. The idea of an original relation of ownership is directly sustained by the philosophical anthropology implicit in the structure of Subject-Predicate-Object. The very fact that the structure of philosophical anthropology namely, the Subject-Predicate-Object sequence, provides a mechanism for the translation of a human into a transcendental subject means that there is a unique relation between the (objective) social world and the individual (human) subject. The unique relation is constituted by means of the essential attributes of the human subject being taken up and transposed into an external, dominant, subject. Similarly, private property starts off by representing a relationship between a human subject and an object but very quickly we find that private property is defined as a relation between subjects, actual and potential proprietors.

For example, private property is a relation of exclusion of all others, a relation which excludes on the condition that it guarantees absolute power of disposal over the object of property, absolute freedom to use and consume that object as one likes. The juridic form of property may vary, for example, from a relation of exclusion (this is essentially true of continental law) to the empirically specifiable restraints on others from interfering in one's property (English common law). Nevertheless, property as a relation is the essential element of private property as is the absolute power over the means of its disposal. To be sure such absolute power may be qualified through a series of specific injunctions but it still operates as a basic premise of private property.

Accordingly, a classic justification of private property rights starts off from the assumption that man, as possessor of himself, is, therefore, possessor of his attributes. For example, his labour power and the products of his labour belong to him. This conception forms the basis of the legal concept of ownership and provides the key to the general form of ownership specified within law. For example, Bentham, Locke, Mill and Green each subscribe to the labour justification of property (Macpherson, 1978). The matter does not rest there, however, for although this original or unique relationship of man to his product may provide a blueprint for other forms of ownership it cannot generate those forms without recourse to the logic of philosophical anthropology. Therefore, this unique connection is transposed into a more elaborate theory of legal rights. Since the relation between subject and object depends upon the fact that the object contains the essence of subjectivity (the attributes of the original subject) then the proprietal relationship can be defined as a relation of subjectivity. If this original relation is to be a prototype then there must be other relations of subjectivity which do not depend upon the fact of creation as a guarantee of ownership but rather recognize the existence of other subjects who may own the object in question. Furthermore, if this original justification of ownership as the possession of ones attributes is to have any meaning then any form of ownership by someone other than the original producer must have the same status. All relations of subjectivity must be identical for private property to be defined as a relationship between formally equal subjects. Furthermore, they each entertain a relationship with an object which contains the resultant of human subjectivity. Therefore, private property is defined as a tripartite relation between subjects with regard to a third real or corporeal product of (human) subjectivity. From there on any relation of private property must have an equal status with any other. Private property can then be defined as the existence of a relation of subjectivity which depends upon the effective exclusion of all other relations of subjectivity. These relations of subjectivity express a package of human attributes and need not reference actual human subjects but can include non-human forms. Although it must be remembered that such apparent versatility depends upon these respective actors being viewed as essential subjects. In this respect Kelsen's work is pertinent to the issue involved especially where he analyses the concept of a legal person. He defines the legal person as follows: "The legal person is not a separate entity besides its' rights and duties, but only their personified unity or—since duties and rights are legal norms—the personified unity of a set of legal norms" (Kelsen, 1945, p. 93) and "The person exists only insofar as he 'has' duties and rights; apart from them the person has no existence whatsoever" (Kelsen, 1945, p. 94). The person is merely the locus or the bearer of rights and duties. Therefore, neither the physical person nor the juristic person is a human being, for this latter concept belongs to biology rather than law. Accordingly, the idea of a prior-subject, an original human being or labouring subject designed to ground the relation of private property and put it beyond man made law, is an evident absurdity. It follows that there is no logical reason why the so called antithesis between natural and fictive persons should persist within law. Furthermore, there is no reason why the subject in question must be a prior-proprietal subject or an epistemological-ontological point that is given to legal discourse (Hirst, 1979). The concept of legal ownership is constructed within legal theory and is not dependent upon the prior existence of economic subjects. There is no necessary reason why the subject of private property must reduce to a pre-given economic subject since it is the legal view and justification of private property rights which establishes the centrality of the subject, however conceived. It is argued, therefore, that this is the way in which law conceives of ownership and not that ownership takes this form because of the prior existence of economic subjects and their role in exchange. Indeed, we shall see below how the logic of philosophical anthropology is both incomplete in itself and inadequate to a proper analysis of ownership.

The basic requirements of a philosophical anthropology of the subject, man, lead on, quite naturally, to the various manifestations of its influence—namely the distortion induced by the structures of Subject-Predicate-Object. Of particular concern here is the manner in which philosophical anthropology impinges on the concept of ownership and the consequences that follow for a general theory of ownership that rests on an implicit philosophical anthropology.

It has been suggested that the concept of private property is characterized by a more or less implicit philosophical anthropology and that the generality of a theory of ownership, dependent upon such a concept, is unnecessarily limited and even a little distorted. But how is the concept of private property imbued with philosophical anthropology and why does this induce a necessary inadequacy? As we have seen, philosophical anthropology inheres in the concept of private property by virtue of the existence of a subject and object of property and the definition of private property as the relation between the two of them. This relation is based on the reification of the essential attributes of the subject. Thus the structure of Subject-Predicate-Object ensures the inherence of philosophical anthropology in the concept of private property. This can be demonstrated quite easily since positivist and common law codes each reinforce the definition of private property as a relation between a person and a thing. The relation is sustained whether private property is defined in terms of a person's absolute power of disposal over a thing; a person's power of exclusion of others from, or a denial of their access to, a thing or, finally, as the empirical specification of unwarranted encroachments on a person's relation to a thing. Even when the relation between a person and a thing is not directly evident, as for instance in the last two (which are often defined as relations between persons), the relation between subject and object is still implied and directly sustained in all three definitions of private property. The central terms of the definition of private property person, thing and relation are thereby established. But what is it that enables the distribution of material reality to be effected in this particular way, as between persons and things? The answer provides us with the first of two particular dependencies of private property with respect to philosophical anthropology.

First of all, the definition of private property as a relation between a person and a thing can only be made on the grounds that persons and things are in fact separate. Private property, therefore, presupposes the prior separation of persons and things, a separation which is supplied by, or achieved within, philosophical anthropology. Thus, the general separation of the subject from his essence and its relocation in an alien object, directly sustains the definition of private property as a relation between a person and a thing. Furthermore, the actual incidence of a legal intervention, which in this case takes the form of the private property relation, is a necessary consequence of the separation of material reality into persons and things, subjects and objects. On this basis alone there exists a profound continuity between philosophical anthropology and the concept of private property. Although if this were all that connected the two then philosophical anthropology would be no more than an abstract condition of defining private property in a particular way and the connection between them would be purely formal—the one acting as the premise of the other. However, private property relies on philosophical anthropology in a more fundamental and immediate sense.

The second concrete dependence of the concept of private property on philosophical anthropology concerns the way in which the actual definition of private property, together with its continued exposition within law, implicitly references the Subject-Predicate-Object structure. This means that the structure of Subject-Predicate-Object is used to establish the ensuing relation between a person and a thing as the all important aspect of private property, as its most developed and articulate form. This is achieved in the following manner. Two basic alternatives are presented to a concept of private property defined as the relation between a person and a thing. It can be argued, first of all, that the relation of persons and things establishes man's domination of the material world. Since the material world is only an extension of his subjective will, man is an absolute constitutive subject. The crucial point being that this dominance is achieved precisely because of man's privileged relation to the material world, he is related to it through the private property relation. Alternatively, the opposite position can be put forward namely, that the external world of objects indexes or interpolates human beings as its agents. In this case the private property relation constitutes the essence of subjectivity and man is its (passive) object. For reasons that will become apparent both of these alternatives are not without problems. Very briefly, whilst the first collapses on the basis that it is hopelessly idealistic, the second invests private property with a will of its own with the result that private property is at once the subject and the guarantor of individual rights.

Contingent upon these specific inadequacies law may attempt an escape route via the notion of the relation as the fundamental concept with which to grasp private property. For example, it is often reiterated that private property is an exclusive individual right in or to some thing and thus represents a privileged relation of the subject to a particular object or else a relation of exclusion of other, would be, proprietors. Assuming this to be a solution, law proceeds to compound the influence of philosophical anthropology and, therefore, the real locus of the inadequacy of private property, by reifying the attributes of man in the abstract specification of the relation of private property—the notion of property rights. At a stroke law fulfills the logic of the structure—(Subject-Predicate-Object) and thereby reinforces, rather than escapes, the problems induced by an implicit philosophical anthropology.

The Corporation and Private Property

The way in which the concept of ownership and in particular that of private property is able to encompass a changed set of socioeconomic relations is central to the issue of legal regulation of corporate affairs and, more especially, to the control of monopoly. For the most part the question is normally asked in two alternative ways. How does the concept of juridic property alter to accommodate a change in economic structure or else how does it manage to stay the same and still adequately express, sanction or structure the changed economic relations? The prior question of whether it is appropriate to view legal and economic relations in such a way is normally absent from any discussion. For example, it is widely assumed that the relations of production characteristic of *laissez-faire* and corporate economies are quite markedly distinct and that the concept of private property is more at home with *laissez-faire* relationships. Depending upon the particular formulation, private property is able to cope with the change or else is hopelessly overwhelmed by it. Alternatively, the change in factual property may engender a corresponding alteration in juridic relations of property. For example, Winkler appears to see the possibility of the corporate economy, or rather 'corporatism', as the harbinger of a distinct corporate law (Winkler, 1976). Pashukanis sets out the elements of a corporate form of law which is in tune with a changed set of relations of production. The partial suppression of commodity exchange which occurs between components of the corporate empire has profound effects on the form of law supposedly based on commodity exchange. This follows since a separation between enterprises is necessary for exchange to proceed in commodity terms. Insofar as this separation is limited—through the growth of conglomerate forms of enterprise—then so too must the notion of equivalence in law be subject to substantial modification, if not actual redundancy. On the other hand Cutler *et al.* (1978) seem to argue that there is no contradiction between the private property form and relations of corporate production providing that the corporation is seen as the agent of possession, providing that it absorbs all the functions of property through the exclusive possession of the means of production. Likewise Renner views it as a change in function, and Tay as an alteration of type. Any conception which sees the compatibility of legal and economic relations in these terms is limited to a finite range of alternatives none of which is any more successful than any other in addressing the complexity of corporate relations. Arguably, this sort of perspective is inherent in a particular way of regarding the relationship between law and economy although its more obvious failings may be revealed in the relationship between the corporation and private property.

We have seen already the conditions under which philosophical anthropology inheres in the concept of private property. What, however, are the limiting and distorting effects induced in a theory of ownership by the inherence of philosophical anthropology in private property? The objections to the philosophical anthropology of the subject, man, are simple. Any theory of ownership informed by an implicit or explicit philosophical anthropology must inevitably be subject to at least two substantive criticisms: firstly, it is inadequate in the face of ownership which is not reducible to an essential subject of a given property right or object. For example, Cutler *et al.* (1977) make the point that religious and corporate enterprises cannot be grasped as subjects in any precise sense. In this it is the problematic of the subject which prevents the proper theorization of corporate forms of ownership and which, therefore, constitutes an obstacle to a truly general typology of ownership. Private property is inadequate because the corporation is not a subject in the traditional sense. Secondly, in equating the essence of man with the products created, exchanged and owned, philosophical anthropology is in a position to cast the corporation in the role of gatekeeper of man's essential attributes. These corporate relations become but different manifestations of the predicates of an essential man and the corporation is able to assume the mantle of the benign subject. Big business comes alive. Therefore, the corporation can be viewed as a subject providing the corporation is regarded as an aggregate of subjective attributes. Therefore, not only is the concept of private property inadequate to specific sorts of social arrangements but it can only approach anything like an adequate portrayal of such relations by distorting the corporation and calling it a subject.

To say that the corporation is a subject is the logical result of the inherence of philosophical anthropology in the concept of private property and the recognition of the central position occupied by private property within a theory of ownership unfolded under the tutelage of legal discourse. But what does it mean to specify the corporation as a subject and what implications follow? Any attempt to grasp the corporation within the concept of private property, through the specification of the corporation as an equivalent subject or indeed as a constellation of human attributes isolated and fixed by the concept of divisible rights in private property, is bound to be inadequate. The attempt is futile because it is impossible to describe possession, control and title by reference to a corporate subject or, for that matter, in terms of a series of human attributes parcelled up as correlates of divisible rights. Furthermore, if this position is held consistently then the corporate subject ends up, in one way or another, as the modern equivalent of the entrepreneurial capitalist. In this formulation the corporation is endowed with a whole series of human attributes and motivations which enable it to be present, in person, on the political and economic stage. Quite simply and unashamedly the corporation is equated with the human essence either as the human essence itself or as the summation of the separate attributes of human essences. Paradoxically, this position is adopted by, amongst others, Cutler *et al.* (1977), who would appear to see no problem in accommodating the corporation within law providing it is seen as a legal subject, and by Frank Pearce (1976), who sees the corporation as the purveyor of human emotions and political sensibilities, big business wanted this, achieved that and resisted the other. To be sure, Cutler *et al.* quite clearly argue that agents should not be seen in terms of possessing universal attributes. For example, they argue that there is no reason why agents need be subjects. But if legal recognition is a condition of existence, of capitalist economic agents, and given that this legal recognition entails the existence of subjects then the agent reappears in the guise of a subject. There is no other option. For example, they claim that "The category of agents capable of operating as a capitalist is a function of the legal system of the social formation in question" (1977, p. 276). Accordingly, the category of capitalist agent is inevitably clothed with the mantle of subjectivity.

The point can be made, however, that law should have little difficulty in construing the corporation as a legal person because it is not necessary to reduce the corporation to the status of an actual human being endowed with human capacities. For example, Kelsen (1945) states the important fact that the corporation is a legal entity which only exists by courtesy of its statute. Moreover, once established the corporation can be said to act in one of two ways: either by imputing human actions to the corporation viewed as a legal person or by establishing the partial legal order which designates human beings as organs of the corporate person. Therefore, Kelsen's statement that only the behaviour of human beings can be regulated by a legal order is circumvented by arguing that duties and rights are represented indirectly to human beings via a partial legal order—a corporate charter or statute. In effect the corporation mediates between human beings and a National legal order.

Kelsen's portrait of the legal person would appear to confirm the way in which law typically construes the corporation by reference to a double standard of responsibility—collective and individual. Kelsen argues that "The attribution of human behaviour determined by the legal order to a community constituted by this same order, is not carried out with consistency because it is not always carried out according to the same criterion" (1967, p. 181). As a statement of the confusion which often surrounds the conception of the corporation within law this is particularly appropriate. Kelsen does not escape the dilemma entirely for he also equivocates before emphasizing the centrality of human beings and the way in which the corporation mediates their rights and duties. Whether the corporation is best viewed as an aggregate of rights and duties pertaining to actual human beings or as a legal person in its own right is clearly important. Irrespective of which perspective prevails there is an important limitation encountered by each. As we have seen already law seems to oscillate between characterizing the corporation as a person—in a variety of senses and with a plethora of consequences—or in terms of the actions of its individual human organs. It has been argued here that neither conception is any more successful than the other in ascertaining or accounting for the complexity of corporate relations. Kelsen's notion of the legal person as a 'personified' unity is hardly an adequate mechanism for grasping the profound interrelationships which make up the corporation. The very idea that the corporation can be conceived as a unity is at the heart of the problem irrespective of whether that unity comprises an aggregate of human actions or legal norms. Whilst clearly distinct from the sort of position which views the corporation as an analogue of an actual human being Kelsen's idea of a legal person is no more successful in this regard.

In one way or another the subject is clearly central to the discussion of private property but whilst it is a basic feature this does not mean that it is the guiding principle, nor is it even a necessary feature of any law. Rather, the subject is inherent in a particular type of law. Likewise, whether or not it is constituted within the legal system in question or whether it depends upon a pre-constituted subject of commodity exchange, whilst important, is irrelevant to the presence of the subject within law and its supposed recursive effect upon the category of agents capable of being a capitalist. Of course, it has been argued here that the concept of private property and its corollary, the category of an essentialist subject, are constructed within law by means of a process which fulfills the logic of philosophical anthropology. But this does not alter the fact that the concept of private property does rely upon a category of the subject and that this has a significant effect upon the way in which capitalist agents are perceived within law namely, in terms of subjective attributes, personified unities and so on.

Concluding Remarks

Having established the distinctive features of the incidence of philosophical anthropology with respect to a theory of ownership, and especially the concept of private property, it is perhaps as well to draw them together by way of a summary. In a very basic sense the specific inadequacies encountered are but direct instances of the more general influence of philosophical anthropology. In splitting material reality into subject and object terms, philosophical anthropology constructs the necessity of establishing some sort of relation between them. For example, the notion of essence or predicate contains exactly such a relation. The exact status of subject and object, person and thing, together with the sort of relation which holds between them, is never satisfactorily resolved within philosophical anthropology. Either, the relation tends to reduce to the subject, in which case the object is only the projection, or at most a locus for the absorption, of the subjective (human) will or conversely, the subject is just an appendage of the object. Both positions are only versions of the same Subject-Predicate-Object structure. The first, since it represents the stage whereby the predicate or subjective essence is fixed in an external object, the essence becoming transposed or translated as the object. The second, because it represents the moment at which the object, being in possession of the human essence, becomes the real subject and the human subject is reduced to the status of a dependent object. Although both positions define the parameters of philosophical anthropology they have, as you might expect, different consequences. Whilst the first option introduces a consistent, albeit absurd, idealism the second is, at least in practice, internally incoherent being unable to resolve the ambiguities introduced by reversing subject and object terms. Perhaps it is because a resolution is not forthcoming between the position, status and relation of subject and object terms that the relation itself is reified as the expression of the essential human existence. The notion of the property right is first of all detached from, and subsequently emerges independently of, the subject and object. Quite simply philosophical anthropology forces the displacement of subject and object terms at the same time as it preserves the idea of their relation as an ideal, all-embracing concept which contains the very essence of subjectivity. The reified concept of a property right, therefore, is the logical result of the consistent application of the logic of philosophical anthropology and, more especially, the structure of Subject-Predicate-Object to the theory of ownership. It follows that the abstract notion of rights does not signal a fundamental departure from, or revision of, the logic of philosophical anthropology for the reason that rights are merely postulated on the reified trajectory of the (human) essence.

Just as the two positions which go to define the limits of philosophical anthropology have effects specific to them so too does this last version. In fact the extension of the logic of philosophical anthropology forms the groundswell for the deification of the property right as the unique form of ownership, as the form which guarantees human freedom. The way is then open for any defence of private property to be justified in the name of human liberty. All incursions on private property can be resisted, by whatever means, for the simple reason that private property contains all that is essentially human and, consequently, the very promise of human freedom. This simple equation of the human essence and the private property right, rooted of course in the theoretical structure of philosophical anthropology, forms the mainspring of one of the most virulent political ideologies of our age and, as we shall see, constitutes the lynchpin of anti-monopoly politics.

It has been established that the reification entailed in the notion of private property rights abstracted from their referrents does not escape the logic of philosophical anthropology. Quite the reverse in fact since in reifying private property rights the logic of philosophical anthropology is simply compounded or completed. But what practical consequences follow on from this more articulate position in terms of an analysis of the corporation? To theorize the corporation on the basis of a distinction between rights and material objects, that is, on the premise of their separation under corporate forms of ownership, is to embrace both a vicious circularity and an inescapable inadequacy *vis-à-vis* the corporation. This follows since rights formulated within the ambit of philosophical anthropology always entail subject and object terms and, therefore, they cannot be totally divorced from the (material) objects and the agents of possession to which they refer. For example, whilst it is quite true that law does isolate the attributes of property from each other, largely through the formation of the trust (common law) or the societas (Roman law), it still defines private property as a relation between a (legal) person and some thing. As we have seen this relation depends upon the fact that it contains the essence of subjectivity. Insofar as this is the case then in separating certain of the attributes of property from each other, Anglo-American Common law, for example, is doing no more than separating the attributes of the (human) subject from each other and introducing a cleavage within the concept of thingness (Patterson, 1979). The essence of subjectivity and the essence of thingness remain intact, it is merely the rights which bring them together which are in any way fractured. This means that there are two principal ways in which the corporation can be regarded from the perspective of private property law. First of all, the corporation may be treated as if it were a giant conglomerate subject, embracing all the pertinent attributes of the individual (human) subject acting in concert as a subject. Or, secondly, the corporation may be viewed in terms of a series of relatively discrete manifestations of subjectivity which may or may not correspond to identifiable officers or shareholders of the corporation. Thus, the corporation is seen in terms of a prospectus of rights and duties. That these twin perspectives do in fact resonate within law can be demonstrated by the existence of two distinct forms of responsibility. First of all, the notion of corporate responsibility indexes the idea of a corporate subject as an appropriate locus for such responsibility. Secondly, the existence of individual liability for corporate decisions references the divisibility of the relationship of subjectivity and its distribution within the corporate hierarchy. It will be argued that neither of these formulations is any more successful than the other in accounting for the basic features of the corporation and that this flaw in the portrait of corporate ownership forestalls the effective regulation of corporate affairs. Furthermore, the way in which responsibility is apportioned in different ways to different types of corporate subjects will have a direct bearing upon the discussion of criminal liability and the existence of a substantive offence under the terms of the Sherman Anti-trust Act. Accordingly, the equation of the human essence with the private property relation, however that equation is conceived, demonstrates the extent to which philosophical anthropology is a necessary support of the private property relation and, in addition, a major reason for the inability to satisfactorily accommodate corporate relations of ownership.

4 Toward a Sociological Typology of Ownership

If it is true that the conventional legal view of ownership falls some way short of a realistic appraisal of the complexity of corporate relations, and it is argued here that it does, then an alternative convention is required for at least two basic reasons. First of all, because it should be a requirement of any constructive criticism that an alternative perspective is suggested. Secondly, because it is necessary to measure the inadequacies of the conventional legal account of ownership against the possibility of a more appropriate analysis of ownership. There is another, perhaps more fundamental, reason for the elaboration of such a typology, one which involves the fact that ownership is so very important for an understanding of the anti-monopoly movement. This importance derives from the unacceptable way in which the conventional portrait of ownership realizes the fundamental distinction between *laissez-faire* and corporate forms of ownership. At most law records a change in the function of private property whilst the actual structure of private property remains intact and competent within changed economic circumstances.

In order that the typology is not merely a local description of the differences between two types of ownership it is necessary to examine the *potential* utility of the typology to describe the bare outlines of other sorts of ownership, namely, feudal and soviet relations of ownership. It has been noted already that the description is not exhaustive but it is, none the less, necessary for the more general grounding of the typology. It should be emphasized also that the typology is not supposed to represent an empirical classification of discrete types of ownership, nor to demarcate a rigorous taxonomy, but to indicate instead the more general principles which isolate forms of ownership from each other.

The basic feature of this typology can be stated in terms of what it is not. For example, just as philosophical anthropology makes man the principle of all theory and practice, so too does man, or the human subject, become the principle of all ownership. It is the central role accorded to man in all this which constitutes the criticisms of philosophical anthropology described in Chapter three. But is it enough to object? Or is a more fundamental break with the entire problematic of philosophical anthropology and a crucial revision of the theory of ownership required? The argument presented in the previous chapter suggests that a revision along radically different lines is both important and necessary. This chapter addresses that objective, but firstly, it remains to reiterate and develop the fundamental distinction between a theory of ownership formulated under the auspices of philosophical anthropology, and one outlined within sociological theory. The distinction can be made by the observation that a completely different premise is required for sociology. A premise which does not separate the subject, man, from his essence and unfold a range of possibilities on the basis of that separation but instead analyses the manner in which production is organized and controlled together with the special capacities which first of all lay hold upon and subsequently set in motion the means of production.

Legal and Sociological Concepts of Ownership

Before embarking upon a delimitation of what is meant by a sociological typology of ownership it is perhaps as well to record the basic differences between this perspective and a more conventional legal account of ownership. A sociological typology of ownership is obviously quite distinct from the more normal account of ownership undertaken on the basis of jurisprudential concerns. Although the two sorts of analysis are different there are, nevertheless, some similarities, most notably in the terminology used—title, possession and ownership. These verbal similarities, however, should not hide the very real difference between the two, particularly since it is argued that the legal concept of ownership often stands in the way of an adequate portrait of the corporate relations under discussion. In order to highlight some, but by no means all, of the differences involved a brief discussion of the respective work of A. M. Honoré and Hans Kelsen concerning the concept of ownership will follow in the hope that it will illuminate some of the more important differences between the two sorts of approach. Needless to say space precludes the discussion from being in any sense an exhaustive appraisal of their work.

A. M. Honoré (1961) has produced a most useful summary of the concept of ownership. He describes a full or liberal concept of ownership which is common to all mature legal systems. This full or liberal ownership, whilst not merely a bundle of rights, is in fact an aggregate of legal incidents or, more simply, a list of elements. He argues that whilst the list is standard, the incidents may vary both in content and in scope. The pertinent incidents are as follows: the right to possess, the right to use, the right to manage, the right to income, the right to capital, the right to security, the power of transmissibility, the absence of term, the prohibition of harmful use, liability to execution, and residuary character. Although all eleven incidents are necessary for full or liberal ownership there are, none the less, different degrees of ownership *per se*, certain definite combinations of incidents which fall short of liberal ownership but which go to make up a sort of ownership. This is clearly a distinctive and persuasive analysis of ownership which parallels certain of the arguments entailed by the typology namely, that ownership is to some extent a general concept which admits of discrete components and degrees which vary. There are two differences, however, the first of which is trivial, the second major. First of all, as far as the typology of ownership is concerned there is no absolute form of liberal ownership common to all legal systems or types of civilization. There is no necessary or universal connection in this regard. It is quite true that Honoré does not argue the necessary place of a liberal concept of ownership, simply the universal presence of the concept within mature legal systems, but this does not detract from the validity of the point. The liberal form of ownership is accorded a priority by Honoré which would be denied by the typology. Secondly, whilst the legal incidents that Honoré has in mind are aggregated to form a full or liberal concept of ownership, the typology admits of no *a priori* form of ownership comprising an exhaustive list of pre-formulated incidents. To be sure, Honoré states that one can own 'things' or 'claims' to different degrees depending upon discrete combinations of legal incidents, and indeed there may be more than one owner, but the possible combinations are finite and the degree of ownership depends upon which legal incidents are aggregated and not primarily upon how they are interrelated. Furthermore, the variation in the degree of ownership is only relative to a prior and definitive combination of incidents namely, full or liberal ownership.

The point of elaborating a typology of ownership is to emphasize, first of all, the content of the relations of ownership, how and what sorts of calculations are made and so on, and, secondly, the manner in which these relations are interrelated to form a definite type of ownership. Honoré is more concerned to establish variations upon a theme of liberal ownership, to specify the restrictions upon full ownership, than to examine the existence of radically different types of ownership. Honoré's vision of ownership entails definite consequences and generates considerable problems regarding the ownership of land. For example, Honoré states that in ". . . the early Middle Ages land in England could not plausibly be said to be 'owned' because the standard incidents of which I shall speak were so divided between Lord and tenant that the position of neither presented a sufficient analogy with the paradigm case of owning a thing" (1961, p. 109). Accordingly, the desire to see the liberal concept of ownership as a paradigm case prevents the proper theorization of a distinct type of feudal ownership. The fault is by no means peculiar to Honoré for similar attempts to regard types of ownership or property as simply variations or restrictions upon a single theme of liberal ownership have been made by Alice Tay (1978), C. B. MacPherson (1975) and Pashukanis (1978).

The main purpose of this exercise is not to criticize Honoré's theory of ownership but merely to describe the basic differences between this sort of theory and a typology of ownership. As we have seen these differences are considerable. There is a further sense, however, in which Honoré's description of ownership is relevant to the issues under discussion. For example, in describing the way in which law can theorize upon different types of ownership and does provide a more or less adequate context for the elaboration of the corporate form, Honoré demonstrates that law is not hopelessly overwhelmed by the inexorable growth of *de facto* concentrations of power. The way in which he describes the corporation in terms of a variable collection of material objects and claims is a case in point. Likewise, his definition of title as the conditions of fact which must be fulfilled in order for a person to acquire a claim to a thing is pertinent. The law does attempt to grapple with the reality of the corporation. But it must be emphasized that in order to account for the corporation, the full concept of ownership is fractured into a series of disaggregated incidences. Similarly, the basic relation of private property is also dissected in order to produce an adequate portrait of the corporate form of ownership. The point at issue, therefore, is whether the manner in which these incidents are interrelated, together with an adequate portrait of precisely what it is which is interrelated, is amenable to Honoré's analysis of ownership. In other words it is arguable that the way in which these incidents are interrelated within different types of ownership accounts for the qualitative difference between them. It is not merely a question of a list of legal incidents and their different aggregation, for the manner of aggregation is fundamentally important as is the content of these incidents and their nearly infinite variability. Moreover, Honoré perhaps sums up the basic limitation of a legal theory of ownership, however complex, when he states that: "The final picture is that of a set of related institutions of great complexity which are best studied against the background of the basic model—a single human being owning, in the full liberal sense, a single material thing" (Honoré, 1961, p. 147). It is argued here that attention to such a background obscures the distinct corporate form of ownership and reduces it to a mere distortion of an ideal type of full liberal ownership; a variation upon a single theme rather than a radical departure.

The example of Hans Kelsen on ownership is perhaps more intriguing. Although not exactly putting forward a theory of ownership, he, nevertheless, makes a number of pertinent remarks upon the so-called distinction between the physical person and the juristic person. As we have seen these remarks pertain both to the concept of private property and to the idea of a corporate personality. Insofar as he talks of ownership *per se*, however, he points out that because an individual actually possesses something this does not mean that he is its legal owner; there is a difference between actual possession and ownership (Kelsen, 1955, p. 93). Furthermore, he argues that Pashukanis must in fact have an extra-juridic concept of ownership simply because individuals 'own' goods prior to exchange and thus prior to the co-incident form of legal ownership. Whether or not this is a proper interpretation of Pashukanis' position—and the problem has been attributed above to the dual determination of law, once by its function and once by its expression of a social relation—Kelsen reaches a conclusion which only holds in an extremely limited sense. He concludes that ownership in an organic and extra-juridic sense is a contradiction in terms. Insofar as this is a tautology then Kelsen is correct. But there is no reason why this must follow, providing the concept of ownership is established in a way which is altogether distinct from the juridical concept of ownership. It is argued here that a distinct concept of ownership is established within the parameters of sociological enquiry.

The Typology

To construct a concept of ownership which is adequate to the corporate form of business organization and inclusive of bourgeois, pre-capitalist, and 'post'-capitalist relations of production is no small endeavour. Above all it involves tracing the various elements of ownership and the form of their interrelation. Whilst the various elements are common to all four types of ownership, their degree of isolation, independence, and development varies directly with the form of their articulation. These basic elements, however, are not intended to exhaust all human history but are merely more or less adequate to the four particular types of social relations outlined above. For example, they are not equivalent to Balibar's universal categories of production with all the 'structuralist' difficulties attendant thereof. Nor is it akin to the demarcation of distinct modes of production, the problems of which have been recounted elsewhere (Hindess and Hirst, 1977). Similarly, the relations of ownership are not entirely discrete for they depend upon their more general articulation with their companion relations. Defining the relations in general is to some extent counter-productive since it would appear to belie their status as determinant relations of ownership dependent upon a specific context. Therefore, the relations of possession, title and control can best be described by reference to specific examples rather than overly general features.

The typology has been sketched in outline already. For example, Chapter two set out a concept of ownership comprising three particular elements; elements which are, depending upon the form of their articulation, more or less discrete. These elements are; title, possession and control. The relation of (private) property can be defined as the interrelation of these three elements without reference to the primacy of rights and without introducing the somewhat difficult distinction between rights, subjects and objects. Instead it is their articulation which accounts for the specific forms of ownership associated with private and corporate property and not the coincidence or separation of rights and material objects. It will be argued that this separation of subject and object and their further coincidence in the concept of private property is ultimately facile. What then is the alternative composition of ownership?

The elements, or the components, which in combination define ownership are as discussed below.

Possession

Relations of ownership are bound up with forms of calculation. In this sense the relation of possession is possible only on the basis of some definite type of calculation which divides tasks and re-assembles them into a process or which calculates the relation of labour to the means of production. For example, it is not so much that possession may depend upon Taylorism or scientific management generally but rather it depends instead upon some form of calculation which ensures that possession of the relevant means of production is possible. This calculation may vary from the elementary forms inherent in estate management through those elaborated by Babbage in 1832 to the more sophisticated forms delineated by Taylor, Gilbreth and modern organizational theory. The process is not necessarily developmental but involves some definite form of the organization of the means of production and the relative control of a distinct labour process. Under certain conditions possession can be equated with the technical function of management. The relation of possession, however, is part of the more general form of ownership which indicates that it is relative to other relations of ownership. For example, Cutler *et al.* use a term possession-in-separation which refers to the fact that managers are also separated from the means of production. It is necessary, however, to distinguish between the management structure, which to some extent defines the relation of possession, and the position of individual managers who are separated from, and therefore cannot possess, the means of production. Possession in this sense may refer to a part of the corporate entity, to the management structure or the function of (relative) control of a certain process, and not to the class location of managers as such. Under other social arrangements, the tenant may also retain actual possession because he is able to use his tenancy in a manner determined by himself. Alternatively, the landlord may retain possession. Thus the crucial element of the relationship of possession consists of the strategies and calculations which comprise the use, or actual operation of any particular process of production irrespective of who is the agent of possession. It is true to say that there is some similarity between this concept of possession and the relation of real appropriation developed by Balibar.

Control

This refers to the distribution of the relevant means of production to a particular use. Despite the unfortunate confusion which often attends the word, control is used in its fullest sense for it refers to the more or less absolute power to dispose of the means of production within the relevant confines imposed by other relations of ownership. For example, we shall see that the source of control of the corporation may be vested in a holding company, the corporate executive, or a constellation of minority shareholders. This last source of control is subject to qualifications imposed by the corporate charter although these qualifications are often eroded in practice. Wherever the relation of control is located, it refers ultimately to the power of disposal of the means of production. The more specific direction of the means of production refers to their actual possession. Similarly, the landlord may be in a position to assign and distribute tenancies and, therefore, control them. More importantly, it is the manner in which control is exercised which constitutes it as a social relation of ownership which may overlap other relations of ownership.

Title

Title does not refer only to the formal legal right to a claim upon a company or an estate but depends also upon the sorts of calculations which govern the circulation of legal titles. It may refer to the system of transfer of assets and to the forms of calculation governing the circulation of capital, stocks, shares and so on. For example, insurance companies, stock market expectations, the world climate, scale of returns and so on, are each important elements in the determination of the transfer of liquid assets between corporate enterprises and investors. In a purely nominal sense the corporation does have the formal legal ownership of itself. It is after all a legal agent and retains the title to its physical assets to which the shareholders may have a claim but only under certain specified conditions.

The conventional wisdom would have it that in return for abrogating control over their capital, investors and stockholders receive a right to a portion of some of the benefits which may accrue to the corporation. But title is far more complex than either the formal relationship of investors to their stake or the companies nominal claim to a separate existence would suggest. Rather, title involves the sort of calculations and conditions which govern the more general provision of finance, the socialization of debt, the exchange of guarantees and the constitutional position of shareholders. The law is part and parcel of that process but does not exhaust it in the nominal or functional sense. It is neither a simple condition nor the sole reality of ownership.

Similarly, there are a number of important calculations governing the existence of the formal tenancy agreement. Calculations which involve the conditions and content of rent together with the more general connection of the tenancy to the estate economy. Circulation of tenancy agreements, the division of plots and so on, is part and parcel of the transfer effected between the estate and any given tenancy. To be sure, these calculations may also constitute the effective possession or even actual control of the tenancy on behalf of the estate. But this merely goes to show how the relations of ownership are interconnected in definite ways. For example, title to land or to a tenancy is not simply a formal condition of rent but is bound up directly with the strategies whereby the estate is organized. It constitutes a basic transfer of resources between the tenant and the estate which is located within the more general ownership of the means of production.

Therefore, there is the general relation of 'ownership of/separation from' the means of production; there are the components or the specifications of that relation, possession, control and title; and there is the arrangement of those relations. It is in this last sense that private property may be defined in terms of the specific coincidence or relation of those elements but not as those elements themselves. Therefore, juridic relations do not reduce to economic relations since private property is a relation between these elements, and consequently, is distinct from them as elements. Similarly, the reduction of law to economy and the ensuing charge of economism can be avoided on this basis.

One particular consequence of regarding ownership in this manner is that the problematic antithesis between public and private property and hence the fundamental terms of the debate concerning nationalized versus free market economies are altered. Instead a series of crucial concepts are introduced, the most important being the relations of ownership of the means of production, the manner of separation of direct and indirect producers from the means of production and, the form of articulation of these relations with each other. These concepts obtain whether ownership is conventionally described as public or private although the form of their interrelation may vary accordingly.

Chapter three clearly rejected the utility of a theory of private property bounded by the concepts of rights, persons and things. But if the notion of property rights and, therefore, the unique relation between the subject and object of those rights is rejected then what is the alternative? First of all, there is a definite and general arrangement of the three basic relations of ownership which ensures that the special character of each is modified by its interconnection with the others. Secondly, there are the separate relations of title, possession and control. Each of these relations both connects and separates certain aspects of the relevant means of production. Accordingly, the general form of ownership does not depend upon a unique relation between an essential subject and object because the concepts of ownership and separation refer to relations and not agents or subjects. Furthermore, since ownership is itself articulated according to three different relations then by definition these relations cannot reduce to a unique connection between a subject and an object. Rather the concept of ownership requires the construction of the respective notions of owner and thingness. As we have seen the concept of private property assumes these items as given on the basis of an implicit philosophical anthropology. Ownership and separation then are relations. Each relation—title, possession and control—refers to a distinct form, or relation, of ownership of/separation from the means of production and to a specific form of calculation. It is manifest that each relation, of which ownership in general is a reflexive outcome, does not primarily refer to a subject who owns and an object which is owned because, in the first instance, the form of ownership of/separation from the means of production is the crucial point, not who owns what. Of course in any particular situation the relations of ownership/separation do refer to specific agents and determinate means of production but this is entirely different from specifying an essential subject on one side relating to an object of which it is the unique subject on the other.

Whereas philosophical anthropology makes man the principle of all ownership and hence man is the basis on which all relations of ownership are predicated, it can be argued that the relations of ownership refer, first and foremost, to each other, to the overall form of their articulation and only then to the means of production and their respective agents. The relations of ownership are dependent upon the social context in which they are generated rather than upon any primarily legal conditions of existence. Thus, corporate forms of ownership do not herald the dissolution of ownership into discrete elements independently of their general articulation and private property does not simply dissolve, leaving an anarchic crystallization of autonomous elements of ownership. The corporate form of ownership is a distinct type of ownership rather than a mutation of the private property form. In addition, this concept of ownership facilitates the proper theorization of transformation, not as an inevitable transfer of the means of production into the hands of the workers, but rather as a highly contingent moment bounded by the internal organization of the form of ownership. As such the form of ownership is a crucial determinant, not an inevitable consequence, of the relations of production. This means that the relations of production occupy a central place for a theory of ownership. But these relations should be understood in the widest sense as the social relations of the reproduction of material existence.

To some extent there is a tradition which supports this view and the work of Henri Lefebvre perhaps exemplifies its basic form. For example he makes the point:

> . . . the concept of 'reproduction' of the relations of production . . . occupies a central position, displacing and substituting itself for certain widely held philosophical notions or scientific specialisations such as 'the subject' (whether individual or collective, cartesian or otherwise) 'the object' ('the thing', 'the sign', etc.), 'structure' and 'function' etc. (Lefebvre, 1976, p. 7/8)

This, together with the work of Godelier (1978) on the dissolution of the base/superstructure metaphor seen as a structured interrelation of levels and perhaps the work of Gurvitch (1947) on forms of sociality and even the writings of Elias (1970) go a long way to display the sort of heritage which may sustain the present enterprise.

The point should be reiterated that this analysis is not intended as an exhaustive study of feudal and bourgeois relations of production. The intention is to demonstrate the adequacy of what is presented as a general typology of ownership in relation to pre-corporatist relations of production and, in particular, to what remains the primary article of faith of anti-monopoly movements —private property. Bearing this point in mind it is possible to embark on such a study. The order of presentation will be sequential—feudal, bourgeois, corporate and soviet but this in no way implies a linear succession of discrete modes of production, nor a necessary path of development one to the next. Further, the mere identification of elements should not be seen as the genesis of a process which has, as its goal, either the radical separation of those same elements or, any other end state, for example, an ideal or reformulated concept of bourgeois private property (Macpherson, 1975; Tay, 1978). The mode of analysis neither implies nor admits of any necessity nor any incipient teleological progression. These caveats having been entered it is possible to address the elements and the form of ownership implied by, or contained in, feudal relations of production.

'Feudal' Ownership

The literature on feudalism is notorious for its disagreement over certain key concepts. Even a cursory examination of the area, however, will reveal that some sort of juridic intervention in the economy is considered basic to the definition of feudal relations of production over and against the apparently economic inclination of capitalist relations of production. Exploitation is couched within legal and political forms of hierarchy when feudalism is in focus but these juridic forms are quickly jettisoned in favour of an economic analysis when capitalism comes within the sights. Accordingly, the notion of a juridic intervention seems to be a basic assumption of the literature on feudalism. This assumption implies, however, that relations which can be assigned to the economic level and those which refer to the juridic level belong to different universes. So much is self-evident if the relation between the two is to be seen as an intervention of law/state or political authority with respect to the economy. This conception of law and economy has been examined already. In this case, however, the juridic level is often brought in to the discussion of feudalism in order to act as a supplementary determinant, or explanation, of the silences for which the economic has no answer. For example, land tenure and ground rent are often construed in this way (Cutler, 1975; Hindess and Hirst, 1975).

An example of just such a political intervention can be detected in the work of Marx. Hindess and Hirst (1975) argue that Marx has recourse to the political instances of coercion in order to account for the fact of exploitation under conditions where the direct producer is not separated from the means of production. A political/legal hierarchy is invoked to account for exploitation under feudal relations of production with the corollary that exploitation is no longer defined primarily as an economic concept but is instead heralded as a political concept. It follows that the form in which rent is paid is irrelevant to the characterization of the precise nature of exploitative relations since those relations are fixed by a political or legal instance and thereby remain unaffected by the form in which rent is paid. Quite simply, the relations of exploitation are directly attributed to the authority of the monarch located at the centre of a feudal retinue of lords and based on their means of political, legal and ideological coercion.

Hindess and Hirst are justified in taking exception to the characterization of exploitation in purely political terms. They also try to steer clear of identifying the economic level in purely technical terms and of demarcating the political level as a space or absence delimited and vacated by the economic. In this last respect they clearly disagree with Balibar. Although Hindess and Hirst castigate Marx for the reliance on a political explanation of exploitation under feudal relations of production it seems difficult to envisage exactly how they can avoid postulating a certain primacy of the political/legal hierarchy, albeit a political/legal hierarchy conceived as a condition of existence of feudal relations of production. And yet this is a position which they vigorously uphold and extend in a later collaborative enterprise (Cutler *et al.*, 1977). This position is upheld notwithstanding the fact that there are considerable problems with the separation of determinate relations of production from their conditions of existence and the separate generation of the social practices whereby those conditions of existence are achieved. Furthermore, by its very nature, this separation would tend to reinforce the characterization of determinate relations of production in purely economic and technical terms leaving their political and legal conditions of existence, not out of account, but out of the reckoning as social relations of production. Hindess and Hirst are then in a position to argue that the political/legal conditions of existence can become primary in the characterization of feudal relations of production. A position which they come close to arguing in the specification of title as a fundament of ownership.

The separation of law and economy implied in most analyses of feudalism mirrors the separation of subject and object achieved within philosophical anthropology. As a result the necessity of legal intervention is derived in much the same way for feudalism as it is for private property. The intersection of philosophical anthropology and the respective positions on the law and economy relation have been outlined already. Therefore, it can be argued that the failure to explain feudal relations of production without reference to an external juridic intervention is a necessary consequence of regarding ownership in a particular way. This means that the specification of separate economic and juridic domains and the influence of philosophical anthropology on the concept of ownership are parallel and find their joint expression in, for example, accounts of feudal relations of production and, in particular, ground rent. We have so far examined the more general account of juridic relations within feudalism. It is necessary, however, to concentrate on the issue of ownership *per se*. For example, there is a considerable tradition which seeks either to accommodate corporate relations in terms which suggest a renascent feudalism or else to deploy the corporation as a simple manifestation of bureaucratic modernity. Admittedly, it seems easy enough to draw a rough parallel between the form of ownership encountered in corporate production and that present in feudal production. After all the tenant or serf does possess the means of production in the sense that it is he who occupies, operates, and uses the tenancy. As Patterson (1979) makes clear the serf is capable of being a proprietor. Furthermore, the feudal lord has a title to the general estate and control over the distribution of tenancies. Any similarities, however, end there. The feudal lord retains for himself—or in some instances a delegated functionary—the direct management of the estate. Estate management, therefore, is lodged within the estate of the feudal lord which thereby becomes the locus of the appropriate decision making calculus. Whether the feudal lord directs in person or through a delegated functionary, the form of calculation remains the same. Effective possession, therefore, is retained by the feudal lord. The tenant on the other hand appears to be separated from all three forms of ownership—control, title and possession, although it is quite true that he does retain a degree of actual possession in the sense that he uses the means of production. As a result, possession is fractured due to the manner of its interrelation with control and title.

Whilst the identification of the different relations of ownership appears easy, the isolation of the form of their articulation is more difficult and possibly more important. To reduce one particular arrangement of the elements of ownership to another on the basis of the similar specification of the components themselves, or the formal or positional parallels in their interrelation, is to commit the cardinal error of enforced historical continuity. On the contrary, it is the particular arrangement of the relations of ownership/separation which is the distinctive feature of any productive relations. It follows that the proper analysis of the specificity and interrelation of the elements of ownership/separation depends upon the adequate isolation of the structure of their articulation.

Starting from the concept of the separation of the direct producer from the means of production Hindess and Hirst, argue the existence of a twofold separation:

1. A legal separation of the direct producer from the means of production, a separation which seems to be a function of title seen as a right of exclusion, a prohibition on others from using the means of production and a condition of rent being paid at all.
2. A real separation of the direct producer from the means of production, a separation which is dependent on the form in which rent is paid. It is by means of the form which rent takes that the ". . . landlord is able to control the direct producers by controlling: (i) the whole economy of the land to which he has title; (ii) crucial elements of the means of production and, therefore, of the access to subsistence of the direct producer; and (iii) the reproduction of the direct producers' means of production" (Hindess and Hirst, 1975, p. 236). For Hindess and Hirst, what they term the legal separation induces a first or preliminary separation between those who own land and those who require land and it is this separation which is a condition of existence of the real separation which is in turn clinched through the actual intervention of the landlord in the process of production. Title and the ability to control the distribution of tenancies and the whole economy of the estate, are vested in the landlord. The tenant, therefore, is left with the actual possession—in exchange for rent—of the means of production, with the ability to work and use them. The form in which rent is paid governs the effective separation of the direct producer from the control of the means of production taken as a whole and thereby ensures that control is lodged elsewhere.

For Hindess and Hirst, legal title is the first condition of the separation of direct producers from the land and it is legal title which establishes what estate management can only confirm/extend. In a basic sense, then, control and possession follow on from legal title, they derive from its primacy and its priority. Legal title is pre-eminent and the process of production can only re-establish it in a more sure, more involved manner.

This position is not without its difficulties. Even Hindess and Hirst appear to equivocate on this issue. On the one hand they argue: "Feudal landed property as title, as an enforced right of exclusion, is a sufficient means to bring free men under feudal exploitative relations" (1975, p. 237). Whilst on the other hand they argue that

> The political/legal instance is limited in its intervention to the determination and defence of property rights in land. The subsumption of the direct producer has been derived only in the first instance from the monopoly ownership of land, from the right of exclusion. Subsumption rests on economic control. Legal title does not make a landlord, and landlordship does not guarantee subsumption. We have not derived subsumption from the political/legal subordination of the direct producers to the landlord—FLP and seignorial power are not equivalents. (1975, p. 241)

This apparent conflict can be resolved only by arguing a strict separation between feudal relations of exploitation and their conditions of existence. Yet these conditions of existence are by definition prior conditions of exploitation. In one sense, then, exploitation is derived from legal separation. Even this limited avenue is denied when they introduce what one suspects was supposed all along, the fact that "It is the economic subsumption of the direct producer on which the feudal mode of production rests" (1975, p. 242). Thus economic subsumption appears to generate its own conditions of existence—the legal separation of the direct producer from the means of production—from whence real economic subsumption is derived. This is indeed a strange circularity which perhaps derives from their attempt to render legal specificity within the confines of a mode of production, an attempt which they later admit was misguided but rectify on the basis of what is seen as an unacceptable extension of the notion of conditions of existence.

This particular way of looking at law and legal title within the parameters delimited by the notion of conditions of existence of determinate relations of production cannot account for the distinct forms of interrelation of the basic relations of ownership. This follows because the relatively formal position accorded to law forestalls the analysis of the complex interconnections within definite relations of ownership and marginalizes the role of law by viewing it as a mere condition of existence. It should be noted, however, that there is an evident contradiction between the apparently general primacy of legal title as a condition of existence and the more specific analysis of control argued by Hindess and Hirst. The analysis of control suggests that the primary feature of feudal landed property is the control of the estate. It is possible that this difficulty is a direct consequence of the inadequacy of the concept of conditions of existence. For example, we have seen that the concept of conditions of existence is inadequate to a persuasive analysis of law and economy, for the reason that it relies on the abstract functionality of the conditions of existence of determinate relations of production for their concrete specification. They are functional therefore they are, is the form of argument employed. This inadequacy is sustained in relation to the analysis of feudal relations of production, for what sense does it make to talk of a legal separation in the first place, when land is ultimately held by force and it is the physical dispossession of potential tenants, and the forms of their perpetual dispossession and separation, which is the basis of the real separation of direct producers from the means of production (Poggi, 1978, p. 30). In the context of a proper analysis of the forms of separation of direct producers from the means of production, taken together with the consequent forms of ownership of the means of production, it makes little sense to talk of dispossession or separation worked out primarily as a distinctly legal separation, as a separation achieved by the intervention of a legal apparatus or a separation worked out within distinctly legal relations or at the level of legal discourse. On the contrary, ownership is an internally articulated concept which cannot be grasped if it is dissected according to its legal and economic aspects each seen separately and linked through the functional concept of conditions of existence.

The specific feature of the relations of feudal production is the interrelation of management and control functions, the autonomy or dependence of the relations of possession and control. Accordingly, the tenant retains the actual possession of the means of production although the particular form in which control and possession are articulated ensures that possession is effectively circumscribed through the efficient control of the estate by the landlord. In other words possession is by no means absolute but is instead limited and subordinated by its structured relationship with control.

If possession is defined as the relative control of a certain labour process then quite clearly the landlord is the agent of possession through the very notion of tenancy. Therefore, it is necessary to attribute specific mechanisms to the functions of control and possession. For example, in assigning the means of production to a particular use, the landlord is quite clearly in a position to control the disposition of the means of production and to some extent to control the extension of credit. Similarly, the tenant is able to determine certain aspects of the work process, method, time scale and so on. But the ability to assign the means of production is closely associated with the effective organization of the estate. For example, the form in which rent is paid is a crucial determinant of the ability to assign the means of production to a particular use. As Hindess and Hirst demonstrate, the payment of rent in kind, through labour expended as non-rented or demesne land, achieves two things: first, it directly relates the landlord to the process of production as the agent of coordination of a labour process and, secondly, through the capacity to balance the proportions of rented and non-rented land, he is able to determine the amount of labour expended in lieu of rent and, indirectly, the labour time available for rented land and the tenants conditions of subsistence. Thus the criteria used to assign the means of production affect the tenants possession of the means of production; control and possession are mutually implicated. Further, since the "... landlord can control the reproduction of the direct 'producers' own units of production through the size of the units let, the form of the tenancy and the level of the rent" (Hindess and Hirst, 1975, p. 239). This means that the size of units rented need not necessarily correspond to viable subsistence plots. The landlord is in a position to control the actual process of production through the supply or coordination of the elements of production essential for subsistence but lacking in the original rented package. Control directly impinges on, or establishes the conditions for, effective possession. Likewise the growth of tenanted units can be checked before or if those units reach a position of independence *vis-à-vis* the 'essential' organizational role of the landlord. The landlord is also in a position to control general requirements—water and pasture—together with large scale capital intensive projects—drainage and mills. Both of these give the landlord considerable leverage over the relative control of the production process and hence establish the basis for the effective possession of the means of production. The provision of credit by the landlord serves only to compound and extend the control exercised by the landlord in the process of production since even under the sharecropping system the landlord rather than the tenant controls the choice of crops. As Marglin notes, even nominal independence was of little value since, "Debt was not a business arrangement but subjugation" (Marglin, 1974, p. 44).

As we can see the forms of calculation associated with possession and control are distinct, as forms of calculation, and interrelated in terms of their effects. The components of ownership whilst they retain a formal or positional similarity with respect to feudal, bourgeois and corporate relations of production are altered by the form of their interrelation. This would seem to indicate that the structure of articulation is the important concept with which to grasp the specificity of any form of ownership of the means of production. As a result of the subordination of possession to control, the forms of calculation associated with possession (management) are, in the first instance, relatively limited, referring only to minor or formal decision-making process and, in the second, hedged about by the more general calculus of the control of the estate. Thus, the decision on the assignment of the means of production to specific uses is closely associated with the decision criteria as to how the means of production should be organized. Similarly, it can be argued that under certain conditions title itself is fractured since it is subject to competing determinants. This division of title between two agents does not affect the specification of title as a component of ownership since there is no unique fusion or association of an agent with each element of ownership. The important point is that the basic elements of ownership are present under feudal relations of production and that the form of their arrangement is, as we shall see, distinct from that encountered under bourgeois and corporate relations of production. Each form of ownership can be adequately grasped through the identification of the distinct structure of articulation of the elements of title, control and possession.

Bourgeois Ownership

Feudal ownership has been defined as a specific articulation of three basic relations, title, possession and control. In order to define bourgeois relations of ownership it is necessary, therefore, to describe the different articulation of the relations of ownership involved in the bourgeois form, to detail the changes in the relations themselves, and, finally, to account for the 'emergence' of a distinct type of ownership. This emergence is perhaps inevitably connected with the so-called developmnet of the factory and manufacture in general. In this sense, an examination of the work of Marglin on the emergence of manufacture provides a summary which is both interesting and pertinent. For Marglin argues that:

> The capitalist division of labour . . . was the result of a search not for a technologically superior organisation of work, but for an organisation which guaranteed to the entrepreneur an essential role in the production process, as integrator of the separate efforts of his workers into a marketable product. (Marglin, 1977, p. 34)

This is a remarkably clear statement of the effective reorganization of the relations of ownership and a useful description of the crystallization of the management function. True, there is perhaps a problem with the idea that entrepreneurs insert themselves into the production process, nevertheless, Marglin does confront the basic question of the forms in which ownership is specified. The development of manufacture indicates that, increasingly, the means of production are removed from the direct producers and stand in a position of relative independence of labour. At the same time possession becomes a definite relation of ownership apart from its relative delimitation by control and is predicated upon the direct management of the means of production. The process is twofold for the re-location of possession away from the direct producers, on one side, and away from a direct implication in the forms of calculation specified by control, on the other, defines the essential feature of the bourgeois form of ownership. Whilst the specific relations of title, possession and control can be defined by forms of calculation which become increasingly distinct, the manner of their articulation with each other describes the space for the insertion of an entrepreneur. In one sense the entrepreneur is no more than a locus for the integration of distinct relations of ownership, he is hedged in by discrete forms of calculation. This locus is more commonly understood in terms of the relation of private property. After all the basic unit of *laissez-faire* economics is the entrepreneur backed up by the concept of private property. Accordingly, bourgeois relations of ownership may be analysed by reference to two major, and essentially competing, tendencies. First of all, the respective isolation of possession, title and control and their re-specification as relations. Secondly, the reunification of the relations of ownership in accordance with 'entrepreneurial stewardship' (which amounts to the effective reorganization of these relations).

Each element of ownership does not necessarily become more developed or complex resulting in an inevitable and complete separation of the relations of ownership from each other. This may be an outcome but most assuredly it is not a developmental process. There is no reason in principle why certain elements cannot regress or remain undeveloped, through being subsumed by another dominant relation of ownership. Similarly, technological superiority is not the criterion for innovation, since innovation depends instead upon economic and social institutions and, in particular, on the control of production and the constraints imposed in turn on control. Far from being part of an inexorable progression from a lower to a higher form of production, capitalist technology is dependent upon the form of ownership of the means of production. In other words, forms of ownership are not forged in the white heat of technological change but are instead the basic parameters of technological development. Thus, the form of ownership is not an automatic reflex nor an inevitable outcome of technology.

A measure of the problematic nature of transformation can be seen in the conditions of crystallization of the relation of possession. As Marglin remarks:

> Without specialisation, the capitalist had no essential role to play in the production process . . . Separating the tasks assigned to each workman was the sole means by which the capitalist could, in the days preceeding costly machinery, ensure that he would remain essential to the production process as integrator of these separate operations into a product for which a wide market existed. (Marglin, 1974, p. 38)

For certain groups of workers effective possession was retained. Accordingly the relation of possession had to first of all emerge and be detached from one particular arrangement of the relations of ownership, and then be affirmed in a distinct relation with title and control, in order for a distinct managerial function to exist. 'Emergence' is not a matter of a one-off leap from one structure of ownership to another, neither is it but one moment in the development of private property. Each relation of ownership and each particular arrangement of the component relations is highly contingent. For example,

> The minute specialisation that was the hallmark of the putting-out system only wiped out one of two aspects of workers' control of production: control over the product. Control of the work process, when and how much the worker would exert himself, remained with the worker—until the coming of the factory. (Marglin, 1974, p. 44)

In short the relation of possession has no unique human subject, agent, associate or correlate. It is truly a relation of ownership seen in terms of other relations which affect it in definite ways. Possession refers to the relative direction of a work process which may, depending upon the general structure of ownership, be vested in the direct producer, the manager, the entrepreneur or indeed in any combination of agents, supports or human subjects. There is no one unique functionary corresponding to the relation of possession. Hence there is not a qualitative leap from feudal to bourgeois to corporate relations of production based upon the insertion or demise of a human entrepreneur. Instead a complex process of conflict, struggle, contradiction and tension governs the form of ownership. This element of conflict and struggle ensures that the mode of ownership is transformed in its very expression. In laying hold of the means of production and setting them in motion it establishes, re-establishes and transforms the balance between the constituent components of ownership. Thus possession is a particular form of the relation between direct producers and the means of production and is the outcome of struggle and tension between the relations of ownership. Ownership, and especially the elements of control and possession, is a fundamental moment in, and of, class struggle. Marglin puts this in context: "The key to the success of the factory . . . was the substitution of capitalists' for workers' control of the production process; discipline and supervision could and did reduce costs without being technologically superior" (1974, p. 46).

Factory discipline, then, is part and parcel of the logic of possession of/separation from the means of production. Scientific management and especially Taylorism, is the form of calculus most often associated with effective possession of the means of production and indeed it is a central part of the extension of control over the labour process through the establishment of the logic of work discipline. Identification of the relation of effective possession of the means of production and the managerial calculus that goes along with possession does not amount to an admission of the validity of the managerialist thesis on the separation of ownership and control. Indeed, there are significant differences between this position and the thesis of managerial autonomy.

The conventional response to the managerialist thesis argues that whilst, under a certain arrangement of the relations of production, managers are a professional salaried strata, their economic and business calculations are, nevertheless, informed by the logic of capital accumulation and profit rather than by a unique constellation of managerial goals. For example, optimizing or satisfying are often quoted as surrogate objectives pursued by management even when in direct contravention of the logic of profit maximization. But the real question is not primarily whether managers follow capitalist logic—a logic which ultimately can induce a certain conformity—but rather involves the status of the decisions which managers are called upon to make. Whilst it is quite true that managers may have an important autonomy *vis-à-vis* control and title and, given that this autonomy is based on the different form of calculation which structures possession independently of title and control, this autonomy only applies to a restricted area of decision-making and a specific form or means of calculation. Of course, the degree of autonomy will depend upon the overall articulation of the relations of ownership and, therefore, will vary as between bourgeois and corporate relations of ownership. The important point, however, is that the status of managerial decisions cannot be reduced to that of decisions affecting control. If that were the case then managers would be independent of other agents of ownership. Nor can management be reduced to the aims of capital accumulation and profit since managers are then seen as more or less automatic reflexes of the abstract logic of capitalism and are denied their specific role in the relative control of the labour process. Broadly speaking the first position is argued by managerialism and the second by its opponents. What is common to both positions is that each, in its own way, denies the existence of the relation of possession and, ironically, the existence of a specific managerial structure governing the possession of the means of production. Possession vanishes into the more general logic of control and, therefore, managerialists and anti-managerialists cannot be distinguished on this basis. For example, Ralph Miliband (1973, p. 34) argues that possession and control are but different strategies within an overall 'capitalist' consensus. On the contrary, managers are no more, no less, than a group of supports for specific forms of calculation implied in the concept of possession of the means of production. They can no more be transposed into a position of absolute control than they can be seen as the incarnation of the spirit of capital accumulation and the profit motive. Both positions fail to realize the essential specificity of the relations involved, particularly the relation of possession, and, therefore, the manner in which they are subject to quite definite rather than general interconnections.

Possession emerges as a discrete form of calculation within bourgeois relations of ownership and may or may not describe an entrepreneurial or a delegated capacity. Whether or not the individual capitalist exercises this capacity or puts it out to a specialized functionary, the logic of possession is established as is the particular articulation of possession, title and control around the personage of the entrepreneurial locus. Accordingly, the relation of possession varies in terms of the more general organization of ownership and in particular depends upon the type of ownership in question. For example, we have established that technological change is bound by the particular form of the organization of the means of production, specifically, by the intervention of management with respect to the possession of the means of production and by the forms of calculation, supervision and discipline associated with the logic of possession, the form of ownership delimits the deployment of technology. To quote Marglin ". . . the primary determinant of basic choices with respect to the organisation of production has not been technology—exogenous and inexorable—but the exercise of power-endogenous and resistible" (1974, p. 60).

Thus, bourgeois forms of ownership can be analysed according to two competing tendencies:

1. The respecification of the relations of ownership and, in particular, the

reformulation of the relation of possession based for the first time on a relation of its relative independence *vis-à-vis* control.

2. The consequent location of a place for the entrepreneurial agent as the locus for the intersection of the various relations of ownership.

As we have seen a particular feature of bourgeois relations of ownership is represented by the advent of scientific management. For example, Taylorism, registered, above all else, the articulation of forms of calculation which could ensure that possession of the means of production was finally and completely removed from the direct producer and secreted in a management structure delimited and sustained by forms of calculation and control. In this sense Sohn-Rethel remarks on Taylor's ". . . singleness of purpose in wanting to transfer the whole skill and experience possessed by the craftsmen of metal trades upon the management". This skill and experience thereby became "a possession of the managers to deal with in the interests of capital; they could carve it up, mechanise the subdivisions and even automate it as a whole" (Sohn-Rethel, 1978, p. 153). Thus the separation of the knowledge from the direct producer constituted a basic condition for the effective possession of the means of production by the managerial structure. It was only on the basis of this prior separation that management gained the means to wield technological coercion on the workers through their control of 'the important decisions and planning which vitally affect the plant'. In effect Taylorism delivered the means whereby management could possess the means of production. Although Sohn-Rethel makes a critical error in arguing that scientific management was necessary to ensure the control of capital over production, since he implies that possession is only a means for exercising control rather than a distinct relation of ownership. He appears to miss the point that scientific management represents a level of decision-making and a form of calculus quite distinct from the criteria which inform and delimit the decision-making concerning capital transfer. As we have seen, decision criteria of possession are quite distinct from those associated with the control of the means of production. Scientific management and possession do not just follow on from, or subordinate themselves to, the establishment of economic control. Possession is neither the form of control nor is it the functional means for the exercise of control. Whilst it is true that control and possession are mutually implicated in an overall articulation of ownership they do not reduce to or collapse into each other. In the end the pitfalls of this reduction can only serve to replicate the exceedingly tortuous reiteration of managerialism and anti-mangerialism.

It will be apparent that scientific management is considered as an index of the theoretical articulation of a movement that took place in the interstices of bourgeois and corporate forms of ownership. Possession, as a form of calculation and criterion of ownership, first emerged within bourgeois forms of ownership only to be developed more completely under corporate forms of ownership.

Scientific management is perhaps properly located as a fundamental thrust of transformation as between bourgeois and corporate forms of ownership. Or, to put it more briefly, scientific management overlaps, or is mapped onto both bourgeois and corporate forms of ownership and it is so mapped precisely because of its intimate relation with possession, a relation which first emerges within bourgeois forms of ownership. For example, elements of what has been termed managerialism date back as far as Adam Smith and Babbage. Therefore, the emphasis upon Taylorism is intended only as an example of managerialism rather than a reflex of the actual influence of Taylor *per se*. In any case, we shall see how Taylorism can be aligned with a form of possession which is intermediary with respect to corporate and bourgeois forms of ownership.

Corporate Ownership

Much has been written on the corporation since the classic work of Berle and Means, *The Modern Corporation and Private Property* (1932), but on the whole the discussion has been characterized by an obsession with three basic themes. First of all, the argument, highlighted by Berle and Means in 1932, that capitalism has been attenuated by the separation of ownership and control, has become the centrepiece of any discussion of the nature of 'managerial capitalism'. For the most part this discussion rests upon the identification of distinct managerial goals. Proponents of managerialism maintain that such goals are socially responsible and the corporation is even regarded by some as basically 'soulful'. The important point for this perspective is that managers do not, necessarily, reflect the requirements of profit maximization and finance capitalism and hence modern industrial society is not, essentially, a capitalist social structure. The dispersal of stock ensures that benefits are widely and generously distributed and the crystallization of managerial goals represents the social and responsible character of the corporation. On the other hand, opponents of managerialism argue two things. First, that even if distinct managerial goals exist they are effectively overruled by the basic requirements of finance capital which are realized through a system of interlocking directorates. Managers are thus forced to comply with the logic of capital accumulation. Secondly, it is often argued that the separation of ownership and control is overdrawn and that managers may own a significant amount of stock and in any case manage in the basic interests of capital accumulation. Thus managerial goals are seen to coincide with those of profit maximization. This argument has been examined in some detail already. Accordingly, it need only be reiterated here that both of these perspectives on managerialism reduce, quite inevitably, to a series of sterile platitudes. The discussion degenerates largely because of the incomplete picture of ownership and control which remain, after all, central to the entire dispute.

A second view of the corporation involves the way in which the social and economic functions of the concept of private property have apparently changed in such a way as to facilitate, rather than hinder, the growth of the corporate empire. Committed, more or less, to an instrumentalist conception of law this position starts off from a particular conception of private property and then seeks to describe the use of the private property form by the corporation. For example, this sort of perspective is implicit in the work of Berle and Means and is made quite explicit in a revised introduction by Berle. He argues that "Increased size and domination of the American corporation has automatically split the package of rights and privileges comprising the old conception of property. Specifically, it splits the personality of the individual beneficial owner away from the enterprise manager" (Berle and Means, 1967, p. xix). Thus, whilst Berle correctly notes part of the tendency, namely the separation of beneficial ownership of rights to a share in corporate profits from the (managerial) ability to determine how those profits are generated, the separation takes place on the basis of the private property form. Accordingly, whilst the corporate assets belong to the corporation as a legal entity the beneficial enjoyment of revenue generated in consequence of those assets is seen as a personal right charged upon the corporation. The corporation is fixed in terms of a package of subjective attributes determined by the basic structure of the concept of private property. The legal concept of private property remains intact but its constituent parts are allocated to several different actors. Above all this represents the quite widespread conviction that the basic structure of law and especially private property are unaltered whilst its social function is fundamentally transformed. This sort of perspective has been examined already in the form of a critique of Karl Renner but perhaps it should be emphasized that this particular perspective is an extremely important determinant of the nature and evident failure of anti-trust legislation.

Finally, there is a more or less consistent attempt to view the corporation as an agency, an actor, or a locus of decision-making seen in its own right. To be sure, there is a great deal of variation in the way in which the corporation is portrayed. For example, the corporation may appear as the incarnation of big business or monopoly capital or, perhaps more modestly, the actual corporate enterprise may be seen as an enterprise subject or agent endowed with the capacity to control, organize and distribute the industrial product. In this respect, the idea that the enterprise unit is a locus of decision making calculus (Cutler *et al.*, 1977/8) is subject to quite specific criticism on the grounds that it fails to realise . . . "that effective possession may rest with any actor, individual or collective, and that the enterprise is not necessarily the only collective actor capable of effective possession" (Scott, 1979, p.34). Scott's concept of social actor is perhaps unnecessarily restrictive and is also subject to precisely the same sorts of criticisms levelled at the concept of an enterprise agent, namely that it dissolves all too readily into some form of surrogate subjectivity. To be fair, Cutler *et al.* do realize that the equivalent of effective possession may reside with any actor since they see the category of agents capable of possession as a function of the legal system in question. Thus the legal system sets up particular agents of (economic) possession which may vary as between legal systems. None the less, the criticism of the general privilege accorded to the enterprise unit or agent is well made. Similarly, the concentration of corporate power within a few major corporations has generated the idea of what Holland (1975) calls a 'meso-economic sector'. This sector of the economy thus becomes the all important actor, a kind of ultra-large 'big business' or the essential form, logic or core of monopoly capital. Accordingly, this sector controls the commanding heights of big business and multinational corporations. There again Perlo (1957) argues that there are strong ties, cemented by interlocking directorates, which link financial institutions in an inner circle of coordinated power. The very notion of interlocking directorates assumes, however, that the interlock has a centre, a single locus which provides the basis for the coordination of industrial affairs, and political and social affairs. Furthermore, Galbraith's (1967) concept of the technostructure assumes that there is a predominant feature of the corporate structure which provides the core of the economy and industrial society generally. The idea that there is a single centre of industrial society, a determinative principle, is subject to quite specific criticisms not least because it reduces all forms of sociality, however discrete, to one fundamental essence. But there is a more compelling reason for rejecting this position as a proper conceptualization of corporate affairs. By its very nature the corporate form of ownership is characterized by a radical disjunction between its composite relations and any connections are quite specific and contingent. To the extent that these portraits of the corporate economy attribute a central importance to the corporation as the predominant actor in industrial society or else isolate one single set of social relations as the primary determinant of industrial organization then they each misunderstand the basic structure of the corporation. For example, even though Stone (1975) argues against the personification of the corporation, he argues that the corporations are the important actors in modern society. To be sure, there are considerable differences between the respective adherents, which is not surprising since there is a long tradition which sustains this particular perspective. Indeed many of these bear a more than passing resemblance to the pioneering work of C. Wright Mills (1956). Nevertheless, insofar as they share the idea that there is some form of coherence to corporate relations and that these relations are constituted around a centre, an essential social actor (the power elite, big business, monopoly capital, the meso-economic structure, the technostructure, the corporate essence, the technological imperative and so on) then they are less than adequate representations of corporate relations.

Over and against those perspectives which attribute a pertinent effectivity, even an anthropomorphic nature, to the corporation it is argued here that the corporation is best understood as a distinct articulation of social relations of ownership. The basic structure of these relations has been described already. Under the corporate form, however, they are organized on a radically different basis and their content as social relations is altered quite significantly.

How then shall we define these relations? The concept of control is a difficult one and it has proved virtually impossible to sustain any agreement over what it means. For example, Scott refers to strategic control as the basic parameters within which corporations act, whereas Berle and Means see control as the power to determine the composition of the board of directors and as such it can be vested in a variety of sources, the formal owners, the effective majority or minority of shareholders, management or, finally, the apex of a pyramid of interlocking corporations. Similarly, the concept of control is often used to refer to the power to determine a quite general set of policy objectives (Parmelee and Goldsmith, 1940; Larner, 1970). Also, there is a more or less consistent attempt to draw a cleavage between strategy and operations as distinct types of decision making (De Vroey, 1975; Eisenberg, 1969). Accordingly, the discussion of control is characterized by incomprehension and even incommensurability. Whatever the particular merits of these perspectives there is a general failure to realize that control is essentially a social relation of ownership. Control is often juxtaposed to ownership in the famous dispute relating to the separation of ownership and control. Likewise Scott (1979), following Giddens (1973) and Clement (1975), argues that strategic control is mediated through legal institutions and relations. Control is even seen as a form or a potential which is inherent in other social relations, possession or ownership. For example, Scott (1979) and Berle and Means (1967) adopt this view.

Over and against this sort of interpretation, it is argued that control is not just a sphere or type of decision-making since decisions invariably result in the making, breaking and reorganization of social relations (debtor, creditor, severance, supervision, subcontracting, redeployment and so on). Therefore, control is a social relation which interconnects definite aspects of the social process of production. Accordingly, control is a genuine relation which brings together resources and uses. To some extent it involves what Poulantzas describes as the ability to assign the means of production to a particular use. For corporate ownership control is constituted through a definite form of calculus which equates diverse factors in a sum which reaches far beyond any unique constellation of boardroom personnel and the corporate entity. For example, the decision to invest or conversely not to invest in a particular product or geographical site carries with it the inevitable restructuring of social relations not formally connected with the identifiable corporation with which we are initially concerned. The relationship of control is much more than control of the corporation or even of the corporate empire since it involves a whole range of factors which affect other social processes. We are not so much concerned with which group has control as with how control is executed. That is to say with the way in which decisions are made, the calculations which inform them, their status *vis-à-vis* other sorts of decisions and their consequences for other relations. Accordingly, whether or not control is by a majority or minority of shareholders or whether a corporation is controlled by management, whilst important, is considerably less so than the social relation of control itself, its scope and its content. Similarly, for Scott to argue that there is a transition from personal to impersonal forms of possession and control tells us next to nothing about the social relations of possession and control. To be fair he does draw a distinction between the modes of control, which appear to designate the author of control (minority, majority, management and constellation of interests) and the mechanisms of control, which describe how control is executed. But it is arguable that the distinction is untenable for there is a very real sense in which the way control is exercised is the proper locus of control, it is the very calculations which inform strategic decisions that are at the heart of control. Who is in control is at best an interesting irrelevance.

Insofar as corporate control is concerned we are talking in terms of the criteria by which calculations are made concerning the choice of locations and products for investment, the division of the overall profit and the general objectives concerning the labour force, finance, and so on. It involves what Aglietta (1979) terms the creation of a head office as an agency of coordination. Likewise, possession is the social relation of direction and use of a determinate process of production involving a complex series of calculations and strategies designed to get production moving. Once production is in motion the relation of possession is necessary to keep it moving. As such it may include all forms of direction of the labour process whether it be through strategies of work study, worker representation/control or by more centralized plant management. Similarly, the level to which possession refers may be that of the enterprise unit, the single production unit (Poulantzas, 1975), the factory, the functional department, or a centre of profit (Aglietta, 1979), depending upon the exact form of industrial organization in question and whether it is more conglomerate than corporate.

Title refers to the system of transfers of liquid assets, to the forms of calculation governing the circulation of capital, stocks, shares, loans and so on. For example, insurance companies, stock market expectations, the world market, scale of returns and so on, are each important elements in determining the transfer of liquid assets between enterprises and sources of finance. As a legal entity the corporation has the formal legal ownership of its assets. After all it is a legal agent independent of its shareholders who do not own the company *per se* but merely hold titles to interest or various claims upon liquidation. For example, in return for parting with their money investors and stockholders receive a right to a portion of some of the benefits which may accrue to the corporation. The relation of title is much more than the fragmentation of private property and the distribution of rights to individual investors and to corporations respectively. As a relation of ownership, title is governed by the logic and the forms of calculation which assign and recycle the market for assets. This form of calculation is distinct from the sorts of calculations which comprise possession and ownership. Although it is true to say that they are interrelated in specific ways. For example, the so-called power of large institutions or investors to buy and sell stock makes itself felt as a factor of calculation by management but not as a hydraulic force impinging upon the corporation. What is important is that the issue of legal ownership and legal rights is bound up with the system of transfers of this particular nature. Law is not just a condition of transfer, nor is it something which facilitates the exchange. The very notion of legal title is bound up with the relation of ownership which we call title. In one sense at least, law is the system of transfer. Conversely, title is not exhausted by its legal constitution since the very notion of a relation of ownership requires the operation of a distinct form of calculus which involves the (legal) transfer of money and division of constitutional rights and so on.

In a very basic sense these three relations of ownership are characteristic of the corporate economy. But the way in which they are interrelated may vary considerably. For example, both Poulantzas (1975) and Aglietta (1979) have noted shifts in the structure of corporations. For Poulantzas, the conglomerate form of business has demonstrated a partial reintegration of separate sub-corporations in a more centralized unit of control. Aglietta detects a shift away from functional subdepartments toward more regionally autonomous centres of profit. They both detect different trends but the main point is that the relations of ownership are inherently relations of tension. Thus the forms of calculation characteristic of the particular relations, as well as their overall configuration, are perpetually shifting. There is a persistent tension between the calculations which inform decisions concerning the transfer of assets and those which determine control and possession respectively. One thing is clear, however, irrespective of the exact interconnection of corporate relations of ownership. Both the concentration and centralization of capital are limited, if not impossible, without the development of management capacities and elaborate forms of calculation relating to the control of the enterprise, the direction of the labour process, the provision of finance, the socialization of debt and the conditions governing it and so on. For example, where monopoly is due to the concentration of capital then it is made possible by the crystallization of a definite managerial calculus. As Braverman (1974) points out, the scale of capitalist enterprises was limited by the availability of management capacities. Similarly, the centralization of capital depends upon an elaborate articulation of the relations of possession, control and title, otherwise the enterprise would simply fall apart.

Soviet Relations of Ownership

In terms of the general typology, Soviet relations of ownership can best be described through a consideration of the work of Charles Bettleheim (1976, 1978). Here the author takes great pains to consider the construction and location of what he calls the enterprise or economic subject. In the process, Bettleheim confronts the nature of state property and forms of legal ownership in a manner which is not without its problems. Indeed, Ralph Miliband (1975) makes a forceful criticism of the consequences of Bettleheim's formulation of economic agents in terms of class relations. These features will be outlined in due course. It is necessary, however, to set out the specific continuities between a general typology of ownership and the work of Bettleheim, insofar as it is an example of one aspect of the more general examination of Soviet relations of production.

At an entirely formal level, it is possible to assign the relations of ownership to positions within Soviet relations of production. Quite simply, title, through the concept of state property, would seem to reside with the state, control too, in the form of economic objectives and resource allocation, is secreted within the state structure and possession is located at the level of the individual enterprise or unit of production. As independent forms of calculation, the criteria for allocating funds to the enterprise as a whole are effectively dissolved on the basis that there can be no external (independent) finance, no elaborate calculation of investment decisions based on revenue, and no independent 'rentier' calculus. For example, "with the early nationalisation of the banks and with the cessation of trading in securities (including the prohibition against payment of dividends and interest) private property rights in intangibles were cut off" (Hazard and Shapiro, 1962, part III, p. 5). Instead these calculations are integrated with other internal decisions over resource allocation and those pertaining to the economic plan involving production priorities. Accordingly, the calculations associated with control and title are mutually implicated under Soviet relations of ownership with the corollary that title is a formal relation of ownership rather than a fully articulated form of calculation. Title is emptied of all but its formal status as a relation of ownership. Thus the abolition of legal title would appear to exhaust the commitment to the abolition of private property. But as Bettleheim is at pains to point out ". . . exploitation can be undertaken as much by those who intervene as 'possessors' of the means of production (the managers of the enterprises), as by those who are supposed to 'control' them in the name of state property" (Bettleheim, 1976, p. 93). And Berman makes the point that ". . . the rights of an enterprise are strongly conditioned by plans and directives of its superior organs . . . Thus rights of possession, use and disposition are only a part of a total process of production and distribution carried on under a plan"

(Berman, 1950, p. 62). Therefore, the crucial aspect of ownership appears to depend upon the interrelation of possession and control. These twin relations of ownership become in turn the axes around which competing definitions of class or classless society seem to revolve.

Whether the USSR is a capitalist state, or an intermediary or even a socialist society is often decided by reference to the further question of whether there is a state bourgeoisie in control of the calculations affecting resource allocation and investment decision-making, and whether the agents who possess the means of production or the enterprise units are part of any such bourgeoisie. Although it can be argued that it is the relations of possession and control which are crucial to an analysis of the structure of ownership under Soviet relations of production, the issue of class position appears to dominate the analysis of the nature of Soviet society. Whether Soviet society is defined as classless, however, depends upon the way in which the relations of ownership constitute the ownership of/separation from the means of reprduction of material existence. The form of ownership is indeed fundamental to a discussion of social relations.

Bettleheim addresses the issue of how to characterize Soviet relations via the question of ownership. He argues that, "In the majority of the 'socialist countries' possession of the means of production reverts to the enterprises" (1976, p. 82). Possession is defined here as the ability to control and put in to operation a determinate process of appropriation of nature (real appropriation). So much is in accord with the general typology of ownership. Where Bettleheim would differ is on the question of the enterprise subject. He argues that "When this possession is consolidated by corresponding legal relations, the enterprise is established as a 'legal subject' . . . (and that) . . . consequently, this possession tends to assume the legal aspects of property" (1976, p. 82). Bettleheim appears to assume that economic and legal relations are distinct because the formulation of the enterprise as a legal subject is contingent upon legal recognition. He also seems to conflate the categories of effective possession and the relation of legal title by assuming that together they constitute a unitary relation of private property. To some extent this is conditioned by the fact that Bettleheim is referring to the remnants of a bourgeois legal form active in constituting the enterprise as a legal subject in post-revolutionary society. But this conceptualization of the relations of transitional society also seems to be trapped within the parameters of an implicit philosophical anthropology. For example, the theory of non-correspondence of certain economic relations with legal relations and the non-coincidence of economic and juridic subjects is at the heart of Bettleheim's dilemma on this issue. For as we have seen, to admit of the former is to argue at least two things. First of all, a purely technicist conception of the relations of production and, secondly, the separation of legal and economic relations in order for one to lag behind or fail to correspond with the other. More importantly, Bettleheim regards economic and juridic subjects as separate forms of subjectivity. Bettleheim recognizes this when he states that:

> In fact, when rights of disposal and control are institutionalised in favour of a limited group of producers (. . .) such rights can give rise to the equivalent of a kind of ownership by this limited group, even though, in theory, the means of production over which these rights are exercised are public property. (1978, p. 54)

Bettleheim confirms this when he goes on to discuss the circumstances under which a juridical personality is conferred on an economic subject (Bettleheim, 1978, p.74). This sort of perspective on Soviet enterprises is by no means unique. Indeed, Berman appears to anticipate it in certain key respects. For example, "The Soviet theory since 1936 has been that rights really do exist, and, in particular, that Soviet economic organs have not merely the functions but also the rights of possession, use, and disposition of the property assigned to them. Yet they do not own that property" (Berman, 1950, p. 61). But it has been argued elsewhere that the concept of the subject is basic to philosophical anthropology and, therefore, is inherent in the form of ownership demarcated by the concept of private property. In this way the concept of the subject and private property provide a continuity between economic and juridic subjects. So much so that to even speak of economic and juridic subjects is perhaps a misnomer. This follows for the reason that the existence of an economic subject often connotes the concept of a juridic subject since in practice they are but two expressions of the same subjective essence formulated under the auspices of philosophical anthropology. It should be evident that the question of the coincidence or divergence of economic and legal entities conceived as subjects is an inappropriate question since the use of the concept of a subject ensures a necessary affinity between the legal and the economic.

The specification of economic subjects in the work of Bettleheim, taken together with the notion of an enterprise subject in Cutler *et al.* each, in their own way, betray the reliance on an implicit philosophical anthropology. Consequently a whole series of essentially false problems are inscribed on the agenda. For example, the question of the lag of legal behind economic relations or the problem of whether an effective possession be defined as a private property right are (to say the least) inappropriate questions. For this perspective, all questions of the respective correspondence of law and economy reduce ultimately to the specification of the conditions under which one mode of discourse is translated into another; economic into legal and vice versa. It follows that the crucial issue is not whether enterprise subjects can be inserted within legal forms and accorded a distinct legal status. The formation of the enterprise, and the economic sphere in general, in terms of subjects ensures the coincidence of economic relations with the categories of legal discourse in advance. Therefore, it is not so much that the relations of ownership are analysed according to the existence of economic and legal realms (such that the coincidence of one with the other can become crucial) it is rather that once economic or enterprise subjects are introduced, this immediately indicates that relations of production can be specified in terms of legal discourse. However, the existence of economic and legal discourse sustains the prior division of material reality into economic and legal realms.

Bettleheim's work on Soviet society has been criticized by Ralph Miliband (1975). Miliband correctly notices the tendency within the work of Bettleheim to derive class relations from the relations of ownership in a manner which affords the subsequent necessity of bringing in purely subjective criteria to determine class membership in Soviet society. For instance, Miliband remarks of Bettleheim "What he seems to be suggesting is that, where there exists a division of labour according to which some people, located in the state or party apparatus, exercise a 'directing function' they constitute a 'state bourgeoisie' engaged in 'class struggle' with 'the proletariat'" (1975, p. 62). Bettleheim clearly recognizes the difficulties of reducing all agents bearing directive functions to a common bourgeois class inheritance. But the recognition is made only on the condition of introducing purely subjective criteria involving the purposes or proletarian practices of party cadres within the administrative apparatus. The criterion of class membership is centred on the question of ideological affinity with the proletariat. This is hardly a sufficient basis on which to construct a class map. Indeed, as Miliband notes of the means used to establish proletarian affinity:

> What these proletarian practices are remains unspecified. But the picture presented here is one where some cadres, lodged in one or other apparatus of power are members of the state bourgeoisie; while others, lodged in the same apparatuses of power are not. But this clearly deprives the notion of state bourgeoisie of any but the most arbitrary and subjective meaning. (1975, p. 62)

The problem of class location is a complex one outside the scope of the present formal indication of Soviet relations of ownership. What is important is the fact that the category of the subject, introduced in order to deal with the complexity of economic centres of decision-making and their further interrelation with juridic subjects and state property, surfaces yet again in the analysis of the class location of managers. Once again whenever economic subjects are introduced it is necessary to indicate the particular bearers of that subjectivity, the location of managers in respect of the class map. But the distribution of class relations depends upon the internalization of competing subjectivities—the subjectivity of the economic subject or the subjectivity of proletarian practices. Class location depends upon the ideological affinity of the bearers of different kinds of subjectivity. As a result the economic subject is determined by the subjective aspirations of individual managers who are but discrete incarnations of a somewhat larger subjective essence. It is no less an economic subject for all that.

Analysis of the work of Bettleheim clearly demonstrates the deep-seated reliance on two major themes. They are, first of all, the idea that enterprises can possess the means of production by virtue of their existence as economic subjects. This particular point appears to parallel Scott's argument that "legal forms cannot have effective possession because they cannot act" (Scott, 1979, p. 33), and the corollary that possession is always an attribute of real social groupings or collective actors. Secondly, the idea that law and economy are separate forms of subjectivity such that the law can establish economic units as more effective legal subjects. It should be apparent that each of these themes registers the effect of an implied philosophical anthropology. Indeed the coincidence between these respective themes (induced by the category of the subject) has been alluded to already. This reliance, however, surfaces more directly in terms of the relation of possession. For Bettleheim the mere existence of a directing function is taken as evidence of the emergence of a state bourgeoisie, evidence which is reinforced by the internalization of the subjective standpoint of the enterprise itself by the bearers of that directing function. Agents of a very specific mode of calculation associated with the relation of possession are therefore confused with a very definite class formation—a state bourgeoisie. A form of calculation is held to denote a discrete sphere of subjectivity, a definite personal support or class position. There are obvious parallels here with the thesis of managerialism, a thesis which likewise supplies an independent class standpoint to a category of agents of ownership, a class standpoint that is supplied with appropriate aspirations and particular affinities and which ultimately rests on the voluntary interaction of competing subjectivities. Further, both Bettleheim and the theorists of managerialism manage to conflate the relations of possession and control. For Bettleheim, agents of possession are just as much a part of the state bourgeoisie as agents of control and, in each case, the sole protection against co-optation into the state bourgeoisie is the preservation of proletarian affinity by the subjects involved. It matters little whether it is a question of an agent of possession or control, all that matters is the ideological standpoint and the appropriate innoculation against integration. Likewise managerialism assumes that agents of possession by virtue of their discrete social status exercise crucial decisions affecting the control of the enterprise. In this the exercise of distinct forms of calculation and decision criteria apparently negates the control of the overall allocation of the means of production. It does so because managers have a discrete subjective standpoint and ideological affinity all of their own, moreover, they are able to achieve this independence because their control is crucial.

This section on Soviet relations of ownership has argued the need to reject all vestiges of philosophical anthropology. The category of the subject, together with the pre-emptive separation of law and economy have specific consequences for any theory of ownership. These consequences are far from abstract since they affect the way in which the social relations of society are confronted. Furthermore, the very possibility of socialist relations depends, in a direct sense, on what it means to own the means of reproduction of material existence. Similarly, the problem of transition from one form of social arrangements to another is dependent upon the form of ownership. This argument has an immediate impact on the very question of anti-monopoly law and, by analogy, upon the analysis of Soviet relations.

Conclusion

The typology highlights the form of ownership as the crucial concept with which to grasp the distinctive features of social relations. The form of ownership is internally articulated and discontinuously ordered rather than essentially uniform and engaged in empirically diverse contexts. It is, therefore, the lynchpin for a proper understanding of the pertinent differences between, for example, entrepreneurial and monopoly capital or between private and corporate property. Insofar as anti-monopoly law is forged on the basis of the reaffirmation of private forms of ownership and *laissez-faire* competition, over and against corporate forms of ownership, then it becomes evident that the form of ownership is at once crucial to the characterization of the anti-monopoly movement and anti-trust law. Given that the form of corporate ownership is the object of anti-monopoly hostility, its persistence goes a long way toward locating and assessing the effects of the anti-monopoly movement, anti-trust legislation and regulation generally. Thus anti-monopoly law can be analysed according to two criteria:

1. The form of ownership.
2. The problem of transition of one form of ownership to another.

The concept of transition is capable of explaining the essential features of anti-monopoly law, the anti-trust movement and regulatory enterprise and, in its adequate specification, is capable of accounting for the basis and the possibility of a legal intervention in economic affairs. It provides a coherent, rather than eclectic, basis on which to analyse anti-monopoly law, the corporation, private property, the anti-monopoly movement and corporate crime. For example, anti-monopoly law concerns the transformation of the bourgeois form of ownership to the corporate form of ownership and is best theorized on the basis of specific instances of resistance to, or reaffirmation of, one form of ownership rather than another.

It should be clear that several things are attempted:

1. To provide a general theory of ownership which specifies three basic relations of ownership.

2. To examine four distinct forms of the articulation of these basic relations of ownership—bourgeois, corporate, feudal and soviet.
3. In so doing to provide a basis for the proper analysis of the parameters of anti-monopoly law namely, bourgeois and corporate forms of ownership.

It is argued that not only is this the most appropriate way of analysing anti-monopoly law, but that it represents the only way a deeper sense can be rendered to anti-monopoly law.

5 *Anti-trust Legislation*

The purposes of this chapter are twofold. First of all, to demonstrate that legal regulation and administrative agency are viewed as interventions within the economy. This much is upheld in the constitutional separation of powers enshrined in Anglo-American political domains and is seen as vital to the independence of law. Furthermore, the idea that law is separate from economic relations is reaffirmed within various Marxist accounts which all hold law to be independent of economic relations, even though it may be conditioned, influenced or ultimately determined by the structure of the economy. Indeed it is this (relative) independence which is seen to be necessary for the function of law as law. At the same time as law and economy are held to be fundamentally distinct they are also supposed to be firmly interrelated—contract, exchange and proprietal right, facilitate and enable economic production. The separation set out as a cornerstone of bourgeois democracy, then, is undermined from the inside. Nevertheless, it does account for much of the attenuation of the legal/administrative review of corporate relations. Thus, law is excluded from a realistic intervention in corporate forms of ownership because of the marginality imposed upon it by the doctrine of separation. It is restricted to the limited role of intervening in corporate affairs and, consequently, is reduced to policing the margins of corporate crime. Secondly, the structure of legal ownership, and its reiteration in the respective concepts of company law and anti-trust legislation, ensures that corporate forms of ownership escape the grasp of legal sanction. The escape is not unequivocal, but it does leave the general relationships of corporate ownership substantially untouched, whilst redrawing corporate boundaries, sacrificing certain corporate personnel and perhaps denting the corporate persona a little. It is argued that this corporate genuflection before the altar of legal regulation is far from a mere gesture. On the contrary, it is a real concession to criminal sanction and civil remedy: the law does have real effects. Although, in the final analysis, insofar as anti-trust legislation is concerned with the form of ownership, and given that this remains intact after nearly a century of anti-trust law, then anti-trust can only be adjudged a relative failure.

To be fair, anti-trust legislation does have its defenders. For example, Rashid (1960) staunchly defends its effectivity. There is, however, a substantial body of opinion which points to its complete failure, particularly during the period under discussion (Reagan, 1963; Arnold, 1937; Pearce, 1976). Furthermore, it will be argued, in due course, that the anti-monopoly movement was directed at the corporate form of business organization which, by its very longevity, signals a major setback to the realization of the anti-monopoly movement's objectives. It is in this sense that the word 'failure' is used and the full sense of the word is not mitigated by the mere inscription of anti-trust legislation upon the Statute book, nor even by its implementation and use.

The assessment of anti-trust legislation takes place against a background of the implicit contest between competition and monopoly and thus between two relatively distinct types of ownership. Whilst it is quite true that specific articles of anti-trust legislation do not always refer to this contest directly, it will be argued that anti-trust legislation should be understood as part of an overall strategy designed to defend free enterprise against the dangers inherent in monopoly. The underlying theme behind the examination of monopoly, price fixing, market division, rebating and so on, is the ongoing change in the form of ownership and the structure of industrial organization which, in a very real sense, permit the almost infinite permutation of monopolistic forms and, thence, monopolistic practices.

The changing form of ownership is important because the specialization of ownership relations entailed by it means that the market is no longer represented directly in terms of independent entrepreneurial units in the manner espoused by neo-classical economic theory. Rather, the form of ownership plays a large part in the organization of both the internal corporate environment and, in various forms of monopoly, the wider market structure. Furthermore, the strategies by which the corporate form structures and dominates the market for a range of products, and by which agreements with formally separate organizations are entered into with regard to the division of these particular markets, are inseparable from the way in which the corporation is organized. To some extent the monopolistic corporation is insulated from market pressures, but far more important is the way in which the market and the corporate form of ownership actually interpenetrate. From the corporate perspective the market is not an external force, endowed with any number of determinative capacities, but is effectively constructed through a series of discrete calculations characteristic of definite relations of corporate ownership.

A consideration of the form of ownership is basic to the assessment of anti-trust legislation. There are, however, a number of specific issues and dilemmas which characterize anti-trust legislation and which must form part of a general discussion of the changing form of ownership. These particular problems will be addressed as issues internal to the more widespread proliferation of what is sometimes termed anti-trust enterprise: the ongoing controversy and organizational basis which sustains and perpetuates the perhaps uniquely American fascination with anti-trust legislation. Accordingly, the question 'can law regulate economic affairs?' assumes an importance all the more exaggerated for not being asked or, more accurately, for not being pursued with any degree of sustained attention. Not only is this sort of question seldom addressed but rather, because it contains the seeds of a particular weakness inherent in the very idea of a specifically legal regulation of economic affairs, it cannot be asked. It is almost as meaningless as it is crucial, because law is constrained by its role as a formally separate apparatus of regulation. Therefore, to ask the question is to invite a negative response.

Broadly speaking, this chapter maps out the general features of anti-trust legislation outlined during a period of rapid change in the form of industrial ownership. It is not so much concerned with the more contemporary use of law to control pollution or to ensure socially responsible corporations (although these issues are considered) as with the historical development of anti-trust legislation during the last years of the nineteenth and the earlier part of the twentieth centuries. This period is chosen because it highlights in a dramatic way the attempted use of law to control a fundamental change in the form of ownership.

What, then, are the pertinent details concerning the structure of anti-trust law? In 1954 Judge Wyzanski made the following, rather revealing, comment in the course of the United States v. United Shoe Machinery Corporation case:

> In the anti-trust field the courts have been accorded, by common consent, an authority they have in no other branch of enacted law . . . They would not have been given, or allowed to keep, such authority . . . if courts were in the habit of proceeding with the surgical ruthlessness that might commend itself to those seeking absolute assurance that there will be workable competition, and to those aiming at immediate realisation of the social, political, and economic advantages of dispersal of power. (US v. United Shoe Machinery Corporation, 110 F. Supp. 295, 348 (D. Mass. 1953); 347. U.S. 521 (1954)

This comment is intriguing for a variety of reasons, not least because Judge Wyzanski would seem to be suggesting that law is a potentially ferocious weapon against monopoly power, and that this ferocity is kept in check by the reasonableness of juridic interpretation and the fearful anticipation of the political backlash which would attend any really ruthless enforcement. The latter part of this particular interpretation is shared by the so-called revisionist historians, and, in particular, by Pearce (1976) and Kolko (1965), but none the less is flawed in certain very important respects. Amongst other things, this chapter will attempt to demonstrate a number of ways in which this interpretation is defective. First of all, it will be argued that the structure of law is such that it places severe limits on the suitability of anti-trust legislation for its avowed purpose of controlling monopoly, irrespective of whether and how such laws are enforced. Secondly, it will be demonstrated that at certain periods the enforcement of anti-trust legislation has been pursued with surgical ruthlessness, and indeed with some measurable success, but that the central feature of monopoly—the structured interrelationship of markets and enterprise units—remains intact. Finally, it will be suggested that the mechanism which inhibits anti-trust legislation is not primarily self-restraint or fear, still less is it a community of reasonable and like-minded men. Rather, the main reason lies with the essential structure of law and, in particular, the legal conception of ownership. The argument is not that law has no effect whatsoever, for palpably law does have very real effects on economic conduct, but that law is prevented from touching the core of corporate relations of ownership. The suppression of law in this respect occurs for quite specific reasons which pertain to the nature and situation of law, rather than to any exogenous and, therefore, resistible variable. For example, power, purpose and conspiracy are often used to explain the apparent failure of anti-trust legislation but such explanations are wanting in a number of respects.

At its base the issue of anti-trust legislation involves two questions. First of all, is the principle of legal intervention an appropriate means for regulating an economic system based on *laissez-faire* assumptions? That is to say, what is the precise role of law with regard to economic affairs? Secondly, are legal categories and concepts relevant to the regulation of economic conduct? Or, in other words, what is the exact scope of law *vis-à-vis* 'economic' relations?

In the first respect, anti-trust legislation does indeed generate a rather perplexing dilemma. It is responsible for maintaining and defending a free enterprise system based on private entrepreneurial interests, decentralized decision-making and on a legal framework which enables free uninhibited contest. But it is also supposed to intervene in order to maintain this apparently automatic self-regulation of the free enterprise system. Setting limits to free enterprise by legal intervention can then be seen as an unwarranted, even illogical, encroachment on the uninhibited pursuit of free competition. There is, of course, a possible distinction to be made between the role of law, insofar as it may provide a series of enabling provisions for the pursuit of entrepreneurial endeavour and the explicitly interventionist stance of law, in the sense that it sets limits to such endeavour. This distinction will be discussed later. Nevertheless, once it is accepted that anti-trust legislation does involve setting limits to economic endeavour (as it does) rather than merely specifying certain enabling provisions which permit or encourage competition, then at least two interpretations of anti-trust legislation are commonly afforded. Anti-trust legislation is viewed either as a comprehensive charter of economic liberty, preserving free and unfettered competition as the rule of trade or, on the contrary, as a "destructive principle

. . . in irreconcilable opposition to the premises and principles of operation of the free enterprise system" (Petro, 1962).

Law would appear to be presented with considerable difficulties even in thinking about intervening in economic affairs. The problem is easily stated. The paradox faced by anti-trust legislation reduces to the requirement that free competitors are preserved at the same time as the effect of their (free) competition is limited. More precisely, the problem is how to assert free enterprise by statutory forms of regulation and state intervention. To be sure, this paradox has taken up a great deal of attention in the interpretation and contextualization of anti-trust legislation. But there is a very real sense in which it stems from a partial conception of the economic as some sort of self-regulating mechanism, against which legal regulation and government intervention in general can only appear as destructive, even as an anathema, to the adherents of neo-classical economic theory. It is arguable, however, that this paradox is merely a result of regarding the relation between law and economy in a particular way. Accordingly, the distrust of legal regulation and statutory involvement is no more than a corollary of the idea that law intervenes in a self-equilibriating economic sphere. Law and economy are, thus, separate instances, for it is only on this condition that (legal) interference can be seen as the *bête noire* of the sovereign economy. Not only does this particular conception of the relationship between law and economy discount the role of law as a framework which sets up economic actors and enables free enterprise but, more importantly, it supposes that a *laissez-faire* economy can be defined, and indeed operate, in exclusively economic terms and, by analogy, as a predominantly economic reality. On the contrary, it has been demonstrated elsewhere that the legal and the economic cannot be represented as separate instances without generating severe problems of priority. In practice the most serious of these problems concerns the way in which anti-trust legislation is regarded as an interventionist apparatus capable of remedying defects generated within a separate economic sphere. The fact that it is less than successful in this objective is seldom traced to the viability of using law in this way but is, all too often, reduced to the fallibility of individuals or institutions and to the corruption of political control.

There is a widespread conviction that, as part and parcel of the law, anti-trust legislation does have an impact on the conduct of economic affairs. This view persists despite the somewhat chequered history of anti-trust legislation in action. But this is not to say that there is no controversy over exactly what law should or should not do. On the contrary, this issue would appear to preoccupy the majority of commentators on anti-trust legislation. There is, however, a degree of complacency with regard to the issue of whether law can achieve a definable objective, once it is agreed upon. For example, the question which appears to haunt any discussion of anti-trust legislation is not so much whether law can regulate economic relations but, rather, in which direction, to what effect and how far law should regulate economic affairs and business conduct in general. Therefore, the determination of the limits which should be placed upon these assumed powers of legal regulation would seem to displace the prior consideration of whether or not law can regulate economic relations with any measure of success or penetration. Accordingly, law is seen as all powerful and ubiquitous, rather than limited and marginal. It is almost as if the regulation of the regulators takes precedence over the regulation of corporate structure.

Of course, the question 'can law regulate economic affairs?' is perhaps contradictory since law and economy cannot be represented as separate instances with any degree of consistency. But it is a question which must be asked if anti-trust legislation is to have any meaning. Otherwise it is seen as a mere gesture by a cynical congress. Whilst this question should preoccupy any discussion of the legal regulation of monopoly, it does betray a questionable heritage since it implies a discrete realm of social structure inhabited solely by law. Accordingly the general discussion of anti-trust legislation seems to ignore the viability of law as a regulatory agency, but even if the question were to be asked, it would appear to depend upon a specific conception of the nature of law which is at best limited and at worst erroneous.

It has been argued, therefore, that law falters before the objective of regulating corporate relations because of the way in which it is regarded; namely, as a separate institutional form able to review and thence to regulate the conduct of economic affairs. But if law cannot be 'baptized' in this way as a separate instance, how then does it become involved in the conduct of economic exchange and in the form of ownership? It was indicated earlier that a distinction could be drawn between the role of law as a regulatory agency and its integration with other social relations. There is a difference between the sort of legal context required for the operation of economic relations and the restriction and limitation of those relations by forms of legal regulation and administrative agency. Law as an appropriate context and law as a regulatory agency are two very different ways of looking at the nature of law. Whereas the existence of the legal structure of private property may enable the furtherance of corporate business forms, insofar as the same structure characterizes the analysis of corporate ownership inherent in anti-monopoly law, it will be argued that it is far from appropriate to its avowed task of regulation. Accordingly, whilst relations of production can operate and, to some extent, exist through the concepts and relations specified in, for example, company law—when law is raised above the level of its mutual implication with the economic and cast as an instrument of regulation or prohibition quite separate from that which it is designed to regulate—the die is cast. It will become apparent that the very separation of law from corporate forms of ownership appears to haunt anti-trust legislation and, in turn, seems to foreclose the possibility of effective legal regulation of corporate relations. Put simply, there is a vast difference between the corporation using the law and using the law to control the corporation.

This, essentially misplaced, faith in the viability of a discrete agency of legal regulation is amply sustained in the constitutional doctrine of the separation of powers. This faith is misplaced in this particular case because it can be argued that corporate relations can be regulated effectively only at the interface of their operation; at possession, title and control relationships. This may involve a discrete regulatory agency but that agency cannot assume the primary responsibility for such regulation, nor can it be a sufficient means for regulation independently of the primary articulation of ownership relations. Thus, company law could be said to work in terms of corporate relations of production because the operating exigencies mean that the primary responsibility is placed with the relations of possession, control and title, but that a residual role is left for law as a form of adjudication and guarantee for title and contract. If this relationship is reversed, as in anti-trust legislation, then the full contradiction of the fallacy of discreteness is revealed with quite disastrous consequences for regulation. Regulation is then endowed with the primary responsibility for controlling the relations of ownership characteristic of corporate structure; preventing monopoly and forestalling collusion. Law is quite simply unable to accept such responsibility and, for that reason alone, is severely limited as a regulatory agency.

If the issue of the legal regulation of economic affairs imposes limits on the role of anti-trust legislation then the content of the particular concepts characteristic of Anglo-American and European theories of legal ownership further restricts the operation of an inappropriate principle, namely, the legal regulation of economic relations. The way in which law is used is as important as the fact that law is used to regulate economic conduct. Chapter four considered the objection to the idea that the corporation can be regarded as a discrete entity derived by analogy with the human subject and assigned all kinds of human attributes, physical capabilities and acting capacities each inserted within legal forms. This essentially anthropomorphic conception of the corporation would appear to confirm the political prejudice that corporations *per se* are capable of political action. Accordingly, the rather unhappy division between legal and natural persons has further facilitated the assimilation of the corporation as a human subject. As Stone remarks, "... whenever the law spoke, expressly or implicitly, in terms of, 'no person shall ...', that rule was smoothly, if unreflectively, transferred to corporations"; (Stone, 1975, p. 28), a sentiment which has been reiterated elsewhere by Hayek (1949). Indeed, the conflation has proceeded to good effect but with precious little justification. For example, this sort of position not only informs sections of the radical left and extreme right, insofar as they drift into rhetorical tirades against big business (analysing social structure as if it is simply the reflex of corporate aspirations) but, it also circumscribes the legal response to corporate relations. This sort of legal response indicates the way in which anti-trust legislation, and the concept of private property, are bound up together, most notably, in the areas of the corporate boundary, conspiracy and the intentional corporate actor respectively.

The Boundary

The boundary is very important for the legal redress of monopoly power and collusion because it is viewed, at one and the same time, as an earmark of size and as a medium for collusion between separate organizations intent on fixing prices or carving up markets. *Laissez-faire* economic theory supposes that within any given industrial or marketing sector there exist several independent companies engaged in competition with each other on a more or less open market. This conception clearly depends upon these companies being separate from each other both in that they are not legally interconnected through formal legal ownership and in that legally separate companies do not in fact act in concert. Therefore, the boundary between these companies is an important indicator of the extent of competition between them. Whether it refers to the simple existence of a barrier between companies or to its condition—whether it can be breached and so on—the boundary is an important determinant of a monopoly. Therefore, the boundary occupies a central, although perhaps unacknowledged, place in the legal regulation of corporate power. But the concept of the boundary is, to say the least, a very uncertain one evincing as it does, a clear space inhabited exclusively by a single corporate essence.

The conventional legal response to the issue of corporate boundaries consists in regarding them as either legitimately or illegitimately drawn, but the question of whether they are relevant measures is seldom even considered. Thus, Justice Brandeis was able to write extensively on the 'curse of bigness' as if it were easily definable and, in turn, the fundamental aspect of monopoly (Bickel, 1967). Where the concept of the boundary becomes more explicit, it is considered as an element necessary to the definition of parallel response, collusion and price fixing. For example, with one notable exception a boundary is essential for collusion between separate organizations. In this respect, it is often noted that treating collusion more severely than size does much to encourage the proliferation of mergers. Boundaries, then, are important for two reasons. First of all, because they appear to demarcate a proper market size, as if boundaries are crucial in this respect rather than contingent and, secondly, they also define separate spheres of business activity such that collusion is meaningful. It will be argued that the concept of the boundary is less than persuasive as a test of competitive behaviour and free enterprise on both of these counts.

If the concept of the boundary is vitiated in respect of corporate relations of production how then can these relations be adequately described? Attention to relations of ownership means that boundaries are not seen as primary forms of demarcation. Dissolving the relevance of legal or factual boundaries serves to enable the analysis of corporate structure as a fluid, changing form of organization. Accordingly, there is no reason why the corporation need be restricted to empirically definable boundaries. The corporation is defined instead in terms of a series of interlocking relations. Although if the corporation is regarded in this manner can it be specified at all, for surely the result of dissolving the privilege according to the boundary is that the corporation becomes inseparable from society at large. All social existence would seem to be predicated upon a ubiquitous corporate family. There are, then, two principal options for this sort of perspective. Either, social structure is a reflex of corporate organization or else, the corporate form of organization is a sociological *a priori* which informs all aspects of sociality, corporate and non-corporate alike. This last alternative is perhaps implicit in the contemporary discussion of corporatism, which sees a widespread proliferation of the corporate form throughout society in general and, in particular, in the conduct of political and economic relations. These options are clearly unacceptable.

In order to avoid the reduction of social structure to corporate relations of ownership it is necessary to be quite clear on the nature of ownership. Obviously some form of demarcation between social structure and corporate organization is required if the worst excesses of what Poulantzas (1975) has described as anti-monopoly politics are to be avoided: the mobilization of a potentially infinite population of all those disadvantaged in some way by monopolies. The problem of demarcation, along with the spectre of some sort of instantiation of spheres of sociality as levels, must appear as important restraining items on the agenda. It is arguable, however, that denigrating the priority of the boundary, whether as a legitimate mechanism appropriate in itself as a form of regulation, as a vantage point from which to define collusion or, finally, as an empirically or legally given state of affairs, is altogether different from arguing the complete identity of big business and social structure. In principle demarcation is perfectly possible on this basis, but it is part and parcel of the definition of relations of ownership. The corporation does not appear as a single entity characterized by a unique corporate essence or personality. Rather, it is considered as an articulation of relations of ownership. In these terms there is no reason why it needs to be a single entity with identifiable boundaries. It is almost as if the corporation degenerates into a series of more or less discrete relations of ownership. Any identity resides in the configuration of these relations, which need not be equivalent to any easily identifiable corporate entity or personality. For example, the structure of Standard Oil, I.T.T. or General Motors is by no means exhausted by their physical being or their formal specification. On the contrary, the relations of ownership generate a whole series of interrelationships which are at once broad and specific, relating particular aspects of possession, title and control to the more general form of calculation characteristic of the market situation.

On the other hand, the issue of demarcation as such does not necessarily prevent the reduction of social structure to the corporate entity. Even as a separate entity, the corporation can be set loose to inscribe its various interests on formally separate political and social institutions. Social structure can then be viewed in terms of asymmetrical power relations, whereby the corporation comes out on top and the rest is reduced to an appendage of corporate aspirations. Therefore, it is the way in which corporate relations of ownership are distinguished from social structure which is important. The fact that anti-trust legislation is saddled with a particularly rigid conception of the monopolistic corporation as constrained within easily identifiable boundaries, together with a specifically legal conception of the conditions whereby boundaries can be breached—collusion, conspiracy and intent—means that the legal response to monopoly is at best limited.

It is apparent that the corporate form of ownership entails the effective suppression of boundaries as physical obstacles to the pursuit of corporate activity. Furthermore, the corporation implies the devaluation of the subject, together with the essentially limited sphere of action open to it. Notwithstanding the necessary structure of corporate relations, the conventional legal/administrative response is twofold. The first response attempts to limit boundary size by preventing mergers and by dissolving monopolies. For example, the provisions of the 1914 Clayton Act are expressly directed at the objective of forestalling mergers. Section 7 of the Clayton Act prohibited the acquisition of the stock or share capital of one corporation by another, wherever the effect may be substantially to lessen competition or tend to create a monopoly. Originally applying only to the acquisition of the stock of another corporation Section 7 was amended by the 1950 Celler-Kefauver Act to include the assets of any corporation. The legislation was seen as a method for preventing major corporations from emerging as 'trusts' through the acquisition of stock, and later assets, of competing corporations and, thereby, dominating the industry through the devices of a holding company. Whilst the Clayton Act was seemingly clear in this objective, the relative lack of action under Section 7 meant that, to all intents and purposes, mergers went on apace. Likewise, the dissolution of monopolies is often regarded as the ultimate sanction behind the Sherman Act. In practice however, things were rather different. For example, the Attorney-General's Committee was moved to state that in the first 60 years of the Sherman Act's history, the . . . "courts have in only 24 litigated cases entered decrees requiring divorcement, divestiture or dissolution" (United States Department of Justice, AGNCAT, 1955, p. 354). Nevertheless, there were three important cases involving the dissolution of so-called single firm monopolies. These were United

States v. Aluminium Co. of America (1945); United States v. Pullman Co. (1943/47); United States v. United Shoe Machinery Corporation (1953/54).

As well as being constrained in principle, anti-trust legislation was considerably restrained in practice. The important point is that even if these provisions had been strictly enforced then their effect would have been at best marginal and at worst irrelevant. This follows for the reason that the boundary generates an inaccurate picture of corporate relations and, in the remedy of dissolution, an inappropriate redress. The second sort of response is to argue that boundaries should be made impermeable and able to countenance neither collusion nor conspiracy. This sort of response will be discussed in more detail later. It is sufficient to say, at this juncture, that the boundary is seen here as the effective guarantor of truly independent spheres of decision-making.

Both sorts of response to the problem of the trusts view the existence of an effective boundary as significant. Whilst the first heralds the boundary as a factor which can limit the extent of monopolization the second attempts to forestall any breaches in the boundary defences. In some respects, then, the boundary is seen to operate both as an hermetic seal and as a site for the counter offensive against monopolization. To an extent the two objectives contradict one another, for the faith vested in the boundary as an important constraint on monopolization is compromised by the existence of strategies designed to secure the boundary against potential abuse. This is a persistent tension within anti-trust legislation. On one side, there is the abiding faith in, and affirmation of, the boundary principle as the guarantor of truly independent arenas of decision-making and entrepreneurial endeavour, both necessary and sufficient for the existence of free enterprise. On the other, there is the gradual recognition that the mere existence of a boundary *per se*, while necessary, is insufficient as a last frontier of private enterprise, unless there is quite considerable protection from abuse. This means that a blind faith in the capacity of free enterprise to regenerate itself is set against the deeply held suspicion that given half a chance autonomous corporations will be compliant in a conspiracy which threatens their very autonomy. For the latter perspective, it is insufficient to provide a context for, and a limit to, private centres of decision-making, since a far more rigorous regulation of their interaction is required if private enterprise and free competition are to be guaranteed. Both types of general response, however, seem to agree upon the fact that law and economy are interrelated, although they differ over the capacity of privately owned production units to conduct themselves according to the dictates of a free enterprise economy. Sylvester Berki summarizes the difference in terms of a question: "Are we interested in competition as a way of life, stressing the role and freedom of each competitor, or are we interested in obtaining the performance associated in theory with competition, the efficient allocation of resources and the implied rates of relative factor returns" (Berki, 1966). There are then two rather more general links at work behind the legal response to monopoly. The first is between a desire to regulate abuse and the demarcation of a role for quasi-legal or bureaucratic intervention in corporate affairs. The second exists between the provision of a legal context (a set of statutory limitations) and the increased circumspection and formality with which the law tends to regard economic conduct. The distinction is by no means clear-cut and it is necessary to examine in more detail the interrelationship of legal and economic interpretations inherent in anti-trust enterprise. In particular, the argument requires a more detailed examination of the trinity of the major federal laws governing interstate activity: the 1890 Sherman Act, the 1914 Clayton Act and the 1914 Federal Trade Commission Act.

Legal and Economic Interpretations of Anti-trust Legislation

The relation between law and economy is indeed complex. So much would be granted by those intimately bound up with the operation and working potential of anti-trust legislation. Lewis observes that ". . . the Sherman Act . . . certainly lacks something as a process for working out the pattern of an economic order" (1948, p. 211), by which he seems to despair of the ability of the Sherman Act to grasp economic reality and to comprehend economic theory. Again the view that economics is a means of keeping anti-trust law from being wholly irrational (Turner, 1963) appears to invert the pessimism of Lewis whilst at the same time reinforcing the general distribution of reality into discrete academic spheres, law and economics. Lewis and Turner succeed in reaffirming the conventional divorce of theory from practice by arguing that anti-trust legislation does not work in practice, rather than the more pertinent fact that it cannot work in principle. Whilst Lewis addresses the Sherman Act as an impossibly abstract theoretical formula, Turner has more faith in the interjection of economics as a dose of reality. What they each seem to imply is that anti-trust legislation is all well and good as a theoretical principle of free enterprise, as a benchmark of free enterprise and as an apparatus of formal prohibition. When it comes down to the practical regulation of contemporary economic reality, however, things are altogether different. Over and against this sort of interpretation, it is argued here that the nature of anti-trust legislation is such that it cannot be sectioned into theory and practice, that the main reasons for the failure of anti-trust legislation are due, respectively, to the strategic choice of law as the mechanism of regulation and to the conceptual inheritance with which law addresses the corporation. It is a distortion, however, to say that the law capitulates in the face of the practical difficulties of dealing with corporate interrelationships. Indeed, the history of anti-trust legislation is littered with any number of genuine attempts at forestalling anti-competitive behaviour. Rather, anti-trust legislation is vitiated in the very process of attempting to get to grips with corporate relations of ownership: first of all, by the idea that law is in some sense a separate agency of review and regulation and, secondly, by the conceptual equipment which provides the parameters of legal regulation namely, intent, conspiracy and private property.

In one respect the contest between legal and economic interpretations of monopoly marks the transition of anti-trust statute law into the burgeoning of anti-trust enterprise. This means that there is an ongoing attempt to square economic requirements, efficiency, expansion, development and so on, with legal regulation; a continuing process of interpretation of anti-trust legislation, together with the development of bureaucratic forms designed to cope with the institutional complex required for active regulation and intervention, rather than the altogether simpler, because formal, process of prohibition. It is notable that the introduction of essentially economic criteria is made relevant in respect of interpretation under the 'rule of reason', whereas the conventional structure of legal thought is more easily situated in relation to the *per se* doctrine. Thus, the controversy surrounding the introduction of greater flexibility under the guise of the rule of reason designed to assess intent, practices and consequences, rather than monopolization *per se*, perhaps encompasses the translation of law into a regulatory machinery equipped to deal with the inevitability of monopoly and required to mitigate only its worst excesses. Additionally, this particular discussion exposes certain contradictions within the basic structure of anti-trust legislation which are responsible, both for its restriction as an effective agency of regulation and for its frustration as an agency of socioeconomic change.

The historical resonance of this debate is found, specifically, in the dislocation between the general thrust of anti-trust statutes, which affirm competition and their interpretation, which is more often than not concerned with the quality of competition than the actual existence of free competitors. There are, of course, certain exceptions to this quite general trend. For example, in the 1936 Robinson–Patman amendment to section two of the 1914 Clayton Act, the juridical concept of intent is so attenuated as to dissolve entirely into an analysis of the commercial effects of price discrimination (Neale, 1966). At the same time, the amendment was expressly designed to protect the existence of small traders from the ravages of wholesale marketing chains and to insulate individual competitors against the full effects of fierce competition. The political exigencies involved in protecting small business, at all costs, to some extent encouraged such apparent peculiarities and will be discussed in a later chapter.

It is still quite common to describe the Sherman Act, ". . . as a charter of freedom (which) has a generality and adaptability comparable to that found to be desirable in constitutional provisions" (Chief Justice Hughes in Appalachian Coals, Inc. v. United States, 288 U.S. 344, 359-360 (1933)). It is this adaptability which apparently enables it to stand, both as a unique expression of economic liberty, a charter of economic freedom, and as a framework for regulatory agencies. This generality in effect spawns the two sides of anti-trust, providing substance for those who would argue for the prohibition of all manifestations of monopoly (but not necessarily monopoly as such) and for those who merely attempt to reserve the benefits incidental to competition within an overall context of oligopoly.

What, then, is meant by the rule of reason and the *per se* doctrine? Interpretation according to the rule of reason and the *per se* doctrine stem from the generality in the phrasing of the Sherman Act. This provides a choice with regard to the meaning of the concepts monopoly power and monopolizing. Whereas interpretation according to the rule of reason refers to zones of legality/illegality, depending upon whether or not the restraint of trade in question is likely to harm the public interest, the *per se* doctrine renders certain restraints of trade illegal outright, for example, price fixing or monopolization. Therefore, the *per se* doctrine heralds a relatively certain, although perhaps rather formal, prohibition of particular sorts of economic arrangements, whilst the rule of reason ushers in wide discretion as to what constitutes the public interest and competitive performance respectively. There is no easy demarcation of the respective warrants of the *per se* doctrine and the rule of reason because each, in its own way, stems from and claims heritage in the Sherman Act. For example, Louis B. Schwartz argues that the Sherman Act appears to state that all restraint of trade is illegal and, therefore, should be prohibited (United States Department of Justice, 1955, p.391). The courts' interpretation, however, tended to restrict the applicability of this prohibition to undue or unreasonable restraints of trade. This is particularly true of the celebrated Standard Oil and Tobacco cases of 1911. Here, the Standard Oil Company of New Jersey and about 70 other corporations and partnerships had been charged with conspiring in restraint of trade and commerce. This conspiracy stemmed from the original collusion of J. D. Rockefeller, W. Rockefeller and H. Flagler in, or about, the year 1870 and involved a number of practices. For example, rebates preferences and other discriminatory practices in favour of the combination by railroad companies; restraint and monopolization by control of pipe lines and unfair practices against competing pipe lines; contracts with competitors in restraint of trade; unfair methods of competition, such as local price cutting at the points where necessary to suppress competition; espionage of the business of competitors, the operation of bogus independent companies, and payment of rebates in oil; the division of the United States into districts so that competition would be entirely eliminated and so on (221 U.S. 344. 1911).

In 1907 the court decided in favour of the United States and against, respectively, seven individual defendants, Standard Oil (New Jersey), 36 domestic companies and one foreign company. Thus, 38 companies were held to be parties to the combination entered into in 1899 in restraint of trade, which was also held to be in violation of Section 2 of the Sherman Act as an attempt to monopolize. The Supreme Court upheld this decision in 1911 and affirmed considerable relief (divestiture) but, nevertheless, qualified the meaning of Sections 1 and 2 of the Sherman Act. Chief Justice White enunciated the pertinent opinion to the effect that only undue restraints of interstate or foreign trade or commerce are prohibited by Sections 1 and 2 of the Sherman Act. Justice Harlan responded, in a partial dissent, that this presumably meant that the defendants could from then on continue to restrain commerce provided that they were reasonable about it and that they took care to ensure that any such restraint was not undue. The meaning of the Sherman Act was contested within the Supreme Court but the so-called rule of reason, none the less, eventually emerged as the more orthodox interpretation. Likewise the judgement in the USA v. American Tobacco Company affirmed that "only acts, contracts, agreements, or combinations which operate to the prejudice of the public interests by unduly restricting competition, or unduly obstructing the due course of trade, or which, either because of their inherent nature or effect, or because of their evident purpose, injuriously restrain trade, fall within the condemnation of the Sherman Act" (221 U.S. 106. No. 118 (1911) S.3).

For the most part, the decisions of the court in this initial period appeared to demonstrate that certain restrictive practices of large combinations could not be stopped because of a *de facto* interpretation according to the rule of reason. It is often argued accordingly, that the Clayton Act of 1914 was designed with the express intention of making mergers, tying agreements, exclusive dealing and price discrimination illegal *per se*, wherever their effect may be to significantly limit competition. Ostensibly at least, this constituted a shift toward the *per se* doctrine, particularly in view of the quite explicit rejection of widespread economic investigation of circumstance as inappropriate. As Walter Adams wrote:

> The Clayton Act is a prohibitory, not a regulatory statute. By its enactment, Congress did not intend to authorise the courts or the (Federal Trade) Commission to determine whether particular mergers are good or bad or in the public interest. Instead, Congress acted on the presumption that a substantial foreclosure or elimination of competition was in itself a derogation of the public interest. (United States Department of Justice, 1955, p.127/8)

But the Act still left considerable discretion as to what constituted a substantial lessening of competition. Conversely, it has been argued that the effect of the Clayton Act was to lead to a reinterpretation of certain restraints of trade specified in the Sherman Act as illegal *per se.* Agreements to fix or influence prices, divide markets or arrange boycotts fell into this category. Whereas under certain circumstances, mergers could be justified, price fixing was apparently illegal *per se*. Accordingly, A. E. Kahn (1953) has argued that there has always been a double standard in the anti-trust laws, in that restrictive agreements between separate firms are treated more severely than proprietary consolidations enjoying the same and even greater market power. Arnold (1937) has gone further and suggested that anti-trust legislation actually encouraged capital centralization because it led to the replacement of 'soft' combinations (collusion, conspiracy) by 'hard' combinations (concrete mergers).

The history of this period of anti-trust legislation is characterized by a more or less explicit contest regarding the meaning of the relevant Acts. Legal historians have indeed dealt with the stages of this contest in considerable detail. For present purposes, however, it is sufficient to demonstrate that there was some sort of contest between two quite general interpretations. On the one side, there was a general approach which apparently made no reference to any sort of economic *gestalt* and, on the other, an approach which assessed 'intent' in relation to economic performance, efficiency and so on.

In relation to the issue of legal and economic interpretations of anti-trust legislation and, in particular, their respective concepts of monopoly, the work of Eugene Rostow (1959) and E. S. Mason (1957) is especially important. For example, Mason seems to be arguing the conventional thesis that legal and economic interpretations of monopoly and hence of anti-trust legislation are distinct if not wholly incompatible. Whereas law is concerned to establish and prevent specific limitations upon competiton, economics is more likely to address itself to questions of market power and control of the market. In this respect it is significant that, for law, the appropriate antithesis is between monopoly and free competition and, for economics, the relevant distinction is between monopoly and pure competition. Free competition is defined as a situation in which no actual or potential competitor is limited in his action by the agreement or harassing tactics of large rivals. Pure competition, on the other hand, is a state of the market whereby no buyer or seller can unilaterally influence the price of goods bought and sold. As Mason puts it, lawyers are preoccupied with rules whereas economists are addicted to models. The difference is real and it should be remembered that monopoly as such has never been illegal under the terms of anti-trust legislation. On the contrary, law has tended to direct itself at the abuse of market power rather than at market power *per se.* The difference is also pertinent, having a number of specific effects upon the interpretation of anti-trust legislation. These effects will be described later. The difference between legal and economic approaches, however, is much more important than it would first appear, for it underlies the far more basic issue of the purpose of anti-trust legislation. As we shall see legal and economic interpretations of monopoly are often associated with radically different policy objectives.

Why then is Mason's work relevant to the discussion of the nature of anti-trust legislation? He argues that even in its earliest common law days, law was more concerned to establish the existence of a monopoly because of the existence of a conspiracy or due to the exclusion of other competitors. This preference was exercised over and against the idea that monopoly was to be found in the control of the market. For example, Mason states that

> . . . whatever are considered to be the evils resulting from monopoly—enhancement of price, deterioration of product, or the like—a monopolistic situation, or an attempt to monopolise, is evidenced to the courts primarily, if not exclusively, by a limitation of the freedom to compete. The original meaning of monopoly, an exclusion of others from the market by a sovereign dispensation in favour of one seller, has continued to mean exclusion, in the broad sense of restriction of competition . . . [he goes on] . . . there has been a growing tendency to declare every contract between competitors which restricts competition unenforceable and, since the Sherman Act, illegal, whatever the extent of the control made possible by the contract. In the case of mergers the monopoly or attempt to monopolise is discovered primarily in predatory practices designed to hamper the competition of outsiders and not in control of the market. (Mason, 1957, p. 344/5)

Thus, for law, monopoly means the restriction of the rights of others to compete through the use of restrictive or abusive practices. Economics, however, holds monopoly to consist of the simple control of the market. From this simple distinction between the two, Mason goes on to assert the superiority of an economic approach to the problem of monopoly. This superiority depends, in part, upon the implicit suggestion that the market may be controlled in ways which escape legal sanction, although far more important is the way in which such an approach is more effective because it is more selective. A properly constructed economic appraisal would be able to ascertain the real, that is the economic concept of, monopolistic situations. Accordingly, the economic interpretation is clearly counterposed to the legal notion of monopoly on the grounds that economics is superior to law in this respect at least. Whereas law is seen as a blunt instrument, "a standard of evaluation in the judgement of public policy", economics is regarded as a finely tuned tool of analysis (Mason, 1957, p.333).

In order for Mason to argue this superiority he would have to demonstrate that economics is more successful in assessing monopoly than law. Not only does Mason admit that economics is no better than law in this respect but where he does insist upon the inherent superiority of an economic approach the argument is entirely circular: economics is better at regulating monopolistic situations because it has an economic concept of monopoly as 'market power'. Furthermore, this concept of market power is itself equivocal. First of all, Mason openly acknowledges that "As a firm grows, transactions that could conceivably be organised through the market's price mechanism are transferred to the administrative organisation of the firm" (Mason, 1957, p. 22). In other words there is a basic difference between the market, which involves "bargaining transactions among legal equals", and the corporation, which encompasses "managerial or rationing transactions involving the relations between administrative superiors and inferiors", and this difference is eclipsed with the growth of the corporation (Mason, 1957, p. 22). This may be all well and good as a description of how the corporation absorbs some of the functions of the market but what sense does it make to then go on and talk about the market power of particular corporations as if the market and the corporation are separate spheres! Secondly, and this is perhaps a similar point, Mason concedes that . . . "firms are not undifferentiated profit maximising agencies which react to given market situations in ways which are independent of their organisation" (Mason, 1957, p. 62). But if the corporation is a complex administrative unit does this not mean that the very concept of market power is attenuated in one very important respect in that it discounts the organizational apparatus in favour of a neo-classical conception of the market as an arena in which one can be powerful?

Finally, and in a somewhat later article, Mason admits that his distinction between legal and economic interpretations of anti-trust legislation is overdrawn. He recognizes that the degree of market control and business performance in general did influence judges decisions, albeit in ways which remained implicit. He then goes on to argue the far more interesting point that so-called economic criteria have been inserted in legal concepts of monopoly and that these have been extended further to encompass considerations normally associated with an economic approach to the issue. The process is both twofold and ongoing. This particular aspect will be discussed later.

So far the argument has been restricted to a rather technical examination of Mason's preference for economic criteria of control and monopoly. It is necessary to ask, however, whether this is really pertinent to a discussion of anti-trust legislation and whether Mason's preference for an economic approach is at odds with the basic structure of anti-trust legislation? The question is important. For example, if anti-trust legislation were merely an attempt to regulate the economy in terms of efficiency and so on then Mason's point would be well made if a little overstated. But it is argued here that anti-trust legislation cannot be reduced to a regulatory apparatus of this kind without generating serious problems concernng the nature of anti-trust law. It is all very well to argue, from the standpoint of economic policy, that competition is good because of its effects and in spite of its consequences, but this needs to be set against the fact that, historically, anti-trust law views competition as an unqualified good in itself and because it guarantees freedom and democracy.[1] This point is quite basic to the argument that anti-trust legislation was above all else concerned with the actual form of corporate ownership which, under certain conditions, generated monopoly.[2] Monopoly was to some extent a secondary issue compared with the form of ownership involved namely, the trust. Mason, therefore, confuses the objective of anti-trust legislation with one of its so-called tests.

As Mason himself points out, anti-trust legislation was never envisaged as a regulatory device designed to use information relating to price, market share and so on, irrespective of the formal arrangements by which prices were fixed and market share achieved. Monopoly, in the sense which Mason describes it, was not the primary concern of anti-trust law. To treat it as if it were is to wholly misconceive it in terms of a purely technical response to the problem of monopoly as defined by neo-classical economic theory. Accordingly, he is restricted to measuring the benefits which are assumed to attach to the notion of competition coupled with the more or less vague overture to the concept of the public interest defined in an economic sense.

Overall, Mason's work is interesting for the way in which he approaches the subject and for the manner in which he differentiates legal and economic interpretations of anti-trust legislation. In treating monopoly as a purely technical problem amenable to administrative regulation, however, he completely misunderstands the basic structure of anti-trust legislation. He even admits as much in the introduction when he concedes that the growth of the corporate form of organization has "played havoc with the ideals and possibilities of Jeffersonian democracy" and that the "techniques of economic analysis are not particularly relevant" to this problem (Mason, 1957, p. 15). Mason does succeed in elaborating some of the ways in which anti-trust law has evolved from a formal apparatus of prohibition into a mere technical device within a general arsenal of administrative regulation. But this does not detract from the more basic point that such a portrait of anti-trust legislation is out of sorts with its original structure.

In the last resort the particular way of regarding anti-trust law cannot be entirely divorced from the manner in which the free-enterprise economy is justified. After all, the supposed defence of free enterprise is to some extent inseparable from the supposed benefits of that which is being defended. It makes sense, therefore, to examine the question of how the free-enterprise system is justified. E. V. Rostow's work is especially important in this respect primarily for the way in which he emphasizes the link between 'democratic freedom' and free enterprise.

There seem to be two distinct but interconnected ways of justifying the free-enterprise economy. First of all, it may be judged in terms of its efficiency and regarded as relatively, if not absolutely, successful, according to criteria concerning output, prices, wages and so on. Secondly, it can be judged by its capacity to generate or secure democratic liberty. These justifications are sometimes used in tandem and at other times in isolation. For example, Rostow clearly recognizes the importance of the latter sort of justification in the following statement:

> In all its arrangements, American society manifests a preoccupation with the problem of power. Persistently, almost instinctively, its policy is always to

> avoid concentrations of authority as a threat to the possibility of freedom. Capitalism stands with federalism, the separation of powers, the disestablishment of religion, the anti-trust tradition, the autonomy of educational bodies, and the other major articles of the American creed, in expressing a deep suspicion of authority. (Rostow, 1959, p. 43)

Although at the same time he tends to dispute the idea that there is an exclusive relationship between *laissez-faire* capitalism and efficiency when he states that there is no logical reason why the state cannot organize production on an efficient basis. Mason, on the other hand, whilst accepting the importance of justifications from the standpoint of political liberty, seems to discount their force and relegate them to a bygone age of Jeffersonian democracy. Indeed the entire thrust of his work confirms his preoccupation with the former sort of argument from efficiency. As we have seen the difference between the two sorts of justifications is important for a proper analysis of anti-trust legislation.

Whatever the particular merits of economic and judicial interpretations of anti-trust legislation (and the discrete justifications which often underscore them), there is a readily definable difference between primarily legal and essentially administrative forms of regulation. To be sure, anti-trust legislation is administered, and the role of the Federal Trade Commission and the anti-trust division of the department of justice are significant institutional forms of administration, just as administration of the economy may take a legal form. But the important point to recognize is that anti-trust law was primarily and unequivocally wedded to the prevention of specified limitations upon competition which, if left unchecked, would subvert democratic freedom. Therefore, the libertarian justification of free competition clearly and unambiguously underpinned the anti-trust tradition. On the other hand, more contemporary issues of regulation, which derive in part from a particular way of interpreting anti-trust law, take as their point of departure the administrative canon of efficiency. The economy is seen in terms of models which generate certain effects which can be mapped onto the performance of the actual economy in the interest of defining the degree of realization of public goals. Accordingly, whereas anti-trust law was originally concerned with the justification of free competition because it was viewed as a necessary bastion of democratic freedom and individualism, administrative regulation is more concerned with the economic justification of free competition on the grounds of its efficiency in terms of growth, price, opportunity, flexibility and so on. The difference is not absolute in any historical sense for the two ways of looking at anti-trust law have intersected in a number of ways. Indeed it can be argued that there has been a variable relationship between the two in which legal concepts may be qualified by so-called economic criteria and economic considerations inserted into legal doctrines of intent, conspiracy and so on. Nevertheless, the fact that the actual course of the anti-trust tradition meandered between typically legal and economic interpretations does not in the end detract from the argument that the strategic ends of the statute were originally linked indissolubly to questions of political liberty.

An example of the interrelation of legal and economic concepts occurs, for Rostow, in the rigorous inference of intent from economic power irrespective of the practices whereby such power was acquired. His argument is twofold. Not only would such a process of inference serve to achieve at least some of the strategic ends of the Sherman Act but he argues that since a number of landmark decisions in 1948—Paramount, Schine and Griffith—these ends have been achieved (Paramount Pictures v. US, 334 U.S. 131, 1948; Schine Chain Theatres, Inc. v. US, 334 U.S. 110, 1948; US v. Griffith, 334 U.S. 100, 1948). It will be argued later that the issues of power, purpose and parallel response are both difficult and openly contested within the anti-trust tradition and that Rostow's interpretation of the developments in 1948 is at best equivocal. Nevertheless, following the logic outlined by Rostow, if intent could and should be read off from the mere existence of economic power this clearly privileges the evidence pertaining to economic power and especially the market to which that power was supposed to refer. As with Mason's argument, this would entail a considerable shift from the original aims of anti-trust legislation by privileging economic interpretations of monopoly over legal concepts of freedom from interference. More importantly, there is no reason to suppose that this approach would be any more successful in combating monopoly nor the corollary—that law is hampered by its failure to embrace economic tests of monopoly power. For example, it can be argued that a reliance upon economic definitions of the market and market power would provide, in Walter Adam's words, a plethora of escape hatches for there are innumerable ways of defining the relevant market and an infinite number of constructions of economic power.

There is a final sense in which the distinction between economic and legal concepts of monopoly may contain within it some indication of the quite limited role of law in combating monopoly. For, if monopoly, industrial concentration, oligopoly and the like are inevitable, in some way or other, then the very idea that law can limit their growth is facile in the extreme. Of course much depends upon how regulation is looked at. If it is merely an attempt to police the unacceptable effects of modern industrial society—whether these are perceived against a moral backcloth of good business conduct or against an economic model of efficient allocation of resources—then regulation may be possible in the quite limited sense of the word. If, on the other hand, regulation refers to the way in which industrial society is organized and to the elimination of the consequences of such organization upon the possibility of independent democratic and entrepreneurial freedom then in being limited regulation is rendered quite useless. Which sort of regulation is held to inform the strategic ends of anti-trust legislation is basic to any assessment of the viability of such regulation.

It is argued here that the aims of anti-trust legislation were quite specific and involved an attempt to prevent the growth of a form of ownership deemed to be an anathema to democratic society. The pioneers of the anti-monopoly movement and anti-trust legislation were loath in the extreme to recognize the inevitability of the corporate form and yet both Mason and Rostow seem to accept some sort of inevitability of oligopoly or industrial concentration as quite natural, and merely seek to regulate its unacceptable consequences. Their commitment to the idea of inevitability is not entirely unequivocal. For example, there are perhaps three different ways of arguing that the inevitability of 'oligopoly' and so on renders legal regulation ambiguous. In the first and the strongest sense, it can be stated simply that if monopoly is inevitable then controls are useless. It is seldom stated as baldly as this and is usually concealed within some statement referring to monopoly as the logical result of free competition and, therefore, controls can at best mitigate its worst effects. Secondly, as Mason (1959, p. 2) argues, if the corporation is fundamental to social life then to touch it deeply is to disturb fundamental social processes. Therefore, regulation can only be marginal. Not only does this discount the role of history in terms of how the corporation came to be fundamental but it also seems to regard the strategic ends of anti-trust legislation in the future anterior. Thirdly, E. V. Rostow makes the point that criminal convictions cannot restructure industrial society and, therefore, administrative regulation is more appropriate. This point is quite typical of the so-called advocates of 'structural' remedy but they seldom consider that these sorts of remedies involving dissolution or simple reduction in the size of the operating units does not, of itself, destroy the corporate form upon which any restraint of trade or monopoly may depend. Furthermore, Rostow's laudatory review of the history of anti-trust enforcement would leave one to doubt his assertion that it has been a history of relative success. This point will be discussed later.

Over and above the specific problems encountered by each of these arguments concerning the inevitability of some sort of industrial concentration or centralization there is a degree to which they miss the point. For example, insofar as it has been argued here that the issue of monopoly is inseparable from that of ownership then the inevitability of monopoly, such as it is, is indissolubly wedded to the inevitability or otherwise of the corporate form of ownership. But it has been argued that the corporate form of ownership is not an inevitable outgrowth of *laissez-faire* ownership. If this is correct it follows, therefore, that monopoly is not inevitable nor is industrial concentration and so on. If this is the case then any limitations of law cannot depend upon the inevitability of that which it is supposed to control or prevent—monopoly and so on—but must refer to the basic structure of anti-trust legislation.

Mason is clearly unhapppy concerning the thesis of inevitability. For example, he evinces a healthy disdain for the concept of 'monopoly' capitalism and argues against the idea that industrial concentration is increasing. First of all, using figures from 1946 he cites the existence of four million independent business units as a countervailing force both to the argument of inevitable or increasing concentration and to the unbridled extent of corporate power. Secondly, he states that there is no evidence that concentration has been increasing. Clearly the two are separate in that concentration may be inevitable but not increasing nor yet total. It is also unclear who Mason has in mind. Whilst Berle and Means did espouse a notion that industrial concentration was increasing it can be argued that the factual basis of concentration is less important than the organizational strategies by which production is conducted. These strategies may subsume so-called independent business units and subvert their incipient status as a countervailing power without any visible sign of concentration or centralization. The thesis of industrial concentration—whether inevitable, increasing, omnipotent or whatever—is perhaps beside the point. Despite reservations about the direction of industrial concentration. Mason still retains an implicit conception of the inevitability of oligopoly. For example, he recognizes that technical and organizational influences may decree oligopoly and, following Schumpeter, that this may be a necessary condition for an effective technological spur to 'real' competition from new products, processes and so on. Therefore, whilst he denies that concentration has been increasingly inexorable he accepts that some sort of oligopoly is inevitable and even beneficial.

It has been argued in this section that whilst there is a substantial difference between legal and economic interpretations of anti-trust legislation and, more especially, in their respective conceptions of monopoly, the distinction is often overdrawn. It is true that the two may herald different sorts of regulation but the connection with one or other heritage is by no means clear cut. Moreover, it is suggested that any greater emphasis upon primarily economic factors would lead neither to more effective regulation nor would it help to attain the strategic ends of the Sherman Act. Indeed the reverse is the case, for greater attention to economic criteria of monopoly would belie the proper and original purpose of anti-trust law. Finally, it is argued that the major limitation of law in respect of the regulation of monopoly consists in the manner in which law conceives of the corporation. The corporation is not seen as an inevitable outgrowth of *laissez-faire* society, nor is it viewed as a peculiarly economic concept beside which law is hopelessly inadequate. On the contrary, it is the way in which law perceives ownership and the concepts which are utilized to combat certain forms of ownership which are at the root of the problem. Anti-trust law would not be strengthened by a greater interjection of economic forms of measurement, it would merely be diverted from its true aim.

Discretion

There may be a temptation to read the contest between so-called legal and economic interpretations of anti-trust legislation in terms of the infringement of fixed and determinate concepts of law by the wholly alien concept of discretion. Not only is the issue more complex than this reading would allow but there is a sense also in which discretion is inherent in law as such (Pepinsky, 1976). Therefore, discretion would appear to be somewhat limited as a means of distinguishing the respective claims of the rule of reason and the *per se* doctrine. On the contrary, the distinction in fact resides in the sort of criteria by which discretion is exercised rather than in the relevance of discretion itself. For example, the rule of reason makes the entire business history of the defendant a relevant topic for consideration by the court. Likewise, there are an almost infinite number of mitigating factors which may allow considerable latitude: the existence of good/bad intentions behind the restraint of trade, the economic consequences of decreeing divestiture or dissolution on the industry in general, the political, military and imperial importance of the defendant and, the essentially contestible nature of expert economic testimony. All of these items may have a bearing on the eventual outcome according to an interpretation construed in terms of the rule of reason. Insofar as anti-trust legislation is governed by this rule, then anti-monopoly policy would seem to be conducted with a view to preserving the benefits incidental to the existence of free competitors. It is perhaps significant that Eugene Rostow makes the following comment "orienting the law around this central axis—the concept of limitation on competition in defined markets—we conclude that by and large our anti-trust law is adequate to its task" (United States Department of Justice, 1955, p. 389). Any practical assessment of the degree of limitation of competition, therefore, is subject to a number of factors which may be held to mitigate the limitation to a significant degree. For example, the way in which the market is defined may result in the balancing of the limiting effect by other factors incidental to competition; technology, performance, efficiency, purpose and so forth. This much indicates that the rule of reason is clearly associated with regulating the complex equation between the assumed benefits of competition, on one side, and the existence of abuse, on the other. It is a regulatory and administrative response to the "development" of the free enterprise economy.

The sort of discretion which attaches to the *per se* doctrine is altogether different. This doctrine is aimed at the formal prohibition of certain acts or market situations in themselves and would appear to be markedly fixed rather than flexible. Nevertheless, the pre-eminence of the concepts of conspiracy and intent involves a measure of discretion in the attachment of authors to any conspiracy in restraint of trade and to the specific intent to monopolize trade. This is particularly true of the Sherman Act discussed below. The *per se* doctrine may seem to bite much harder on anti-competitive behaviour than does the rule of reason, but the reliance upon essentially legal criteria means that the issue of legal regulation of economic affairs is posed even more starkly.

The Sherman Act

The Sherman Act comprises two basic sections. Section 1 states that every contract, combination in the form of trust or otherwise, or conspiracy in restraint of trade or commerce among the several states, or with foreign nations, is hereby declared to be illegal. Section 2 states that every person who shall monopolize or attempt to monopolize, or combine or conspire with any other person or persons, to monopolize any part of the trade or commerce among the several states, or with foreign nations, shall be deemed guilty of a misdemeanour. Moreover, Section 3 states that, every contract, combination or conspiracy in restraint of trade is illegal in itself and Section 8 makes it clear that person or persons includes corporations and associations. On the face of it this would seem to provide persuasive evidence of a *per se* interpretation of anti-trust legislation. The particular warrant for the encroaching popularity of the rule of reason is to be found in the use of the common law to interpret the underlying meaning of the Sherman Act. This is especially true of the judicial construction of Chief Justice White in the Standard Oil case described above. Although it is equally clear that Section 1 of the Sherman Act still depends upon the concept of conspiracy and that Section 2 points up the importance of the concept of intent. In this sense the twin concepts of conspiracy and intent are important supports of the Sherman Act irrespective of any particular construction thereof.

Conspiracy

So far as anti-trust legislation is concerned the concept of conspiracy has two main referrents: intra-enterprise conspiracy and inter-enterprise conspiracy. Intra-enterprise conspiracy refers to the fact that the corporation can conspire with itself in three ways. First of all, it is entirely plausible that as an independent legal subject, the corporation may conspire with officers acting on its behalf or, again, a conspiracy may be formed between officers who belong to the corporation. Secondly, a parent corporation may conspire with a subsidiary or else a number of subsidiaries may conspire with each other. Finally, intra-enterprise conspiracy includes the possibility that a person or persons (including corporations) may own stock in two or more separate corporations and can, therefore, form the basis of a conspiracy between them. Each conspiracy refers, of course, to some definite restraint of trade or attempt at monopolization. It is quite clear that each form of intra-enterprise conspiracy depends upon the identification of certain subjective predicates of the corporation. This much holds whether these predicates are condensed as the corporate subject, dispersed to discrete representatives of the corporation (its officers in other words) or else exercised by stockholders. In each case the accurate specification of these predicates is absolutely essential to the finding of a conspiracy. This is also the case for inter-enterprise conspiracy. Quite simply, conspiracy requires certain subjective supports capable of conspiring. Insofar as the corporation itself is viewed as an active agent of the conspiracy then it is as a subjective conspirator. If, on the other hand, corporate personnel are involved then it is in their capacity as bearers of the corporate subject, specific supports of the predicates of the corporate essence. That is to say, in their role as corporate personnel (managers) or title holders (stockholders) and not in their capacity as free individuals.

The importance of the corporate role is often crucial. As Stone remarks "... the law goes even beyond demanding proof of wrongdoing of any corporate agent, and insists on a connection (proved by a preponderance of the evidence) with someone fairly high up in the corporate hierarchy" (Stone, 1975, p. 53). Therefore, there is a clearly delineated attempt to penetrate to the heart of the corporate essence, insofar as it is to be found in certain key guardians, namely, top management. The attempt is far from successful, for example the Delaware Supreme Court made the following comment:

> ... it appears that directors are entitled to rely on the honesty and integrity of their subordinates until something occurs to put them on suspicion that something is wrong. If such occurs and goes unheeded, then liability of the directors might well follow, but absent cause for suspicion there is no duty upon the directors to install and operate a corporate system of espionage to ferret out wrongdoing which they have no reason to suspect exists. (Graham v. Aliss-Chalmers, 188. A2d. 125, 130, Del. 1963)

Insofar as there is a tendency to insulate top management from the unacceptable face of corporate activity, on the grounds that they cannot be held responsible for what they do not know (Stone) and, given that there is a fundamental cleavage between possession and control relations, this particular strategy is perhaps less than successful in fixing corporate responsibility to identifiable authors.

Section 1 of the Sherman Act requires a plurality of actors, a convocation of co-conspirators, before it can be violated. The Act depicts the corporation either as a subject or as an aggregate of subjective predicates. This follows because the Sherman Act does not proscribe restraint of trade as such but only every contract, conspiracy or trust in restraint of trade. Under the provisions of the

Sherman Act restraint of trade cannot be a substantive offence, with the result that some form of identifiable collusion between separate actors is essential for a successful prosecution under Section 1 of the Act. It is commonly understood that if a corporation commits a substantive offence then the agents of the corporation responsible for the perpetration of the crime are guilty of conspiracy. It does not follow, however, that restraint of trade by a corporation implies a similar conspiracy between discrete layers of the corporate hierarchy. In short, it is by no means clear that a corporation can conspire with itself in restraint of trade and in violation of a Section 1 offence. This doubt would seem to be borne out by the fact that by 1955 there had been no recorded decision in favour of a Section 1 charge of intra-enterprise conspiracy by a corporation and its officers. In over 60 years not one charge succeeded unless it was accompanied by other charges and accompanying evidence of overt conspiracy in restraint of trade.

Section 2 offences are rather different since monopolization is a substantive offence with the result that corporate personnel can be found guilty of a conspiracy to monopolize trade. Likewise, conspiracy between subsidiaries, or between a subsidiary and the parent company, and a conspiracy resulting from commonly held title to the stock of discrete corporations, can be upheld as Section 1 offences. Thus the court held that

> The test of illegality under the Act is the presence or absence of an unreasonable restraint on interstate commerce. Such a restraint may result as readily from a conspiracy among those who are affiliated or integrated under common ownership as from a conspiracy among those who are otherwise independent. Similarly, an affiliation or integration flowing from an illegal conspiracy cannot insulate the conspirators from the sanctions which congress has imposed. The corporate interrelationships of the conspirators . . . are not determinative of the applicability of the Sherman Act. (U.S. v. Yellow Cab Co. 322 U.S. 218, 1947)

A very clear statement which seems to mark out an extremely far reaching role for the Sherman Act. Nevertheless, this potency is predicated upon the concept of conspiracy. As we have seen the concept of conspiracy would appear to dissolve the relevance of corporate interrelationships and, arguably, the most secure basis for any form of regulation. Instead, restraint of trade by corporations is viewed entirely as a matter of conspiracy between distinct actors. Even if the provisions of anti-trust legislation are interpreted strictly, in a way which enables law to bite hard on anti-competitive behaviour, then the attempt is perhaps unnecessarily restrained by the conceptual equipment available, respectively, conspiracy and intent. Further, when the concept of conspiracy depends upon the existence of some sort of boundary between a parent and a subsidiary company, or between subsidiaries or between a corporation and its executive officers, then the picture of corporate interrelations implied therein merely confirms the inadequacy of law as an agency of regulation.

The discussion of intra-enterprise conspiracy highlights the difficulties involved in conceiving of the corporation as a subject in its own right as well as viewing it as an aggregate of discrete subjective attributes. These difficulties are compounded when law attempts to describe the basis of a conspiracy between one or more permutations of these respective subjects. It is with regard to inter-enterprise conspiracy, however, that the potentiality of law as a regulatory agency faces a more important test. Inter-enterprise conspiracy involves what has come to be known as the issue of conscious parallelism, the idea that companies may pursue a parallel course of action without recourse to an overt conspiracy. This course of action may include such items as pricing policy, output level, market share and so on. Conscious parallelism is so called because it involves two aspects; first, a knowledge of competitors conduct and, secondly, uniformity of business behaviour or, what amounts to the real manifestation of a suitable synonym for collusion. This particular issue penetrates to the heart of anti-trust policy since it raises the question of whether conspiracy can be read off from the presence of economic effects normally indicative of overt collusion or, conversely, whether an active conspiracy, a genuine meeting of the minds, is essential for the finding of conspiracy under the anti-trust laws. A question which appears to crop up again and again, therefore, is "should law bite on uncompetitive situations without being restricted by rigid legal concepts" (Neale, 1966).

Interpretation of inter-enterprise conspiracy is far from uniform. For example, in 1948 the Federal Trade Commission announced that ". . . when a number of enterprises follow a parallel course of action in the knowledge and contemplation of the fact that all are acting alike, they have, in effect, formed an agreement" (FTC, 1948). An interpretation which had been upheld by the Supreme Court in the same year to the effect that concerted action constituted a combination within the meaning of the Sherman Act (FTC v. Cement Inst., 333 U.S. 683, 716n. 17, 1948). On the other hand, the Supreme Court made the following declaration in 1954:

> But this Court has never held that proof of parallel business behaviour conclusively establishes agreement or, phrased differently, that such behaviour itself constitutes a Sherman Act offence. Circumstantial evidence of consciously parallel behaviour may have made heavy inroads into the traditional judicial attitude toward conspiracy but 'conscious parallelism' has not yet read conspiracy out of the Sherman Act entirely. (Theatre Enterprises Inc. v. Paramount Film Distributing Corp. *et al.*, 346 U.S. 537, 541-542, 1954)

The implied dispute is between two rather fragile contestants. As Rostow (1955) remarked, a case of purely tacit or conventional collusion devoid of such additional evidence as formal/informal understandings, policing measures, correspondence, and so on has never reached the courts. Moreover, Neale (1966) indicates that reading off collusion from the mere existence of economic effects indicative of parallel action is largely restricted to a charge under Section 5 of the Federal Trade Commission Act. It constituted an alternative means of preventing the continuation of a tacit agreement after conspiracy is established by more conventional (legal) means. Any inclusion of a comprehensive analysis of the economic effects of a restraint of trade is thereby subordinated to the primary finding of an overt conspiracy in the normal (legal) manner. Accordingly, conscious parallelism is restricted to secondary relevance. By the same token there were no primary charges relating to individual sellers following the lead of a more powerful competitor in the absence of any separate agreement or conspiracy established at law.

There is a rather perplexing array of opinions on the early interpretation of conscious parallelism. Neale (1966) provides a summary of the position which is both useful and to the point. He argues that agreement or conspiracy in restraint of trade can be proved conclusively by circumstantial evidence, "so long as a chain of evidence can be built up for which the only plausible explanation is a common understanding or plan". That much is established at law. Anti-trust law, however, knows no doctrine of constructive conspiracy, "the existence of a restrictive agreement cannot be proved simply by showing that the effects usually associated with such an agreement have occurred". A great deal of discretion exists between these two interpretations of the basis of a conspiracy. But conspiracy still requires a genuine meeting of the minds. Indeed, it is often suggested that the best form of defence to a charge of conspiracy would be to offer a plausible alternative interpretation of the basis of parallel action rather than to challenge the fact of parallel action as such.

At bottom the issue of conscious parallelism involves the more general contest between those who would view the impairment of competition as actionable *per se* and those who would restrict anti-trust legislation to the apparently rigid concepts of conspiracy and intent. In order to rely on the impairment of competition *per se* as a criterion of illegality, it is necessary to countenance an exhaustive analysis of the consequences of particular actions in the light of some model of perfect or workable competition. It is not just a matter of outlawing price fixing *per se*, since the whole essence of conscious parallelism involves a detailed assessment of the market in order to define parallel action and then to infer an implicit conspiracy. This sort of strict approach is characterized by a basic concern for the regulation of competition and the preservation of a series of benefits which, it is assumed, adhere to free competition; growth, efficiency and adaptability. As such it ceases to be a distinctly legal regulation of economic affairs becoming instead a bureaucratic response to the free enterprise system.

To some extent this bureaucratic administrative response describes the role of the Federal Trade Commission in its dealings with the problem of restraint of trade. Whilst this sort of perspective may have left a few high tide marks inscribed in the history of anti-trust legislation, it has not achieved any deeper resonance within anti-trust legislation. For example, the Milgram v. Loew judgement ruled that consciously parallel practices demonstrated the existence of conspiracy. Also, this approach to some extent replaced the meeting of the minds (deemed essential for the finding of conspiracy in earlier interpretations) with the notion of a constructive conspiracy. Although on appeal certain reservations were entered along with a wholesale dissent. In effect the Appeal Court argued that parallel action was still insufficient by itself but that in the absence of an attempt by the defence to put forward a plausible alternative interpretation it was sufficient in this particular case (Milgram v. Loew's Inc., 192 F. 2d 579, 583 (3rd Cir. 1951) and 343 (U.S. 929 (1952)). At most, this sort of response has appeared as an adjunct to a properly constructed legal appraisal of economic affairs and, therefore, has been subordinated to the dictates of legal concepts like conspiracy and intent. The rigid steel conduit case, often quoted as a landmark in the rigid pursuit of parallel action, in fact involved only a secondary charge under Section 5 of the Federal Trade Commission Act abutting a primary finding of conspiracy and aimed at preventing its renewal (Triangle Conduit & Cable Co. Inc. *et al.* v. Federal Trade Commission, 168 F. 2d 175 (48) and 336 U.S. 956 (1949)). Furthermore, even if this response advocating constructive conspiracy constituted the prevailing interpretation, then the attendant reliance upon economic consequences would divert attention from the issue of economic ownership and thus would change the nature of anti-trust legislation entirely. It would make relevant a potentially infinite number of essentially contestible economic variables prior to the assessment and balancing of matters incidental to the existence of free competitors. On this reading of anti-trust legislation all that it could achieve would be the regulation of abuse within an overall framework of oligopoly designed to meet certain criteria of performance rather than to eliminate monopoly. The issue of industrial concentration and centralization would be relevant only insofar as they impeded or increased performance. Therefore, the opportunities for the defence of restraint of trade, on the grounds of technological or strategic importance, efficiency and so on, would be potentially boundless and the scope of law at best uncertain and at worst secondary.

The argument is not between the sort of general approach which would abandon legal concepts, in an attempt to foreclose monopolistic effects, and the strict criminalization of corporate activity. Nor is it between the greater exercise of discretion and the more rigid imposition of legal sanctions. Both sorts of response overlap to some extent and each is flawed in very specific ways. Over and above these particular problems, what is important is that these two quite general responses supply the paradigm for legal regulation. That each is based on certain fundamental, although quite unacceptable, assumptions goes a long way toward explaining the comparative difficulties encountered by both legal and bureaucratic forms of regulation. If these twin forms of regulation overlap then the problem of priority becomes apparent. As we have seen the evidence of the earlier part of the development of anti-trust legislation resolves this dilemma by inserting economic criteria within sharply delineated legal concepts. Thus, intent may be read off from the existence of certain consequences and a conspiracy may be constructed by reference to market behaviour. Accordingly, the denegration of corporate structure, inherent in the conventional analysis of competition, is compounded by being absorbed within a form of legal analysis which views corporate structure in terms of a subjective essence and sees criminal action as the responsibility of individual authors.

As we have seen, the concept of conspiracy in restraint of trade characteristic of Section 1 of the Sherman Act indexes the notion of a subjective agreement between conspirators and also demarcates discrete corporate spheres capable of entering into a conspiracy as co-conspirators. The charge of conspiracy requires the specification of actors who are in fact authors of the conspiracy. Insofar as the charge derives from the Sherman Act, these parts are played either by the corporate subject itself or by identifiable bearers of the predicates of the corporate subject, corporate personnel in other words. The Sherman Act clearly specifies that person or persons can include (legal) corporations. Further, if restraint of trade is to be defined then the criteria by which it is to be assessed are admitted only as an adjunct of the concept of conspiracy. Restraint of trade is not an offence *per se* but requires a conspiracy to activate the process of legal sanction. Consideration problems attend the specification of the corporation as an economic subject or as a constellation of economic actors. Additionally, the concept of any sort of equilibrium between free producers and consumers, through free exchange in the market, is a less than accurate portrayal of the corporate economy. Therefore, the concepts of restraint of trade and conspiracy are inappropriate regulatory mechanisms. This much becomes plain with regard to their separate capacities, but when each is taken in tandem with the other then the possibility of effective legal regulation of economic affairs recedes into the background.

Corporate Agency and Intent

Section 1 of the Sherman Act depends upon the identification of a conspiracy in restraint of trade. Similarly, Section 2 of the Act is sustained by an equal reliance upon the concept of intent. Monopoly *per se* is not illegal. What is illegal is the monopolization of trade. This special offence of monopolization involves two distinct aspects: first, monopoly, which is defined as the power to fix prices or exclude competition and, secondly, a deliberate use of, or attempt to preserve or acquire, such power. This is represented by the conventional contraction of these two aspects as power and purpose. Intent is essential for the finding of a charge under Section 2, but it implies two component parts. First of all, because the Sherman Act is a criminal statute it requires specific criteria of guilt. Secondly, it is necessary to identify specific actors capable of crystallizing and exercising an intent. In order to establish authors of criminal intent, it is necessary to specify the corporation as a collective subject or aggregate of subjects. Whilst it is quite true that these subjects need not be human they must, nevertheless, express the requisite subjective attributes. Accordingly, this reliance upon a subjective caricature of the corporation cannot help but miss its central feature: the fact that it is a highly complex organizational structure. So-called structural features, however, have not escaped attention entirely. Kaysen makes it clear that the basic issue is one of structure. It is the structure of the market which inspires, even requires, parallel action or agreements to agree. But the preoccupation with the definition of parallel action fails to consider the structure which seems to enforce parallel action namely, the domination of the market by and for the few (Kaysen, 1951). This sort of interpretation may have much to commend it, but the solution advocated by Kaysen appears to imply an unnecessarily restrictive definition of structure. Divestment, divorcement and dissolution are seen to constitute an effective relief against monopoly. Whilst it is quite true, as far as it goes, that behaviour is a function of market structure, there is no guarantee that this will be altered by redistributing the boundaries of the corporate enterprise. Nor is oligopoly or market structure a problem of legal ownership, to be remedied by redrawing the profile of stock ownership. To be sure, the call for structural remedies necessarily implies that oligopoly, or the corporation as such, are not in fact prohibited. This much is perhaps obvious, and the point is often made that monopoly is not actually illegal. Nevertheless, there is a clear presumption, within anti-trust legislation and, especially within the anti-monopoly movement, that the law is used to regulate the increasing dominance of the corporate form through an attack on what it sees as its unacceptable consequences. Therefore, the spectre of monopoly and the promise of competition inform every moment of anti-trust legislation, even though monopoly as such is not quite illegal.

A Section 2 charge requires more than a demonstrable intention, it requires evidence of the necessary power to fix prices. The definition of market power in question depends upon how the relevant market is construed. The assertion that "size is of course an earmark of monopoly power" was set forth in United States v. Griffith *et al.* (334 U.S. 100 (1948) 107 n.10). Thus, under certain circumstances, the offence of monopolization may be inferred from the mere existence of a near or total monopoly on the grounds laid out in United States v. Aluminium Company of America, that "no monopolist monopolises unconscious of what he is doing" (2 Cir., 148 F 2d. 416, 432). Perhaps more importantly, the Griffith case established, further, that "monopoly power, whether lawfully or unlawfully acquired, may itself constitute an evil and stand condemned under section two even though it remains unexercised" (334 U.S. 100 (1948) 107). There is, then, a clear presumption that size is an important criterion of monopoly power and, at times, even a direct determinant of the offence of monopolization. Although size is seldom regarded as being actionable *per se* (United States v. United States Steel Corporation 251 U.S. 417 states that mere size is not outlawed by Section 2) it is, none the less, an implicit determinant of action under the anti-trust laws. Furthermore, size is an important factor in determining whether or not a monopoly exists. For example, Justice Hand in the Alcoa case delineated the following rough and ready tariff: 90% of supply is sufficient to constitute a monopoly; 60-64% of supply is doubtful and 33% of supply is clearly not enough (United States v. Aluminium Company of America, 148 F 2d. 416). Of course, by itself the issue of size is seldom conclusive and US v. Columbia Steel, demonstrated that the ". . . relative effect of percentage command of a market varies with the setting in which that factor is placed" (334 U.S. 49r, 527-8, 1948).

As we have seen, economic criteria are undoubtedly important for any determination of monopolization. How the market is defined, its overall size, the strength of competitors, prevailing business trends, the freedom of entry, specific capital requirements for the participation in the market, geographical area, the levels of advertising and consumer demands, each of these has an important bearing on the definition of the power to monopolize. Furthermore, evidence relating to the way that prices are formed and decisions made, their course, flexibility, relation to prices in general, price competition and customary procedures, is an important criterion of purpose. The typically flexible requirements, necessary for a demonstration of a positive purpose to monopolize trade, stem from the considerable latitude involved in defining any particular restraint of trade and from the broadly based discretion as to whether such a restraint of trade is against the public interest. As Neale puts it, "Intent is assessed in the light of power" (1966, p. 129).

It is true that the requisite intent is not normally the specific intent to monopolize, although such an intent does exist under anti-trust legislation, but rather a conclusion based on how monopoly power was acquired, maintained and used. Accordingly, the entire history and business policy of a corporation may be scrutinized and made relevant for the proof of a general deliberation and intention to monopolize in violation of Section 2. The charge of monopolization may be sustained if a subjective intent to acquire and keep a monopoly position characterizes business policy or, if an objective intent can be inferred from the continued existence of a monopoly. Objective intent is formed by analogy with the legal notion that human action, and thus corporate action, is intentional in the absence of evidence to the contrary. For example, the famous dictum enunciated by Judge Hand that no monopolist monopolizes unconscious of what he is doing demonstrates one sort of objective intent (United States v. Aluminium Co. of America, 148, F. 2d 416 (1945)). However, reading off intent from market consequences does not necessarily salvage the concept of intent as an effective means of regulation. On the contrary, it tends to reinforce the concept of intent by compounding it in a reference to an equilibrium between neo-classical (economic) subjects as an implicit measure of monopoly or restraint of trade (Aglietta, 1979, p. 13).

As we have seen, the definition of monopoly power in a specific market situation and the construction of a deliberate attempt to secure such market power intermesh to provide typically flexible interpretations of monopolization. A monopoly need not violate Section 2 of the Sherman Act, wherever market demand is so low that reasons of efficiency deem monopoly to be the most practical means of meeting it. Likewise, where a dramatic change in demand or cost leaves but a single supplier or, where a sole company survives by dint of superior skill, foresight and industry or by pre-empting demand by developing an entirely new product, then these situations may justify the existence of a monopoly. Therefore, if monopoly is thrust upon a corporation by market forces or by any one of the above factors, providing that this is the only reason for the existence of a monopoly, the corporation is not in contravention of Section 2 of the Sherman Act. This position has been upheld in a number of cases which affirm the right of a corporation to have a monopoly but, nevertheless, introduce sanctions because of the way in which that monopoly has been exercised. For example, United States v. Terminal Railroad Association of St. Louis (1912); Gamco v. Providence Fruit & Produce Building (1952) and United States v. Lorain Journal Company (1951), all suggest that it is only the misuse of monopoly power which is likely to infringe Section 2. Even then, the issue of misuse may be decided by the definition of the relevant market, as in the Times Picayune Company v. United States (1953). Here, the Supreme Court returned a majority verdict in favour of Times Picayune on the grounds that, whilst the newspaper held a monopoly of the morning market, it did not have a monopoly of the combined morning and evening market and that its attempt to contract advertisers to a package deal was not tantamount to an offence of monopolization. Nevertheless, this last case is not typical of the majority of cases of this nature.

There exists, then, a clear presumption that monopoly *per se* is not in fact illegal and that the offence of monopolization requires some form of proof regarding business malpractice which is essentially unfair in itself. The progressive aspects of monopoly, development, expansion, efficiency, do not invoke the wrath of legal sanction, but rather the deliberate frustration and calculated exclusion of potential new entrants is necessary in order to precipitate action under Section 2. This general theme persists with reference to the specific

Section 2 charges of attempting to monopolize trade and combining or conspiring to monopolize trade. Neither of these special offences requires any evidence of monopoly power at all. In the former, proof of the requisite intent can be found in documents pertaining to the attempt, or in an assessment of the industrial backcloth to the attempt. Whereas for the latter, proof of intent can be regarded largely as a proof of conspiracy. The specific intention to monopolize is not consummated in the simple act of merger, but requires conclusive proof of a larger, altogether more sinister, plan to dominate the entire industry. Even where the attempt failed, the offence can still be proved, that is to say, monopoly power is irrelevant. For example, this has been upheld in the Columbia Steel case of 1948 and in the Yellow Cab case of 1949.

Consideration of the Sherman Act demonstrates that it falls rather uneasily between two sorts of general criteria. First of all, economic criteria are relevant to various stages and, in particular, with regard to the more uncertain interpretation normally associated with the rule of reason. The exercise is designed to assess the consequences of specific market conditions. These consequences do not, necessarily, adhere to identifiable acts nor, for that matter, do they attach to particular actors. But rather, under certain circumstances, specific acts such as conspiracy or monopolization can be linked with individual authors, largely through the notion of intent, and both may be inferred from market structure. Thus, economic criteria are inserted into legal concepts and become an essential part of the determination of an infraction. Secondly, legal criteria are involved in ascertaining intentional acts (conspiracy, monopolization) or specific practices (price fixing) which may limit competition. These acts or practices are outlawed in themselves and, whilst there may be some scope for discretionary definition of these acts or practices, once found they are outlawed *per se*. In practice, of course, these two sorts of criteria become intertwined. The essentially legalistic language of anti-trust statutes - which refer to intent and conspiracy as fundamental to the finding of a violation—together with the basically economic analysis of market structure, which finds the concept of monopolization utterly incomprehensible, often overlap. As might be expected, they do not prove to be happy bedmates. There is a persistent tension between the two with regard to judicial interpretation which has only partially been resolved in favour of legal criteria. Thus, the Attorney General's National Committee stated that ". . . The anti-trust laws establish criminal guilt or civil responsibility; here as in all other phases of the law, legal responsibility is individual" (1955, p. 340). Hence, actual behaviour cannot be deduced from general market structure, since legal responsibility has to be induced from direct evidence pertaining to the individual involvement and perpetration of a legally prohibited act, price fixing, monopolization and so on. This interpretation is by no means clear cut, however. For example, the former Assistant Attorney-General Wendell Berge said in 1940: "The rights of the accused which are of the utmost importance when liberty of an individual is in jeopardy, are irrelevant symbols when the real issue in the arrangement under which corporations in industry must compete" (United States Department of Justice, 1955, p.353). In other words, the corporations were treated unfairly according to a systematic violation of fundamental principles of justice. It would appear that the suspension of legal rights, and the greater reliance upon bureaucratic intervention, did indeed have some effect, particularly in view of the somewhat strained reaction of the former Assistant Attorney-General. It would be wrong, however, to conclude that bureaucratic intervention fared any better than a more legalistic form of economic regulation. They each have substantial failings. Whereas law is limited by its reliance upon the concepts of conspiracy, intent and private property, bureaucratic intervention is perhaps preoccupied by an analysis of market structure in terms of ideal types (perfect or workable competition, monopoly and oligopoly), which cannot help but discount material structures of ownership in favour of an hypothesized equilibrium between economic actors. In this sense, any restraint of trade is measured against a purely imaginary equation. As Pepinsky argues, the injury caused by price fixing is impossible to arrive at from the point of view of economic theory or economic practice: "From the point of view of economic theory, the injury caused by price fixing is shown by models contrasting oligopolistic or monopolistic markets to competitive ones. The problem with this comparison is that a competitive market, as an abstraction, cannot exist in reality" (Pepinsky, 1976, p. 30). Also, the definition of economic injury from an empirical point of view is impossible because the simultaneous existence in the same economy of two markets for the same product with similar buyers and sellers is impossible. There is no basis for a comparison. Accordingly, the *ad hoc* basis of bureaucratic regulation would appear to lack any clear-cut criteria for arriving at restraint of trade and, therefore, would seem to be without a sound basis for a sustained regulation of economic conduct. Furthermore, legal and bureaucratic forms of regulation are each hampered by their respective roles as independent agencies of regulation.

The Sherman Act represents the major thrust of anti-monopoly law, especially in view of the resolution of statutory doubts in favour of its basic directives. Nevertheless, anti-monopoly law is far from exhausted by a consideration of this alone. Section 7 of the Clayton Act, as amended in 1950, is the primary provision to which the department of Justice and the Federal Trade Commission resort on the question of mergers. The clear intention of this section, which the 1950 amendment strengthened, was to halt undue concentrations of economic power and monopoly in their infancy; to nip mergers in the bud before an action under the Sherman Act became appropriate. Walter Adams makes this point abundantly clear "The Clayton Act is a prohibitory, not a regulatory statute. By its enactment, Congress did not intend to authorise the courts or the commission to determine whether particular mergers are good or bad or in the public interest. Instead, Congress acted on the presumption that a substantial foreclosure or elimination of competition was in itself a derogation of the public interest" (United States Department of Justice, 1955, p.127-128). As we have seen this is a *per se* interpretation of restraint which denies not only the relevance of intent, the ethical basis of an acquiring firms business practice, but also price fixing and the exclusion or destruction of competitors. Instead, it is sufficient to demonstrate the reasonable probability that a substantial lessening of competition or a clear drift toward monopoly would accompany a merger in order to secure its prohibition under the provisions of the Act. However, as the Federal Trade Commission made clear in 1953, ". . . competition cannot be directly measured; no single set of standards can be applied to the whole range of American industries. No single characteristic of an acquisition (would in all cases) . . . of itself be sufficient to determine its effect on competition" (FTC. Dkt. 6000, p. 9). Instead, a case-by-case examination of all the relevant factors is necessary to ascertain the probable economic consequences. Whilst not directly equivalent to a Sherman Act test (the Clayton Act requires a less stringent burden of proof) it none the less describes a substantial area of discretion and a tendency to submit to a rule of reason interpretation. The latter sort of interpretation is further reinforced by the idea that under certain circumstances a merger can lead to increased and more effective competition and, consequently, the proliferation of oligopoly can be beneficial to vigorous competition between equals. This, coupled with the indeterminacy associated with the questions of how substantial must any foreclosure of competition be in order to constitute a restraint, and at precisely what stage a merger constitutes an incipient derogation of competition, makes the case for the rule of reason approach. Furthermore, as Neale points out, the purely quantitative test of the substantiality of any decrease in competition is apparently insensitive to motive. Nevertheless, the preference of the courts for the concept of intent tends to ensure the convergence of the Sherman and Clayton Acts on this particular issue, with the result that intent is still the earmark of an offence for the courts, if not for the Federal Trade Commission (Neale, 1966, p. 473). For example, the foreclosure of competition through vertical integration has not been successfully prosecuted in the absence of intent to monopolize. Moreover, the impact of the Clayton Act seems to be limited to the imposition of a sliding scale whereby gratuitous size requires less stringent proof of intent, coercion and interference and, vice versa, small is innocent (Neale, 1966, p. 440). Therefore, size appears yet again as an implicit determinant of action under anti-trust legislation, at once affirming the prevailing distrust of bigness and also forestalling the appropriate grasp of corporate relations. It is almost as if a theory of the corporate 'bully' stands instead of an accurate portrayal of corporate ownership.

It would be entirely incorrect to make the assumption that these general propositions are in any way definitive statements concerning the complex nature of anti-trust law. This is particularly true of the more contemporary use of anti-trust legislation as a rather different form of regulatory agency, tied much more explicitly to a type of cost benefit analysis based on levels of price formation. A consideration of these developments would be out of place here, particularly in view of the fact that they appear to change the complexion of anti-trust legislation quite dramatically, in a direction at odds with its original structure. What was once a perhaps uniquely American attempt to get to grips with 'bigness' and defend free enterprise, has passed over into but another 'tool' for the ostensible regulation of prices. Although, even with regard to the earlier course of anti-trust legislation, with which we are primarily concerned, the process of interpretation is complex and it would be as true to say that an equal case could be, and indeed has been, made out for an alternative interpretation of anti-trust legislation. The important point, however, is that at bottom anti-trust legislation, and the ensuing process of interpretation thereof, is bounded by two quite fundamental persuasions. First of all, economic consequences are viewed as irrelevant to the successful prosecution of a conspiracy in restraint of trade, monopolization of trade or mergers. Secondly, there is a persistent tendency to attribute a great deal of importance to economic context, performance, business practice and history. So much so that at times economic context may even be a crucial determinant of any action under the anti-trust laws. As Miller puts it: ". . . there is on the one hand a legislative-administrative process which provides a degree of flexibility in detailed application of the law in the face of different situations and changing attitudes, and on the other hand a judicial process which provides for substantial consistency and continuity in broad principles" (Miller, 1962).

These two alternative perspectives on anti-trust legislation provide for a substantial contest sufficient in itself to account for the wholesale proliferation of anti-trust enterprise as a dialectical exercise. Irrespective of which persuasion prevails (with a few exceptions the evidence is largely equivocal), it can be stated quite plainly that each is entirely inadequate as an agency of prohibition and potentially flawed as an instrument of regulation *vis-à-vis* economic affairs in general and corporate structure in particular. In combination their respective weakness' tend to be compounded and, in isolation, their marginality in respect of corporate relations vitiates any potentiality which they may have to a degree which perhaps overshadows their particular failings.

Punishment

The issue of enforcement of anti-trust legislation and the punishment of offenders has taken second place to the examination of the structure of anti-trust legislation. This is understandable given that the structure of anti-trust legislation is prior to its enforcement. There are, however, a number of important details concerning the actual enforcement of anti-trust legislation which amplify the argument concerning how it portrays the corporation.

The bare outline of enforcement is easily described. There are three principle enforcement mechanisms. First of all, the Department of Justice, secondly, the Federal Trade Commission and, finally, the pursuit of private action by treble-damage litigants. Obviously, the process of investigation is complex, involving the sort of decision-making criterion which inhere in any criminal justice system. Anti-trust legislation is no exception on this issue. The process, however, is subject to quite specific problems. For example, a comprehensive process of investigation is necessary in order to determine the existence of a probable violation; an investigation uncovers a violation rather than being stimulated by a criminal act into the process of finding a responsible author. Since resources are scarce there is a necessary process of selection and concentration at work and hence a wide ambit for the exercise of discretion. Over and above this fully comprehensive investigatory procedure employed prior to the instigation of formal criminal or civil proceedings, there is the additional selection of the appropriate penalties (criminal action), equitable relief (civil action) or voluntary agreement (diversion process). In short the proper channelling of legal/administrative action occupies a pivotal place in the determination of action under the anti-trust laws. Although formally impressive, the strategies for obtaining information are in practice attenuated, particularly with regard to civil cases. This is especially important given the relevance placed on information to the investigatory and dispersal procedure and the general priority accorded the collation of facts in the judicial process. Indeed, the emphasis on facts is often held to be a direct consequence of the apparent generality of the statute law which comprises the anti-trust field. On this particular issue the Attorney-General's National Committee was moved to recommend that, precisely because the complexities of business life govern the unpredictable nature of executive action, the criminal process should only be used where the law is clear and the facts reveal a flagrant offence and a plain intent to restrain trade unreasonably. One might add, also, that the existence of an effective relief, other than the empty reiteration of anti-trust's statutory provisions, is in part a determinant of action under the anti-trust laws. As Miller says of the 1946 American Tobacco Case "The government after winning the case was hard pressed to find any effective remedy since, in view of the structure of the market, instructing the firms not to conspire is of little significance" (Miller, 1962, p. 231). The establishment of precedents of this nature plays a large part in determining whether or not any action will be taken in future and, if action is to ensue, what sort it will be. In addition to the issues of investigation, dispersal and enforcement, the Departure of Justice also claims some competence in relation to the provision of advance clearances and releases for proposed mergers.

Section 11 of the 1914 Clayton Act empowered the Federal Trade Commission with the authority to enforce compliance with the Clayton Act provisions. Thus, the FTC was endowed as an auxiliary organ of anti-trust enforcement. As such the FTC has no criminal jurisdiction but is instead a quasi-judicial administrative tribunal able, in theory, to hold hearings into suspected violations, to issue cease and desist orders and, contingent upon subsequent infringement of such orders, to refer a case to an appellate court for enforcement. The cease and desist order is basically an injunction comparable to a civil remedy in a Sherman Act case. The FTC also has power to investigate the operation of a department of Justice decree and, on presidential or congressional authority, to investigate violations of anti-trust statutes. In addition, there is an apparatus of informal settlements, trade practice conferences and voluntary compliance in general. The FTC has statutory powers to obtain information necessary to its function which are set out at Section 6 of the FTC Act.

Finally, the incidence and success rate of private suits for damage, held to be a result of anti-trust violations, has increased dramatically since the end of the second world war. One problem with such suits is caused by the plea of *nolo contendere* to a criminal charge. The advantage of such a plea is that, whilst it does not dispute the charge, it nevertheless forestalls the establishment of specific violations, which can form valuable precedents for any number of private treble damage suits. Likewise, it avoids the publication of what the corporation was up to, in terms of establishing specific factual transgressions. The advantages of suppressing publicity of corporate malpractice are fairly obvious and need not detain us here.

So much for the formal structure of enforcement. The actual patterns of punishment and discipline, however, which these diverse practices exemplify, are more important determinants of the efficacy of legal and administrative regulation. Without doubt the most far reaching remedy available under the anti-trust laws is the civil motion in equity to decree the dissolution of a monopoly. Although potentially powerful, the measure is vitiated, in practice, by the general reluctance of courts to take what they regard as extreme action to restructure an industry. As Neale makes abundantly clear "Neither in the Alcoa case nor in that of the United Shoe Machinery Company would the courts accept, as a practical matter, the physical dissolution of the organisation concerned" (Neale, 1966, p. 406).

This reluctance is compounded by the practical problems involved in ordering the dissolution of monopolies and, as Neale goes on to point out "In some cases the practical difficulties of dissolution seem to have frustrated the search for effective remedies altogether" (1966, p. 406). The supreme reluctance of courts to take this form of drastic action, except where the absolute necessity of such a decree is overwhelmingly compelling and its execution practicable and fair, is sustained by empirical evidence. For example, in over 60 years of the Sherman Act only 24 litigated cases decreed divestiture or dissolution (United States

Department of Justice, 1955, p.354). Apart from this empirical manifestation, the supreme reluctance betokens a dilemma close to the heart of anti-trust law; a dilemma which Justice Hand joined in enunciating in the Alcoa case of 1945 that ". . . the Sherman Act does not mean to condemn the resultant of those very forces which it is its prime object to foster: *finis opus coronat*. The successful competitor must not be turned upon when he wins" (148 F. 2d. 416 (12)). Thus, as we have seen already, whilst the efficiency and dynamism of large enterprises may be viewed with pride and applauded accordingly, the power of unchecked monopoly is viewed with suspicion and cynicism. Ambivalence of this magnitude is adequately summarized thus: "To have the 'power condemned in the courts as illegal, and its exercise beset by complex injunctions, while the organisation itself remains intact, is a solution which reflects this ambivalence of attitude pretty closely " (Neale, 1966, p. 436). Such ambivalence reflects the basic irrelevance of criminal sanctions, especially with regard to their essentially retrospective character and the fact that even quite substantial financial penalties wither in embarrassment beside the corporate budget. This fundamental irrelevance contrasts markedly with the apparently all too relevant civil remedy, in that decrees granting divestiture or dissolution are almost too radical even to contemplate as a solution. The answer to this evident discrepancy between criminal and civil sanction, seems to be to embrace some form of behaviour or conduct modification whereby the courts decree detailed injunctions relating to specific practices, a kind of prospectus of rights and duties designed to regulate business conduct without changing the structure of ownership which may inspire such conduct in the first place. In this respect Neale makes the following remark "In a sense the real purpose of all that goes before the Court's decree—the complaint and trial—is to obtain jurisdiction over the parties for the purpose of regulating their business conduct" (1966, p. 396). As far as real structural remedy goes, an interesting variant of the prospectus approach has recently been recycled by Ralf Nader (1976) to the effect that corporate charters should include specific restraints on corporate conduct. Although such solutions have long been decried by the advocates of so-called structural remedy (Kaysen, Turner) who seem to imply that one cannot instruct a corporation to throw off the market pressures which produce monopoly situations. Finally, even in the rare cases where the formal structure of legal ownership is altered by dissolution, the actual structure of ownership may alter very little and the relationships between the component parts of the former corporate empire remain substantially similar. This much is admitted in law by the inherent suspicion that even independent firms may in fact conspire to produce what amounts to a monopoly situation. It is further sustained in practice by the assessment of the famous dissolution of Standard Oil in 1911. Despite being fragmented, the various independent 'Standard Oils' continued to respect each others' marketing zones and acted in concert to suppress the independents, at least until such time as new international conditions provided even greater scope for monopoly and thus new arrangements with competitors.

The options open to law are considerably restricted. Even supposing that the courts manage to overcome their supreme reluctance to penalize enterprise, the efficacy of what appears to be an extreme remedy, dissolution, is vitiated in the extreme. If, on the other hand, the interrelationships between independent corporations are taken into account in assessing restraint of trade, then the arsenal which is made available is hampered by the concepts of conspiracy, intent and private property. Either way, the room for manoeuvre is blocked with the result that truly effective legal regulation would appear to have been a dead letter from the start.

Anti-trust legislation sets out two main sorts of sanction, namely criminal and civil. Whilst both sorts of sanction point to the centrality of legal process they, none the less, each index quite different types of discipline. Whereas criminal sanction points up the centrality of punishment and of retrospective penalties for specific transgression of statute law, civil sanction forces the issue of the appropriate remedy of restructuring, intervention, injunction or private damages to the forefront. What they share in common is some implicit conception of corporate relations. Criminal sanction relies upon the feasibility of comprehending corporate structure through the concepts of conspiracy, intent and private property which reinforce the picture of the corporation in terms of human subjects and individual authors. Therefore, the application of monetary sanctions is designed to affect the behaviour of the corporation in the same way that individuals are held to be deterred from re-offending. The corporation is seen as a rational economic actor, capable of calculating the simple equation between profit and cost, pleasure and pain. As Stone points out, "The underlying reasoning is pretty much the same 'bad bargain' analysis that we have brought forward from theorists like Bentham and have simply transferred from people to corporations without reflection" (1975, p. 36). Not only are such classical conceptions of criminality suspect in themselves but, further, there is very little warrant for supposing that the corporation would act in the same way as an individual in any case. The 'behaviour' of corporations is in no way reducible to individuals, so why should it behave as if it were? Why should anti-trust legislation assume that the corporation is a unified essential subject which can both experience sanctions in the same way as individuals and act upon that negative experience to modify its conduct in the way that individuals are supposed to? The answers to these questions are exceedingly pertinent, for they penetrate to the heart of the entire notion of legal regulation and expose glaring faults.

Conversely, civil remedy assumes that to beset the corporation with a host of complex injunctions, each referring to specific practices from which the corporation must desist, means that the relations which sustain and inspire such practices will modify accordingly, if not immediately then in due course. If they do not, and given that dissolution is practicable, then the courts have recourse to the ultimate sanction. They are able to decree some form of dissolution and thereby redraw the corporate boundary. But, as we have seen, this may leave intact the interrelationships between operating units together with the more or less ubiquitous forms of calculation which may ensure parallel response.

Civil remedy is caught between dissolution and regulation which reflects the very marginality of law, able to intervene only at the margins of formal ownership and openly exhibited conduct. Criminal sanction is construed in terms of individual authors and identifiable practices. This is confirmed in the parallel reluctance to use the imprisonment clause provided in the Sherman Act. For example "The very few cases in which jail sentences have been imposed have mostly featured some special element of racketeering or fraud which aroused moral indignation" (Neale, 1966, p. 394). Therefore, the law is more concerned with attaching penalties to individual or corporate authors than with effective regulation. To be sure, these monetary sanctions may be more burdensome to the individual than to the corporate subject, but they are not necessarily any the more effective for regulating the structure of corporate interrelationships. Particularly in view of the fact that corporations can find ways of indemnifying its officers from all but the hard end of criminal sanction and, even there, can find alternative ways of reimbursing its officers. Even if these penalties were substantial, there is no guarantee that they would result in any changed practices. Finally, it is often argued that the real value of anti-trust legislation lies not in what it does but in what it does not. That is to say, in its capacity as a general deterrent. It is argued that the abhorrence associated with the stigma of criminal prosecution is such that it deters all but the hard core of corporate criminals. As Wendell Berge argued "The stigma of indictment tends to be the real punishment" (United States Department of Justice, 1955, p. 353). This is a little disingenuous given the relative attenuation of criminal sanction and the marginality of the human subjects apparently capable of espousing such feelings. Moreover, even if the responsibility for corporate crime can be traced to readily identifiable personnel within the corporation, this does not imply that they or, more importantly for the stigma argument, their contemporaries, will actually perceive the offence as real crime to be viewed with genuine abhorrence. There is much evidence to suggest that such an expectation, is, at best, equivocal and, at worst, wholly misleading.

There are, however, a number of more recent proposals which suggest that it is possible to regulate corporations, not by sanctioning their unacceptable consequences, nor by carving up the corporate empire but by radically redrawing the corporations conditions of existence. Both Nader and Stone have argued the case for more rigorously defined corporate constitutions; Nader, by putting forward proposals for federal rather than state charters and Stone, by arguing for greater attention to social values in the structure of corporate decision-making (Stone, 1975; Nader *et al.*, 1976). Clearly, the charter is a very important lynchpin. Once it is accepted that the corporation is a legal entity, brought into existence by state law and replete with a state charter, then removal of the charter is tantamount to execution. The efficacy of using the charter in this way has been recognized for some time as an unacceptable solution to the problem of corporate excess. The merit of Nader and others is that they refuse to accept this verdict and wish to re-open the question of the potency of chartering. One cannot doubt the serious intention behind the idea of more rigorous chartering, nor the historical case to be made for the role of rogue states like New Jersey and, more recently, Delaware in enabling the growth of corporations. These states did indeed provide tailor-made conditions for the unimpeded growth of large corporations. But the point has been made repeatedly that the law should not be regarded as a separate agency of review and regulation, nor as a discrete condition of existence of the corporation. Altering the conditions whereby a corporation may retain its charter does not have an automatic effect upon the vast concentrations of industrial power which are supposed to underlie or co-exist with the corporaton as a legal entity.

This is not to say that the case for chartering is absurd, merely to recognize that the interrelationship of law and economy is more complex than is allowed by the chartering argument and that altering the terms of incorporation need not have any necessary effects upon the organizational arrangements under discussion. Sewing up the corporation within a restrictive and accountable charter imposes a role upon law for which, arguably, it remains unfit. It assumes a definite status for the law and a causal relationship between law and economy which enables the case for chartering to be made. Quite simply, the case for federal chartering depends upon the idea that the law can restrict economic activity within certain constitutionally defined limits. Whilst clearly superior to the open-ended charters which sustain corporations there is no evidence, nor even any suspicion, that this process would be any more successful in controlling conglomerate organizations.

Whatever its more general merits the case for chartering is diminished by its advocates choices of practical remedies. For example, Nader argues that corporate officers found to be in wilful violation of the relevant Act should be disbarred from office, that fines be calibrated according to offenders' means and the gravity of the offence and that penalties be increased for corporate recidivists on the grounds that the alleged deterrent effect is demonstrably weak. The gross inadequacy of these sorts of sanctions has been examined already and their use here merely undermines any credibility which may be attached to the argument in principle. Stone is especially disparaging about the case for federal chartering. Whilst he sympathizes with their aims he makes the point that

> . . . what is written in a corporation's charter plays a very limited role in regulating most corporate activity today; most of the regulations to which corporations are subject are imposed through law, and any corporation that could be made subject to federal charter requirements is right now constitutionally amenable to ordinary federal legislation. The advocates of federal chartering have to show that whatever they would accomplish via federal charters could not be accomplished directly by tougher federal laws. (Stone, 1975, p. 71 n.)

Stone's work is altogether more incisive and a great deal more sensitive than that of Nader. The idea that corporations should be made more responsible is buttressed by a range of specific reforms directly designed to affect the decision-making process and to increase public accountability. Whereas Stone embraces an admirable scepticism with regard to the more conventional mechanisms of control and punishment it is, nevertheless, suspended when he comes to unfold his own prospectus of reforms. Whatever effects general and special public directors may have on safety, pollution and financial respectability, Stone offers little in the way of suggesting their actual success in addressing corporate size and interlocking networks of control. The specific issue of ownership would appear to escape altogether from the rather pathetic array of well-intentioned regulatory mechanisms designed to increase corporate responsibility. This is especially saddening given the insight which Stone offers on the limits of regulation and it is a pity that this insight does not carry over into the reforms he suggests. For example, whilst Stone is correct to argue for the necessity of altering the structure of corporate decision-making he is perhaps wrong to assign this to a regulatory relationship which is sadly lacking in the wherewithal to effect such changes. In any case, injecting personnel into the corporation prior to the finding of an infraction would at most parallel the greater reliance upon intervention in the criminal justice network in general, the success of which hardly inspires unbounded optimism. One thing is clear, however, and it is the fact that it is regulation *per se* which contains inherent difficulties irrespective of the content of such regulation or, indeed, how it is achieved.

Conclusion

There is nothing impossibly abstract about law which prevents it from regulating monopoly in any but a marginal sense. The failings of anti-trust legislation are specific and hinge upon the way in which monopoly is viewed. In assuming that monopoly is a question of over large corporations or covert action between corporations, anti-trust legislation has a definite view of how corporations can be defined as well as an idea of the ways in which they may gang up together. It is this definite way of regarding monopoly which reinforces the prevalent legal conception of the corporation. The limits encountered by law derive from the particular way in which anti-trust law represents the role of the corporation in any monopoly situation. This particular failing is an example of the more general way in which the law perceives the corporation, the most pertinent aspect of which concerns the conception of ownership. Accordingly, the limits of legal regulation derive as much from the specific nature of anti-trust legislation as from the more general legal account of ownership and the corporation.

Notes

1. This does not indicate an acceptance of the equation of competition and freedom, merely the fact that this equation was seen as central to the existence of anti-trust legislation. For an interesting discussion of, and disagreement with, the logic of equating freedom with competition see Cohen, G. A. (1981). *New Left Review* **126**.
2. The point should be made that there is no necessary correspondence between the corporate form and the existence of monopoly but that monopoly cannot be understood properly outwith the parameters delimited by the concept of the 'corporation'.

6 *The Anti-monopoly Movement*

We have seen how anti-trust legislation is often regarded with a certain degree of cynicism. This cynicism has many sources but chief among them is a sense of frustration brought on by the utter failure to do anything significant about the trusts. This frustration is sometimes accompanied by the suspicion that the actual agencies of regulation have themselves become co-opted in the service of the corporations they were designed to control. Then again it may break into outright paranoia because the agencies of regulation are seen to have spawned yet more agencies in what appears to a veritable orgy of state control. This last source bears witness to the contemporary obsession with 'de-regulation', both in the USA and, more recently, in Great Britain. The evident frustration with anti-trust legislation clearly references discrete sources of grievance, but what they share in common is the tendency to discount the historical role played by the anti-monopoly movement. It is almost as if the movement is ignored in what has become the celebration of an American failure; the counterpoint to the success story of business and enterprise. Or, worse still, the movement is regarded as but a pawn in a ploy by cynical plutocrats to fettle the opposition.

This chapter aims to restore a certain authenticity to the anti-monopoly movement and to describe the arterial network which formed the basis for its construction. It is argued that the anti-monopoly movement can best be analysed as a genuinely independent movement irrespective of the particular fate of anti-trust legislation. This fate has its own origins which do not concern the motives or the structure of the anti-monopoly movement as such but refer to the nature of law *per se*.

In Chapter one there is an implicit indication that the anti-monopoly movement was both authentic and, in some respects, even potent. This belief has been sustained by the demonstration of distinct reasons for the failure of anti-trust legislation, reasons which relate to the structure of law rather than, for example, to the omnipotence of big business. The existence of specific reasons for the relative failure of anti-trust legislation to control monopoly relieves the anti-monopoly movement and, to some extent, anti-trust legislation of any necessary status as purely instrumental tools of big business or the capitalist class in general. Therefore, the argument evinces a clear rejection of any attempt to reduce anti-trust legislation to the abstract requirements of capitalism or, again, of those tendencies which seek to remove the arena of political tension and class conflict from the agenda. Eschewing these tendencies, however, does mean that the issue of political struggle and strategy is forced to the surface. It is necessary, therefore, to demonstrate an appropriate framework which allows for the specificity of political strategy.

Political Organization

There are a number of ways in which the specificity of political practice may be realised. Two recent examples of attempts to grapple with this problem will be examined in some detail. The first, largely associated with the work of Louis Althusser, grants the political a measure of autonomy, albeit within a context in which its ultimate impotence is induced by the coming of the last instance. For this perspective, the state somehow ensures the final coherence of ruling class interests and, in this particular case, manages to negate any residual hostility toward monopoly capital. The second, involves a discussion of the work of Hindess (1978) and Hirst (1977). Here, the radical independence of politics is ensured in a way which dissolves altogether the privileged relation of political representation and economic interests. For example, there is no reason why political issues need represent supposedly more basic economic interests. Indeed, it is argued further that the conditions which allow economic interests to be theorized separately entail unacceptable consequences.

There are other ways of ensuring the independence of politics. For example, the work of Max Weber represents just such a tendency toward highlighting political specificity. The two accounts discussed here, however, are of particular interest precisely because they address the problem of the interrelation of the political and the economic in a way which claims to solve the twin problems of independence and representation. Furthermore, these issues are central to the existence of an independent anti-monopoly movement.

In a traditional sense, then, the problem of political specificity is invariably seen in one of three basic ways. First of all, the political is viewed in terms of a series of instances which are each integrated within a totality. Secondly, it is seen as one third of a tripartite division of powers which are somehow fixed in splendid isolation and interdependence. Finally, and in the interests of avoiding idealism, it is seen as an indirect expression of formally separate economic interests. The imagery may vary but the political tends to be analysed in terms of one or other of these perspectives. But if they are to be sustained then each must involve some sort of mechanism which can explain the eventual coincidence of initially or relatively separate instances of sociality. Otherwise politics becomes autonomous in an absolute sense with the result that the political manifesto carries the seeds of its own fruition and the conditions of its gestation. To the extent that this coherence mechanism is specified, however, it imposes a necessary but unacceptable uniformity upon social relations. On the other hand, if this mechanism is not specified then the problem is either ignored or the conclusion rendered absurd: politics is liberated from society altogether. This paradox stems from the way in which the problem is posed in the first place. For example, the concept of a totality of social relations, the idea that politics can represent ultimate or proximate economic interests and the idea that politics is an independent medium of fulfillment, far from meeting the conditions for political specificity, serve to forestall them.

This introductory section aims to establish the boundaries which allow the anti-trust movement a substantial measure of authenticity, on the basis of the existence of specific reasons for the failure of the movement to achieve its objectives. These reasons clearly involve the use of law as such. For example, even if it were true to say that the federal institutions of legal regulation converge around the requirements of monopoly capital, or the needs of capitalism in general, it would explain nothing without recourse to some conception of an expressive causality whereby the requirements are smoothly conveyed to the appropriate organs of state. This conception both depends upon the sort of coherence provided by the concept of a totality and, also, reinforces the alleged coincidence involved in reducing political action to economic, and essentially capitalist, interests. Of course, there have been many attempts to avoid the consequences of conceiving the anti-trust movement in this way but these attempts are, sooner or later, presented with a variation of the more general paradox. To the extent that one or other of these explanations is seemingly rejected, then the underlying account of the failure of anti-trust legislation becomes meaningless because it still depends upon an implicit convergence of interests. On the other hand, if they are retained, then the corollary is an entirely unacceptable portrait of the social formation as a series of levels linked by some form of expressive causality. If this paradox is to be avoided then an alternative way of dealing with the independence of the political is required. It must be said, however, that this is not an easy task. At the very least, an appropriate alternative would have to forestall the *a priori* distribution of social space into economic and political instances, production relations and social relations. In addition, it would need to avoid reducing political positions to economically derived interests. Finally, it would have to render highly ambiguous the concept of the control of the state apparatus by capital or one of its fractions, monopoly capital.

Once anti-trust legislation is regarded in terms which suggest the structural relations of monopoly capital, on one side, and the phenomenal effects of legal regulation, on the other, then the twin problems of determinism and causality appear on the agenda. How do we connect the omnipotence of monopoly capital with the impotence of legal regulation? Althusser manages to avoid this problem by arguing an essentially Spinozian concept of structural causality. In effect the structure is present in its effects which thereby obviates the need for any mechanical connection. There is at least one problem with this conception. Althusser's work is characterized by a rigorous polemic against all forms of economism, historicism and idealism and yet we find here an obvious reliance upon an implicit determinative principle which underlies and ensures certain necessary effects. Thus his work is gripped by a form which he seeks to eradicate, with the inevitable result that the political appears to vanish into the overarching coherence of the totality. There appears to be no other option available to Althusser.

Cutler *et al.* argue the radical separation of determinate relations of production from their conditions of existence. This has the merit of reintroducing the problem of determinism but, nevertheless, fails to specify any sort of general solution. Where there is an indication of the mechanism which connects conditions of existence to determinate relations of production, it seems to hinge upon the fact that determinate relations of production 'possess' conditions of existence. These conditions of existence are uniquely theirs. As we have seen this involves an exceedingly formal type of functionalist explanation. Exactly how this conclusion accords with the simultaneous denial of all forms of causality is not entirely clear. This is especially confusing since the denial of causality seems to depend upon a rejection of the twin problems of causal agency and the cleavage of social space into instances.

In attempting to accord politics the independence it deserves both Althusser and, to a much lesser extent, Hindess and Hirst are each forced into a position which they would regard as unacceptable. Despite their intention to render a theory of political specificity the problem of political independence remains unsolved. If political actors are granted a measure of independence and they are not simply reduced to the immanence of the structure in its effects or analysed in terms of their representation of the interests of big business, farmers or entrepreneurs, then the problems inherent in the concept of interests and the issue of what it is that they represent, are crucial. For example, to state that a political position, platform, party or argument is in the interests of big business is to specify those interests independently of the means of their representation. It is to locate an abstract arena where interests can be crystallized unambiguously. The actual course of politics can then be measured against this abstract spectrum. As Hirst (1977) makes clear, however, in the absence of any attempt to account for the distortion or non-representation of fundamental class interests the analysis is short-circuited and, once again, politics becomes more or less a direct expression of basic class interests. Both the concept of totality, and that of interests, appear to grant a measure of autonomy to the political but, as we have seen, inserting that autonomy into a coherent social formation or, constantly referring it back to more basic and, therefore, more real class interests or potentialities, produces one of two results: either the concept is made redundant and once again politics reflects economic forces directly, or the distortion is entirely accidental and, therefore, beyond analysis. At the very least this is a questionable basis on which to conduct an examination of, what will be argued is, the specificity of political action and that of the anti-monopoly movement in particular.

Even if the concept of an expressive totality and the notion of interests and their representation in politics are rejected, the manner in which the problem is posed reduces, still further, the likelihood of a proper solution. To state that monopoly capital has certain requirements and that these requirements are represented in particular forms of political action, even if such representation or reproduction is imperfect, qualified or independently determined, is to indicate an underlying motor of history, which allows monopoly capital to be the fundamental dynamic of historical change, together with a functional correspondence between phenomenon and essence, politics and interests, which enables those requirements to be met. Both Hindess (1978) and Hirst (1977), reject the concept of interests as representations of Svengali-like forces and they refuse the necessity of any correspondence. But, for all that, the concept of determinate relations of production, their conditions of existence and the means and practices which achieve them cannot, at least on the face of it, avoid specifying a functional relation between production and its conditions of existence and a contingent connection between political practice and conditions of existence. They both assert the radical autonomy of political practice and, hence, the possibility of addressing political movements and strategies in their specificity, rather than in their capacity as manifestations of a more basic essence. In asserting such autonomy, however, they allow for the possibility, even the necessity, of some form of their general interconnection. In this sense it seems quite inevitable that there is some prior allocation of social space involved. But the warrant for such a division appears to be arbitrarily decided and, as we have seen, presents problems which are perhaps unnecessary.

These various renditions of the relative independence of political practice appear to depend upon an implicit concept of class. To be sure, the concept exhibits considerable internal variation, but it does occupy a privileged position. For example, it may be used to secure a positive relation between political representation and economic interests. Or else it may be more of a vision, an ultimate reference point for and a proximate site of, a whole host of intersecting, relatively autonomous determinations. Witness the way in which the class struggle is often invoked to account for particular discrepancies. But, as Poulantzas and Althusser have made abundantly clear, there are no social classes prior to their opposition in struggle, classes do not exist first and foremost and only then join in struggle. Classes can only be identified in the process of struggle and, more importantly, only come into existence in forms of struggle and conflict. Therefore, struggle would appear to assume priority over classes and the associated problem of their structural determination. Hence the elegant, albeit excessively formal, typologies of class determination produced by Erik Olin Wright (1978) are to some extent secondary problems. On the contrary, the actual forms of struggle, conflict, tensions, strategies, political articulations, issues and arguments, are of paramount importance—they are not just secondary to some real arena of class struggle situated within structural parameters or on the terrain of history. In short, attention cannot centre on an essential theatre of class struggle demarcated by orthodox Marxism, of which particular issues are but phenomenal manifestations, without in turn heralding the relative denegation of particular political strategies. To assert the specificity of political struggles in this context is an essentially stillborn enterprise which, at the very least, forestalls a proper analysis of the anti-monopoly movement.

In terms of the analysis of anti-trust law, however, the foregoing argument has a number of specific consequences. On this basis, the anti-trust movement can be viewed as an articulation of discrete forms of political practice which comprise distinct organizational forms and definite structurations of political issues. The political forms are not condensations of some abstract class struggle nor are they mere requirements of specific fractions of capital or functional necessities of determinate relations of production. Of course, a number of issues remain unresolved by this form of argument namely, what is the relation between the apparently real adjustment of the form of ownership and the forms of political opposition/defence entailed in the anti-trust movement? If there is a genuine independence of politics from pure class positions and interests, a genuine liberation of the political from the artificial insemination by the economic instance, then, a radical separation is entailed along the lines advocated by Cutler *et al.* (1977) with all the attendant difficulties thereof. Alternatively if there is no distinction to be made between political and economic instances, and there are simply organizational complexes which defy classification as economic/political items, then the question of representation is redundant. Everything is determined by its essential existence as a social relation. This would appear to mean that the anti-monopoly movement is inseparable from *laissez-faire* capitalism and entrepreneurial forms of ownership and that *laissez-faire* capital reappears in person on the political stage. Given the form of the critique employed here, this solution is clearly unacceptable. Although it is by no means certain that it is the inevitable conclusion to the radical dissolution of instances. This is partly a question of how to draw the distinction between the economic and the political and indeed of how they are defined. For example, it is perfectly consistent to argue for the non-reduction of political organization to economic interests on the grounds that the traditional distinctions between what is political and what is economic are untenable. This does not mean, however, that politics is reduced to economics or vice versa. On the contrary, the distinction is bound to be somewhat arbitrary and so it is a question of the sort of distinction and the criteria involved. The anti-monopoly movement was clearly designed to defend a definite type of social organization characterized by a form of *laissez-faire* ownership. But because it is regarded as a basic constituent of sociality, ownership is not seen as an economic or legal form which it falls to the anti-monopoly movement to defend. Nor is it the political manifestation of economic liberalism. The movement depended upon a number of clearly defined organizational contingencies which were bound up with the type of ownership involved. Both the form of ownership and the organizational contingencies of the anti-monopoly movement are truly social relations. Therefore, the twin questions of economic reductionism and political idealism are inappropriate.

Once fought for and won, the independence of political conditions from economic relations is not easily relinquished. For example, let us reconsider the position espoused by Cutler *et al.* (1977). Determinate relations of production have specific conditions of existence secured by distinct forms of political and social practice. But why must determinate relations of production have priority over their conditions of existence and the ensuing relation take a functional form? No doubt the answer is that materialism necessarily implies some form of priority for relations of production, although as we have seen, such a conception of the relations of production is restrictive in the extreme. Which leads on to the second doubt: why distribute social relations into determinate and conditional relations, especially in view of the simultaneous denial of the validity of distributing social space underlying the rejection of discrete instances and the criticism of general doctrines of causality? Surely the logical outcome would be a seamless web in which causal priority is denied, rather than a surrogate form of conditional and determinate instances (Wright, 1979, p. 72).

The present argument is conducted in terms of accepting the logic of radical discontinuity whilst, at the same time, recognizing the more fundamental and particular continuities which characterize all forms of sociality. Since it is impossible, for a genuinely social analysis, to separate instances, items and forms without at some stage reintroducing a general means for their subsequent interrelation, then, a truly radical separation of forms or the assertion of political specificity, is possible only on the basis of a completely different form of continuity. Discontinuity presupposes continuity and therefore, it is a question of the sort of continuity which characterizes social relations. To state the specific convergence between the social form of ownership (a particular strategy of political organization, a series of constitutional premises and so on) and the construction of a political platform of anti-monopoly politics is very different from countenancing a general relationship between class determination, real or potential interests, and their political expression; a long way from reading off political positions from class or economic locations. In short, there are a whole series of contingencies which comprise the anti-trust movement. There is a complex network of social relations, law, forms of calculation and technical criteria which govern the existence of *laissez-faire* capitalism and, therefore, the basis of anti-monopolism; a whole series of sociocultural residues which cannot be adequately comprehended via the distribution of sociality into determinate and conditional relations.

A number of objections may be made to this sort of argument not least because it appears to be a form of pluralism. Whilst there may be a plurality of contingencies, one element crucial to a definition of pluralism—the demarcation of a given social item, the state, from the range of forces which influence it—is quite definitely absent. Accordingly, the tendency to drift into a general theory of multiple-causality or a concept of political plasticity is muted. At the very least the conception of the state as but a special type of organization of social relations would prevent the state from being regarded as an instance with the capacity to condense separate and politically diverse interests. Likewise, the companion charge of historicism or essentialism would also be misplaced. In the absence of any fundamental, unifying or determinative principle earmarked by a spirit, epoch or totality which forces its imprint on all social relations it seems difficult to envisage how such a charge could be sustained.

It is perhaps inevitable that the argument has, so far, remained rather defensive. It is possible, however, to assert the analysis more forcefully. It is argued in Chapter four that each of the relations of ownership contains a fundamental tension or conflict, it is this tension which characterizes the dynamic of the relations of ownership and their capacity to change. Thus, title is governed by a persistent tension between sale/income and between corporate and stockholder claims; possession is gripped by a struggle over the conditions of the labour process, strategies and counter-strategies are evolved as problems of organization, research is undertaken, innovation countenanced and various human relations and organization theories invoked, stimulated and commissioned as practical and theoretical responses to problems generated by the tension inherent in the relation of possession/exclusion; control is engrossed by larger issues of national/international climate. All three relations are articulated together in a complex, wholly interactive manner and, as such, define the relevant form of ownership. Determination of particular classes is not a primary aim. Tension and conflict exist independently of specifying the class location of the supports of such struggle. Thus, the general relation, ownership of/separation from, replicated in discrete ways in each relation of ownership, describes the source of a fundamental conflict without requiring the actual presence of wholly unambiguous classes at each and every point. The reference is to elements of struggle, rather than to completely formed historical agents each embodying some pure class position diametrically opposed to, and inextricably set upon a collision course with another pure class location. The fundamental problem of agency is not resolved by the resort to contradictory class locations, which serves only to demonstrate the facility with which basic categories admix themselves in ever more infinite permutations. On the contrary, it is necessary to dissolve the trajectory of an essentialist form of class struggle in order to realize the particular character of regional struggles, tensions and conflicts. Accordingly, interests are defined, not as quasi-automatic reflections of neo-class positions but, in terms of organizational forms and strategies constituted in the very interstices of ownership. For example, this procedure bears directly upon the notion of whether there exists a distinct managerial elite unified by a series of interests which separate managers, as a distinct class, from the narrower range of capitalist interests. As Hindess (1978) and Hirst (1977) respectively point out, it is not so much an issue of groups, positions and classes but rather, strategies, political sediments and legal residues. In short, it is unnecessary to identify interests and, therefore, authors of such interests, since it is sufficient to locate political forces and arguments in as much as they are constructed through definite forms of political practice and organizational strategy.

It is not so much that ownership is real, and that legal and ideological forms are predicated upon, or indeed lag behind, that prior reality but rather, that the relations of ownership are inextricably tied up with so-called ideological and decision-making frames, which in part constitute those relations. But this is not the structural determination of class position or an economistic derivation of ideology, state and law because, first of all, the form of ownership is not a structure, nor is it yet a totality, still less is it a constellation of positions and, secondly, ideology, law and state are not conditions of ownership, nor are they reflections of ownership, they are quite simply mutually implicated in forms of ownership. The form of ownership is defined by the organizational strategies and relations which do not necessarily form a unity, and, therefore, cannot be reduced to an essential principle of ownership/separation, nor can they be fixed as a static, functional complex. But neither are they radically distinct in the sense of being assigned a priori to particular social destinations—the economic, the political, the legal—such that their autonomy becomes problematic and ultimately reduces to some concept of overall or final convergence. This may be a hard option but, since relative autonomy is ultimately meaningless and radical autonomy virtually impossible, there is no alternative but to consider ways in which specific discontinuities are rendered in a general context of continuity. To be sure, the danger of conflation applies an important limitation to this conception and, whilst it is quite true that such an argument provides no prior grounds for distinguishing levels, or types of social relations, the organizational relations are, nevertheless, discrete orders. But they are not discrete in a way which draws rationalist cleavages between real adjuncts of academic disciplines;

law and economics, or which assign certain types of sociality to discrete levels of the social formation. This argument is perhaps the logical outcome of a systematic denial of epistemology and hence of the relation between existence and discourse (Hindess and Hirst, 1977), and the attempt to take seriously the notion of structuration (Giddens, 1979) as a genuine alternative to structure.

Anti-monopolism

It is now possible to describe the constituents of what may be termed anti-monopolism. Whilst falling considerably short of prescribing free competition and enjoining business to compete under the threat of injunction or criminal sanction, the federal anti-trust laws are, none the less, inextricably bound up with a particular set of social arrangements based on the theme of free competition and *laissez-faire* capitalism. The connection is forged in at least two particular ways. Not only does the Sherman Act fail to make any sense outside a context which records an implicit faith in some sort of free enterprise system, but the central protagonists on the political stage, and the final assessment of anti-trust law, can only be regarded in the interstices of two general types of social arrangements. For example, to talk of monopoly points inevitably to a distinct type of ownership in which a substantial proportion of any local, national, or international market is brought under the auspices of a common organizational complex. Whether the components of a corporation are formally separate or organizationally integrated, the fact that it has a monopoly means that the form of control is distinct from that entailed under free competition and that the relations of ownership are different in consequence. These two general sets of social arrangements define the extent of the anti-trust movement and anti-trust law respectively.

The fundamental provisions of anti-trust law have considerable common law precedents/antecedents dating back to seventeenth century English law. These provisions, however, become all the more opaque when viewed as the systematic outcome of a process of rationalization and legal change or as the advance which signals the essential mutability of law in the wake of complex industrial and social change. For this sort of perspective, law is counterposed to other forms of sociality as an item governed by an internal dynamic of advance, rupture or response to external exigencies, rather than being looked at as a complex element fully integral to the organization of social relationships. For the present, anti-trust law is not seen primarily as a rational administrative response to the erosion of enterprise by a wholly alien and apparently spontaneous outburst of monopolization or merger mania, but is instead viewed as a strategy undertaken as a challenge to a particular sort of social organization which involves, as a matter of course, a defence of certain sets of social relations. That the strategy was authentic and sincere is very far from implying that it was necessarily successful or that it echoed some basic revolutionary chord in the class struggle. Of course, this procedure necessarily points to some form of class struggle, but it is far from being the sort of original class struggle which maps out all social relations or which provides the motor of history; far from the struggle between classes which at once characterizes the totality which in turn structures class position and thence, in true circularity, class struggle. On the contrary, it is viewed in terms of a highly specific strategy which involves the tensions and contradictions engendered by the form of ownership and the form of organization of social relations.

A cautionary note should be sounded in relation to the substance of this chapter. The argument presented here depends upon the precise determination of what happened in the run up to the Sherman Act of 1890. Otherwise there is an equally powerful argument to the effect that anti-trust legislation was the result of an entirely cynical manipulation of concessions formulated and granted at the conscious level by political leaders or hypothesized as entirely responsive to the interests of the ruling class or big business. There is, however, a sense in which 'what happened' is beyond us. The empiricist denegation of the past as non-existent, and history as thereby impossible, carries considerable weight, particularly in view of the historians' reliance on empirical analogues—accounts, reconstructed events and so on—materials which are publicly contestible but, none the less, empirical artefacts. The analysis must hinge upon something other than the actuality of historical evidence. In the absence of absolute guarantees concerning the past, whether sustained by rationalist or empiricist forms of discourse, attention must turn to other sorts of requirement. For example, Popper's (1968) assertion that elegance may, under certain circumstances, stand as a criterion of scientific acceptability, or Thompson's (1978) insistence on the unique quality of historical logic, would at least appear to allow for alternative guarantees of scientificity. What is clear is that history can in no sense provide an independent crucible wherein the competing claims of historical interpretation can be resolved. On the contrary, historical explanation of this kind touches the very core constituents of any social theory—what kind of social portrait does a particular historical explanation imply, what are the implications for social analysis entailed therein? These are the sorts of issues which separate out competing interpretations of the anti-trust movement. Not a claim to absolute truth, nor even to relative acceptability or to purity of purpose, but to the consequences and coherence of social theory entailed in any analysis of anti-trust law, legal regulation and control.

The orthodox liberal historian's view of anti-trust, gently satirized by Hofstadter and pedalled more or less intact by Pearce, unfolds as follows: "In 1890, as a largely meaningless and cynical gesture to appease public sentiment, an ultra-conservative Congress passed the Sherman Anti-trust Act" (Hofstadter,

1967, p. 190). The gesture was so vague as to be almost unintelligible and neglected to such a degree that it became dormant, if not actually impotent. Far from controlling combinations in pursuance of monopoly power, the law was used to far greater effect in hounding labour unions; a reversal of intent later consolidated during the 1920s when the Federal Trade Commission was turned, from an agency designed to control business, to an agency dominated by business interests. Whilst Hofstadter refrains from suggesting that such a portrait is entirely false, he, none the less, concludes that it is substantially misleading, largely because it tends to discount the . . . "honest if ineffectual concern with the problems of size and monopoly, and genuine doubts about the proper means of solving them" (1967, p. 191-2). The view of anti-trust portrayed here stems, in part, from telescoping the undoubted failure of anti-trust law to such an extent that it overlaps and, ultimately, denigrates the validity of the anti-monopoly movement altogether. Accordingly, the anti-monopoly movement is considered only insofar as it presents the necessity of being assuaged, sold out to, or manipulated by, cynical plutocrats. It will be readily apparent that the logical result of this reduction is the anti-monopoly movement is denied any organizational integrity what so ever.

Over and against the view portrayed above, the thesis advanced here is really very simple. There are specific reasons which account for the failure of anti-monopoly law, reasons which belong to the structure of law and the manner in which law conventionally addresses the corporate form of enterprise. These reasons more than account for the failure of anti-trust law without having recourse to a conspiracy view of history or to a conception of an omniscient plutocracy; the specific failings of each of these accounts have been recorded in Chapter one. Moreover, in the final analysis, a theory of plutocratic omniscience, can only gain credence through a cynical disregard or distortion of the organizational basis of anti-monopolism.

The present chapter attempts to give expression to the organizational basis of anti-monopolism. The intention is not so much to gauge the extent of anti-monopoly feeling, nor the somewhat intangible relation between popular sentiment and legislative activity, but rather to record the rudimentary nexus which sustained anti-monopolism in the first place. The organizational nexus is important for the reason that political sentiment should not be viewed as an automatic reflex of productive status but instead, as something which requires specific means for its articulation. Therefore, it is insufficient to point to the relative disadvantage of certain economic groups in relation to, and largely as a result of, the growth of the corporate economy, and thence to infer the inevitable tide of anti-monopolism. On the contrary, sentiment of this character requires substantial organization, since it does not simply issue forth from the underlying dislocation of economic forces. This much should not be taken as a denial of any link between economic organization and political action, merely that the link, if link is an appropriate word, is forged in a very special manner. Thus, the heart of the matter is the organization of so called economic activity and the struggle to preserve one set of social arrangements over another. The form of organization of ownership and the organization of anti-monopolism are, in this sense, inseparable—since they each depend upon the other—with the result that the concept of representation is hardly a relevant method with which to grasp the phenomenon of anti-monopolism. Accordingly, the organization of ownership and the organization of anti-monopolism are continuous, not in the sense that pressure groups are held to be continuous with economic groups and thus to represent their interests, but in the sense that the arrangements entailed under one form of ownership and the positions articulated or generated within a particular type of political organization are inseparable as types of social relations. The organized defence of entrepreneurial ownership is a necessary part of the continued existence of that form of ownership, which is not to say that such a defence is secured automatically by the form of ownership merely that, for analytical purposes, the two cannot be separated out because they are continuous.

What then is the organizational basis of anti-monopoly politics? The roots of organized anti-monopolism are to be found in the agrarian campaigns of the late nineteenth century and, in particular, those directed against the railroads. For example, the Granger movement of the 1870s resulted, albeit indirectly, in the Granger laws designed to regulate the railroads. The importance of agrarian discontent is usually registered in a curiously abstract way as a generalized discontent with the economic and political changes of the late nineteenth century. Thus, it is often argued that, whilst these campaigns focused upon the specific inadequacies of the rate rebate system or the currency issue, these deficiencies were less important than the basic "immorality of the system as a whole" (Miller, 1971, p. 162). Without in any way wishing to deny the force of this disgruntled reaction it must be stressed, however, that anti-monopolism was not just a generalized response to a shift in the principles of democratic government or, to a perceived interruption of 'the American Dream', still less was it purely a spontaneous outburst of popular sentiment. On the contrary, anti-monopolism contained exceedingly specific points of reference and particular grievances and, moreover, a distinct organizational structure. As Thorelli indicates

> Opposition to the malpractices of transportation agencies and other 'natural monopolies' was always a significant part of the anti-monopoly movement in post-bellum years; in fact, until at least 1880 the outcry against the railroads constituted the core of that movement. Short-term exorbitance and flagrant discriminations of many varieties formed the focus of opposition to the railroads. Only secondarily were the farmers of the West and South, the Grangers, the independent, Reform and Anti-monopoly parties antagonised by the forms of railroad organisation. (1954, p. 568-9)

It is true to say, however, that these particular grievances did engage more fundamental issues, in the sense that the deficiencies of the rate rebate system, for example, were inseparable from the issue of monopoly *per se* and, therefore, the form of organization involved in their perpetration. But it is not the case that these specific grievances were but manifestations of some more basic morality play or, that the form of organization was simply a secondary consideration. The relationship between actual grievances and more abstract issues is far more profound than is credited by either Miller or Thorelli involving, as it does, the implication of so-called abstract issues in the actual formulation and even identification of grievances.

The importance of organization in this respect is vital but it is a consideration which is all too easily forgotten. For example, Hofstadter remarks that ". . . it is too little realised that the farmers, who were quite impotent as a special interest when they were numerous, competing, and unorganised, grew stronger as they grew relatively fewer, became more concerted, more tenaciously organised and self centred" (1955, p. 7-8). This is indeed a compelling indication of the limitations involved in reducing political influence to a question of numbers and a persuasive indictment of the contraction of politics to the mere expression of economic position.

The organization of anti-monopoly politics was by no means clear cut. Indeed the organization of the anti-monopoly movement, in defence of what amounts to the right to remain unorganized, contains an apparent paradox. Whilst it is quite true that the process of organization in defence of individual enterprise against the encroachment of opportunity by organized conglomerates of wealth engendered tensions within anti-monopolism this did not detract from the importance of organization to the anti-monopoly movement. What these tensions did affect is the particular organizational objectives and, more importantly, the choice of legalistic remedies designed more to enable competition than to interfere with free choice.

It is perhaps a commonplace to assert that the organization of political movements can only take place according to a set of more or less explicit premises and on the basis of a series of ideological/cultural conditions. It is these conditions and premises which provide a clue to the unique thread which joins entrepreneurial endeavour and political democracy in a seemingly unbreakable weave. The link, once forged, proves an exceedingly versatile and inclusive tool in the construction of anti-monopolism as an organized movement. What, then, are these premises and conditions? In terms of the agrarian movement, undoubtedly the most important premise concerns the physical possession and use of land as a necessary and sufficient condition of valid ownership, legal title and property right. This commonwealth of land owning producers can then be protected by a form of minimalist state given over to sanctifying and guaranteeing the rights of separate producers. These components go to make up what

Hofstadter entitles the Agrarian Myth, according to which Americans pay homage to the 'fancied innocence of their origins'. Its importance for us stems from the common vocabulary which the myth spells out, enabling a variety of disparate groups to coalesce in organized anti-monopolism. Furthermore, the consensual quality of the vocabulary of the agrarian myth denotes an important convergence between the exigencies of organizing anti-monopolism and the essential features of entrepreneurial ownership—since they both depend upon the same cultural artefacts. Therefore, it is this coincidence of structural features which heralds the form of ownership as an organizing principle of anti-monopolism, rather than any clear-cut relationship based on the interests of the victims of economic disruption.

It has been indicated already that anti-trust legislation presents a certain paradox with regard to the regulation of free enterprise. Likewise, the central place accorded to the collective organization of anti-monopolism would appear to be at variance with its avowed intention; the preservation of individual entrepreneurs. It might be expected, also, that the position of the farmer, within the anti-monopoly movement, is not exactly unambiguous, poised as he is between the dignity of labour, on the one hand, and the claims of independent ownership, on the other. Indeed, Hofstadter goes as far as to argue that the character of the American farmer evinced a dual structure, espousing at one and the same time solid entrepreneurial values embracing opportunity, progress, profit and commercial values and a form of agrarian radicalism, which vented his yeoman inheritance, betokening a solidarity with labour rather than capital. Far from manifesting a fundamental contradiction, this dual aspect of agrarian character demonstrates what Hofstadter, in another context, called the co-existence of reform and reaction in American politics; the fact that anti-monopolism was organized around entrepreneurial or conservative principles against the encroachment of opportunity by big business. It is deeply significant, therefore, that the opposition to big business was based upon the idea of a privileged relationship between entrepreneurial endeavour and political democracy. As a political faith this relationship was useful in combining diverse political organizations and, as an organizational principle, it demonstrated the cleavage between entrepreneurial and corporate forms of ownership. In addition, anti-monopolism demonstrated the profound coincidence between political organization and the form of ownership. Thus the growth of land speculation in the latter half of the nineteenth century, unrelieved by the Homestead Act and facilitated by unrestricted entry until 1888, indicated a fundamental change in the form of ownership. The absentee-owner of land displaced the yeoman farmer as the prototype of agrarian America and the pattern of tenancy, entailed in absentee ownership, was consolidated accordingly. The Farmers Alliance and, more especially, the Populist movement can, then, be seen as organized expressions of the principles of entrepreneurial ownership and, therefore, a direct defence of its actual structure. For Hofstadter at least, the Populist movement was but ". . . another episode in the well established tradition of American entrepreneurial radicalism", an expression which well sums up the organizational principles of anti-monopolism (Hofstadter, 1955, p. 58).

The importance of Populism for the anti-monopoly movement lay principally in the way that Populism sustained the idea of a single all-important struggle, between the allied hosts of monopolies, the money power, great trusts and railroad corporations, in one corner, and the farmers, labourers and merchants, who produced wealth and paid their taxes, in the other. The struggle was viewed as fierce, the stakes as high and, above all, the contest as one which admitted of no middle way. Thus anti-monopolism was clearly defined as *the* opposition in American society and the price of failure as absolute depotism and/or the end of civilization. The link between routing the plutocrats and the preservation of democratic freedom could scarcely have been made any stronger; a factor which perhaps accounts for the inclusive character of Populism. This particular link has always been regarded as an essential feature of anti-trust legislation. For example, the Attorney-General's Committee stated that "Anti-trust is a distinctive American means for assuring the competitive economy on which our political and social freedom under representative government in part depend" (United States Department of Justice, 1955, p. 2). The inclusive appeal of this sentiment, for Populism, was further reinforced by the unique crystallizing power of the merest suspicion of conspiracy. Whether the locus of the conspiracy is alcohol, communism or big business, it has always received its fair share of heated invective. Indeed, the corporate conspiracy was deemed to be so omnipotent that the farmers' alliances, initially distrustful of all forms of government regulation, eventually countenanced almost any federal measure that would shift the balance away from the corporate economy. Even where such measures appeared to contradict fundamental principles of *laissez-faire* society, they seemed admissible given the deep cleavage riven by the polarization of corporate and anti-corporate organization. Whereas the Granger movement, or rather the Granger laws of the 1870s, limited intervention to state level, the Alliance movement of the 1880s effectively paved the way for federal regulation and control of the corporate economy. As a result, the mere fact of federal action against the trusts was by no means as contradictory as it may seem to some contemporary observers. Although it must be reiterated that in this respect the Granger movement vested little faith in the idea of regulation *per se*. As Miller makes clear the farmer ". . . showed little confidence in legislative control and continued to look to competition from waterways and more railways for a solution to some of his problems. The state and law, the farmer believed, were too easily perverted into instruments of advantage for the commercial classes" (Miller, 1971, p. 162). A disquiet which was echoed in the very failure of the Granger laws to achieve their, admittedly limited, objectives. What this line of thinking demonstrates very clearly is the need to account for the resort to the legal regulation of monopolies or railroads since the actuality of legal regulation cannot be induced from the prevalence of a public clamour for a distinctly legal form of regulation. If for no other reason than because the clamour was not so much for legal regulation as for political and social annihilation. At the same time though, Miller does argue that the railroads preferred to make their stand in the federal courts for a number of reasons. In the first place, "the companies seriously doubted the impartiality of the state courts, and it is true that these courts were highly responsive to popular pressures" (1971, p. 175). An idea which has been recycled by Pearce in the sense that local political organization threatened the railroads in a way in which federal regulation could not and which would appear to indicate preference for the least ineffectual of two equally ineffective remedies.

The various agrarian organizations were by no means the sole basis of the anti-monopoly movement. Indeed, it was characteristic of the Populist movement in general that an organizational nexus was formulated which embraced a diverse range of causes. Not least important of these alliances was that between yeoman and labourer, agrarian and proletarian organization. Thus, rural and civic labour were equivalent forms for the Populist movement engaging, as it did, both the Knights of Labor and the Farmers alliance. That these groups later diverged, labour toward more collectivist programmes under the aegis of the American Federation of Labor from 1886 onwards, and the farmers to commercial and even corporate forms of organization, does not in any way belie the potency of the alliance at the time. In this respect Millis and Montgomery make it clear that the demands of organized labour before the first world war were . . . "of an individualistic, anti-monopoly, personal rights, uplift character rather than protection of the job and security of tenure" (Thorelli, 1954, p. 147). Again, Thorelli appears to suggest that this anti-monopolism was perhaps a result of the effective separation of labour from the possession and control of its conditions of production (1954, p. 150). Notwithstanding the apparent ease with which anti-monopoly sentiment emerged, the task involved in uniting these various groups under one umbrella should not be underestimated. In this respect the professional experience of the Populist leadership, albeit much of it an experience of failure, is a significant example of the organized structure of Populism. In this sense, Hofstadter (1967) details the previous involvement of the Populist leadership in a succession of lost causes. Likewise, the pre-eminence of merchants and business men, rather than farmers, in the reform movement of the 1870s perhaps highlights the importance of the organization of interests rather than their simple transmission from economic position to legislative outcome (Miller, 1971). The fact that the farmers were organized on a different and more self-consciously commercial basis by 1919, when the Farm Bureau Federation was founded or, that the farmers themselves began to fall foul of the anti-trust laws, that is until their partial exemption along with labour organizations under the Clayton Act in 1914, in no way detracts from their vital and radical role in the latter half of the nineteenth century. Furthermore, and this is possibly the basic point, welding together seemingly diverse causes into a coherent movement, characterized above all by a deeply held consensus against the trusts, could scarcely have been achieved spontaneously.

In addition to organized labour and agrarian groups, the place of small and medium sized business should not be ignored. After all, these firms expressed the prototype of *laissez-faire* enterprise and as such, could be expected to be in the forefront of anti-monopolist organization. Even an apparent reluctance on behalf of businessmen to engage in an organized defence of free market forces does not detract from the role of enterprise in anti-monopolism. Of course, their reluctance was not always a relevant factor given the priority of organization over sentiment. In this respect the role of the Sovereigns of Industry cannot be overestimated. This organization ". . . during the 1870's successfully, if temporarily, brought such diverse elements as farmers, labourers and urban middle class together for purposes of political and economic reform" (Thorelli, 1954, p. 149). This organization was stridently anti-monopolist and provided an effective framework for the crystallization of entrepreneurial values, together with a programme for their defence. Likewise, the anti-trust league provided an important forum for independent businessmen.

At various times, then, the Granger and Reform movements of the 1870s organized the campaign against the railroads and the farmers alliance orchestrated anti-monopolism which, by 1890, and buttressed by various Labour and business groups, was at the forefront of a national campaign against the trusts. W. S. Morgan noted the organized opinion of the farmers as follows: "Monopolies exist by law are chartered by law, and should be controlled by law. A trust is a conspiracy against legitimate trade . . . It is demoralising in its influence, inconsistent with free institutions and dangerous to our liberties. To participate in a trust should be a crime subject to severe punishment" (Thorelli, 1954, p. 144). Likewise, a farmers congress of the United States in 1889 reiterated its opposition to all combinations of capital which control the market, whether those combinations were in the form of trusts or not. Whilst the form of agrarian organization was at least maintained by the Greenback movement, that is until 1888, the organization of local farm labour groups successfully articulated more explicit demands for state action on the trust question. Such action, on the issue of trusts in general, betokened a much wider alliance with, for example, the Knights of Labor; an organization which, during the 1880s, addressed itself to, amongst other objectives, the problem of strangling monopoly. The demands for constitutional action on the issue of the trusts, initiated rather falteringly and perhaps unwillingly within agrarian farmers at first, were later furthered under the auspices of the national Anti-monopoly Party formed in 1884 out of an amalgamation of various state equivalents or predecessors. Together with the Sovereigns of Industry, the Anti-trust League and the National Labor unions, these were the diverse components of anti-monopolism in its first, largely populist, phase. The campaigns instituted under the banner of anti-monopolism were not, in the final analysis, unconnected with the Interstate Commerce Act of 1887 and the Sherman Act of 1890. Although it must be said that the connection, between popular sentiment and legislative remedy, is by no means clear cut. Whilst reaching a crescendo in the 1880s anti-monopolism did not recede after this apparent victory, indeed Hofstadter argues that it was at its most intense until 1914 (1967, p. 193). Nevertheless, anti-monopolism underwent a subtle change of form as a result perhaps of its articulation within the provisions of Progressivism.

It is not feasible to examine progressivism in any great detail, nor is it essential to chart the precise demise of populism and the exact germination of the progressive movement. Indeed, a precise distinction between Populism and Progressivism is difficult to achieve. Perhaps the most that can be said, at this juncture, is that whilst Populism was characterized by a marked consensus, Progressivism heralded ambivalence on many crucial issues. Thus, Hofstadter is able to remark that . . . "the Populists had tended to be of one mind on most broad social issues, and that mind was rather narrow and predictable" (1955, p. 134). Whereas the progressive movement attempted to realign the benefits and limitations of corporate size, by means of a distinction between responsible and irresponsible wealth, the populist movement was unremitting in its hostility to big business *per se.* To be sure, the progressive movement attempted to draw the equation between private property and political freedom ever more tightly, as George Mowry observed, progressivism was opposed to . . . "the impersonal, concentrated, and supposedly privileged property represented by the behemoth corporation. Looking backward to an older America (they) sought to recapture and reaffirm the older individualistic values in all the strata of political, economic and social life" (Mowry, 1951, p. 88-9). In this they were at one with the Populists and, as one observer put it, the Progressives succeeded in enacting one after another of the Populist demands or, rather less charitably, they stole much of the Populists underwear and clothed it in more respectable garments.

Although founded on a clear commitment to *laissez-faire* philosophy, the Progressive movement underwent a substantial modification ultimately perhaps aspiring to a form of leadership which Appleman Williams would describe as class conscious; a form of enlightened self-interest or reformism prepared to hold the ring between corporate excesses and Collective Trade unionism (Appleman-Williams, 1961). As has been seen already the progressive movement was to have a very important effect upon the unfolding of anti-trust enterprise, with the most obvious connections being the distinction between good and bad trusts and, the introduction of the rule of reason and the concept of abuse. There is, then, a distinction between Populism, which was vigorously anti-monopoly and of undoubted importance in generating the 'possibility' of the 1887 Interstate Commerce Act and the 1890 Sherman Act, and Progressivism, which sought an operating equation between *laissez-faire* and industrial concentration and, needless to say, failed abysmally in terms of its anti-monopolism (whatever its more limited successes as a harbinger of regulation).

We have, so far, seen the substantial organizational basis of anti-monopolism, but the force of anti-monopoly sentiment presents us with a perplexing paradox. If Populism was as fervently anti-monopolist as is claimed, and given the sincerity of congressional intent in passing the 1887 and 1890 anti-monopoly laws, how then can we account for the failure of so laudable an attempt? Some have attempted to explain the underachievement of anti-trust legislation. Thus, Thorelli observes that "It has been held that business regarded the anti-trust bill as completely innocuous or even favoured it as a means of pacifying the general disquietude without doing any serious damage to business interests" (1954, p. 215). An opinion which resonates at varying amplitudes within the work of revisionist historians, for example, Kolko, Weinstein and latterly Pearce. This position has been criticized in Chapter one and, at this juncture, it need only be argued, along with Thorelli, that business was not as homogeneous as it appeared and that small business and agrarian representatives were scarcely invisible in their opposition to monopoly and in their support of the bill. For example, "The records of legislative debates furnish abundant proof that the direct and specific aim of Congress was to eliminate and prevent restrictions on competition" (1954, p. 571). Likewise, it is clear that in passing the Sherman Act "Congress meant to go to the utmost extent of its Constitutional power in restraining trust and monopoly agreements" (U.S. v. South-Eastern Underwriters Assn. 322 U.S. 533, 558 (1944)). Although it must be conceded that the question of intent is not crucial to this sort of argument. For example, it is perfectly possible to argue the complete sincerity of congressional intent and to account for the failure of anti-trust legislation by reference to its subsequent manipulation by corporate interests. This has been argued by many commentators. For example, Neale (1966) argues a similar point to the effect that a tradition of dissolving monopolies during the 1911 period of structural remedy was abrogated in favour of the mere regulation of business conduct. As some would put it 'disillusion instead of dissolution' summed up the change in direction. Again this sort of argument ignores the defects inherent in law, which were written, or incorporated, into the provisions of anti-trust legislation. But the question still remains, why did anti-monopolism adopt a regulatory form so ill-suited to its task, namely that of the legal regulation of monopoly? This is indeed the crux of the issue, for if anti-monopolism had a strong organizational base, and if congress was at least not uninterested in passing a measure to control monopoly, then why was the Sherman Act so constrained in principle, let alone in practice?

The reasons for anti-monopolism using the law as a regulatory agency are exceedingly complex and could be accounted for by ascribing an attitude of legalism to the social structure of late nineteenth century America. Thus the law is seen as an essentially bourgeois construction, the anti-trust movement is viewed as a bourgeois organization and anti-trust legislation is seen as an eminently suitable remedy. This sort of account may have its attractions, perhaps chief among them being its apparently all inclusive character. There are, though, more direct components which can be assembled into a more persuasive explanation of the legalistic draft of anti-monopolism. It must be remembered that the opposition to the corporations was based upon a strongly individualist conception of ownership and democracy. Accordingly, whilst the corporations were seen as impersonal assaults on individual liberty and opportunity they were, nevertheless, reduced to individual terms, whether as corporate entities or as constellations of personal characteristics. For example, the so called muck-raking magazines of the progressive era were able ". . . not merely to name the malpractices in American business and politics, but to name the malpractitioners and their specific misdeeds" (Hofstadter, 1955, p. 188). Thus, the individualistic conception of the corporation in terms of individual agencies of malpractice made a resort to law appear eminently practicable. As we have seen, the extension of personal responsibility to include corporate behaviour was afforded by the general conception of the corporation as a legal person. Furthermore, if it were possible for the muckraking magazines to name the actual perpetrators of particular misdeeds, it was perhaps not unreasonable to accept that the law would be capable of doing likewise. In this sense, then, it would seem that the legal conception of the corporation and the journalistic arsenal interlocked to provide typical explanations of the roots of the trust problem. It was individual agents or individual corporations which were responsible for steering these vast conglomerates of corporate wealth to the brink of total domination and control of american society. Accordingly, not only was the law required to do something, it was seen as capable of doing something.

An example of the individualistic thrust of much exposé journalism can be seen in the history of Standard Oil written by Ida Tarbell (1966). This history was serialized by McClures magazine, between 1903 and 1904, and undoubtedly focused upon the particular exploits of John D. Rockefeller and his associates, principally, Henry Flagler, Samuel Andrews, Stephen Harkness and William Rockefeller. Thus Rockefeller was singled out as the symbol of the trust problem. With such powerful individualistic imagery it is perhaps a small step from exposure to enforcement. Therefore, this sort of journalistic foray undoubtedly contributed, in some sense, to the belief in the efficacy of legal sanction. To the extent that the sort of muckraking characteristic of the progressive era marks the culmination of a long process of expose journalism dating back to the 1870s, it is perhaps not unreasonable to suppose that it shaped the way that corporations were viewed and, in turn, paved the way for the acceptance of a legal remedy. This much perhaps indicates the way in which the form of law accorded with the way in which the problem was popularly conceived, but it does not tell us why there was a resort to legal remedy.

The idea that the trust problem should be approached by way of a strict application of the doctrine of personal responsibility has been renovated and put forward more recently. For example, it is possible to detect very similar currents at work in the vigorous campaigns of Ralph Nader (1973, 1976) which appear to centre upon the accountability of corporate personnel. The idea depends upon the enforcement of law relating to personal responsibility. Whether or not this would work is open to grave doubts, especially in view of the criticisms detailed in Chapter five. But what is important is that it reveals the feasibility of such an approach and, therefore, the basic individualistic structure of anti-trust legislation. Accordingly, as long as the trust problem is viewed in terms of the perpetration of individual acts by specific authors it carries the strong possibility that a legalistic remedy is seen as appropriate. Undoubtedly such an approach to the problem would have, and indeed has had, some effect, but whether it succeeds in restructuring corporate relationships, and thereby alleviating the problem of monopoly, would have to be examined in the light of the constraints on law recorded already. In that regard it is possible to state that any effect would be at best limited.

A similar conception of individual responsibility was broached by Ross (1907) at the turn of the century. In the context of an argument which suggested that sin had become corporate and impersonal with the onset of the corporate economy, Ross put forward the idea that corporate directors should be held personally responsible for every preventable corporate abuse. Thus, the solution to the problem of corporate malpractice was, yet again, viewed in terms of individual accountability.

A persistent fear within the anti-monopoly movement was that at some stage a combination of the combinations would emerge to dominate every facet of American society, including government. This fear clearly hinged upon corporations getting together in a conspiracy to defraud the American public of its birthright. The importance of conspiracy for the anti-monopoly movement and anti-trust legislation has been recorded in some detail. There is, though, an important connection between the two. If the basic threat was seen to be conspiracy, then it is not unlikely that the law would be used as a means of dealing with the problem and that the concept of conspiracy would be accorded a central place within any ensuing legislation. Therefore, there is a congruence between the conception of the trust problem and the basic structure of law. From there it is but a short step to arguing that this congruence may explain the use of law as a regulatory remedy and also the basis of its relative failure.

If law is seen in some sense or other as a guarantee or condition of private property then again it is not unreasonable to suppose that the law would be used to ensure the persistence of private centres of decision-making, based on private property. To the extent that big business is regarded as eclipsing the freedoms associated with private property, then the corollary would appear to be that the law should defend those freedoms. Hence it is possible to infer the genesis of anti-trust legislation from the concept of private ownership. Thus, the prevalence of, what Hofstadter refers to as, Anglo-Saxon and Yankee thinking is often held to account, for the resort to legislation and legal enforcement as the appropriate redress for corporate wrongs. For example, in order for the concepts of personal freedom and guilt to have any meaning it is necessary to defend the context in which they operate from the incursion of corporate disregard. Accordingly, it is possible to argue, not only that law should control monopoly, but that it can control monopoly both in principle and, if given enough attention and men of good will, in practice as well.

These partial accounts of the resort to the law may have much to commend them. For example, they each demonstrate the clear coincidence of legal and popular conceptions of the trust problem. But what they fail to do is to explain why the law was used. This is a particular problem given the initial lack of faith in legal remedies described above. There is, however, one overriding sense in which the resort to the law can be explained persuasively. That is to say, short of a radical restructuring of American society what other option was available but the use of anti-trust legislation?

We have seen already how the link between anti-trust legislation and democracy was seen to depend upon the preservation of private centres of decision-making within American society. This constitutional link, however, is important for another reason. For example, the separation of powers, the balancing act whereby relatively distinct bodies are charged with the responsibility for reviewing other organs of state, is quite basic to any account of anti-trust legislation. In this scheme the law is charged with the responsibility both for controlling and proscribing behaviour and for reviewing and regulating the conduct of other social orders. Thus, the law is regarded in terms of a separate agency of review and regulation. It has been argued that this conception affects the ability of anti-trust legislation to achieve any significant alteration of corporate relations. This very same portrait of law, as a separate agency of review, also explains why the anti-monopoly movement was faced with no other option than that of legal regulation. Within the constitutional separation of powers where else could the movement look for the regulation of monopoly but the law? Law was the body responsible for the review and regulation of other social orders. Moreover, given that the trust problem was popularly conceived in terms of the need for greater personal accountability and predicated upon the dangers of conspiracy, the law was more than likely to be the prime candidate for the regulation of monopoly. This candidacy was further reinforced by the anti-monopoly movement's basically conservative commitment to private property.

Conclusion

It has been suggested that the anti-monopoly movement had a strong organizational basis which, for a time, provided a radical critique of the emerging corporate economy. That this radicalism was enveloped by an essentially conservative commitment to *laissez-faire* economics, entrepreneurial freedom and private property, in no way detracts from its critical vigour. This commitment did, however, severely limit the range of solutions which were adoptable and thence, in the long run, served to vitiate the radical potential of anti-monopolism. Nevertheless, the existence of a strong organizational basis for anti-monopolism does not necessarily imply that such strength was automatically reflected in legislative activity. In this sense the implied disagreement between those who insist upon discounting the strength and depth of anti-monopolism in the run up to the Sherman Act, for example, John Clark (1931) and those who, like Oswald Knauth (1914), detect a profound uproar and frenzy concerning the trust issue prior to the Sherman Act, is misplaced. Both perspectives seem to assume that popular sentiment is important; for the former, by its apparent absence or neutralization by cynical plutocrats and, for the latter, by an overriding presence which enables a more or less automatic translation of sentiment into legislative effect. They each appear to assume either, that legislative activity is insulated from popular sentiment (sentiment which is in any case grossly exaggerated) through some form of cynical manipulation by conservative or business interests or else, that legislative activity reflects public opinion in a wholly representative fashion. It is argued here that anti-monopolism cannot be reduced to the status of pressure politics and, therefore, to an adjunct of legislative outcome, without in some way colouring anti-monopolism with the all too evident failure of anti-trust legislation; a failure which has precise rather than plutocratic determinants. Furthermore, preoccupation with the presence, absence or extent of popular sentiment inevitably discounts the organizational basis and principles of anti-monopolism, reducing them to the preamble of what amounts to the sale of the century. On the contrary, the anti-monopoly movement had an authentic organizational basis which, for specific reasons, adopted a legislative approach, which was genuinely designed to do something about the trusts but which failed for reasons of its very design namely, its use of law as a prospective remedy.

Conclusion

Ideas concerning how law and economy are supposed to cohabit are as important today as they were in the nineteenth century. Where held they appear to underpin a return to a somewhat older belief in *laissez-faire* society and economic liberalism or else reiterate the basic reduction of law to economic and essentially capitalist interests. The former views regulation as an unnecessary fetter upon enterprise and initiative and the proper task of government and law as simple; to unleash the innate power inherent in economic freedom. Far from protecting free enterprise from itself, regulation is seen as a burden upon the competitive instinct. The role of the state is to ensure the conditions of economic freedom and not to eliminate its unacceptable consequences. Conversely, the latter views regulation as irrelevant or as a necessary feature of the restructuring of capital. In one way or another law is seen as some sort of reflex of economic forces. Both perspectives discount legal regulation, the first by seeing in it a potent symbol of government interference, the second by regarding it as a gesture of liberal equality.

The new found conservatism which appears to have captured both sides of the Atlantic has the merit of articulating the idea of deregulation or privatization. It has a very clear, if somewhat naive and retrospective, view of the economy as a vital force which requires a minimum of conditions in order for it to deliver a feast of opportunity. Accordingly, with the exception of the closed shop and trade union power, it no longer attempts to outlaw certain types of economic arrangements as intrinsically bad. On the contrary, if the economy is left to its own devices then the market will ensure that monopoly is, at worst, temporary and, at best, logically impossible. Monopoly, according to Friedman, is everywhere a result of government interference not forces intrinsic to capitalism or the market.

This marks a clear departure from a tradition of regulation founded more than half a century ago. Whereas the development of anti-trust law succeeded in altering the purpose and indeed the manner of regulation, substituting a form of cost-benefit analysis for the prohibition of economic arrangements, modern exponents of conservative philosophy appear to question the validity of regulation. They do so not because it does not work, cannot work or works in an indirect way, but because it is wrong. In effect they have refurbished a very old idea relating to the illogicality of controlling free enterprise. But then, as now, the argument is curiously one-sided, accepting the role of law, private property and so on as a protector of economic liberalism but rejecting it as a regulatory device. Therefore, it is the type of regulation which is at stake. The law is all well and good as an abstract condition of economic opportunity but insofar as it attempts to enforce the possibility of opportunity through restricting corporate excess then it becomes an anathema. As we have seen this sort of perspective ignores the deeper sense in which law is integrated within socioeconomic relations. Furthermore, the idea that corporations are inherently competitive or that the market is an independent mechanism equipped to force free competition upon unwilling or reluctant competitors is an evident absurdity. On the contrary, legal and economic relations form a complex unity and this carries with it the corollary that using law as an external device to regulate or ensure economic competition is a fundamental misapprehension of the law. The economy is not a self-sustaining entity which depends upon legal conditions and which fights off legal interference. Similarly, the law is not an independent mechanism of review and regulation and using it as if it were puts the law at a considerable disadvantage *vis-à-vis* corporate relations of ownership.

If classical economics suggests a somewhat limited role for legal regulation then Marxism fares little better. In assuming that the economy is determinant and that law is an independent but secondary sphere, the economy, first of all, is endowed with the capacity to engineer its requirements in the field of law, state, politics, ideology and so on and, secondly, forms a discrete object or entity in some sense relatively secluded from its effects upon other social relations. For the new conservatives the economy is supposed to engineer freedom and progress whilst for Marxists it engenders a separate realm of determined relations. Both endow the economy with an independent power. The Right marginalizes law as a condition of economic progress whilst Marxism suspends law as secondary and determined. To be fair, this is a caricature of Marxism and there are more sophisticated examples of how it can be used to show the essential class bias of law, but we have seen how they all depend upon an artificial distinction between law and economy. The difference between the new conservatives and Marxists is in the machinery which is supposed to interconnect law and economy, not in the belief that they are related. This means that they are each prevented from comprehending the essence of the legal regulation of the economy.

Anti-trust legislation provides the opportunity for a unique insight into the possibility of legal regulation and an example of the relationship between law and economy. Whilst clearly representing a specific form of regulation it, none the less, displays some of the more pertinent difficulties attendant upon a more general regulation of economic affairs. In this respect the relative failure of anti-trust legislation in the United States is significant because it depends upon two main factors. First of all, in attributing the process of regulation to law—by framing it as anti-trust legislation, referencing certain acts as criminal and by attaching definite penalties to the violation of the relevant statutes—law is clearly seen as an independent agency of review and regulation. Whatever its more general merits, this sort of perspective contains two main weaknesses. Not only is there very little justification for distributing particular sorts of social relations to distinct and separate orders but, also, the very process of separation, which is supposed to guarantee independence, means that law is placed in a position which makes it very difficult to comprehend the complexity of that which it is supposed to regulate. The very existence of anti-trust legislation indicates that law is separated out from other sorts of social processes and cast as an independent review body. Indeed, this separation is seen as vital to its proper function. But there are immense problems involved in analysing society in this way, problems which are insurmountable when law is supposed to regulate the complex equation between free enterprise and monopoly. Secondly, irrespective of the fact that law is placed in the untenable position of having to regulate the corporate form of ownership, the way in which law conventionally portrays the corporation, together with the strategies designed to achieve its regulation, are further indices of the failure of anti-trust legislation to fulfill its avowed objective. The corporation cannot be viewed as an extended and distorted analogue of the concept of private property. Moreover, in treating the corporation as if it would respond, either collectively or in person, in the way in which individuals are supposed to behave is to court disaster. Fines, imprisonment and decrees are, at best, inappropriate and, at worst, irrelevant mechanisms of regulation. Even if the arsenal of available sanctions were improved, and there is much scope for improvement, the way in which the corporation is seen to operate would place severe constraints on the viability of law as an agency of regulation. Strong sanctions are set to nothing against the impossibility of ascertaining those corporate relations which sustain or indeed constitute criminal offences.

Of course this does not mean that law has no effects, nor even that it has unintended effects. Rather any effects which can be attributed to the existence of anti-trust legislation do not involve what must be its fundamental tenet namely, the form of ownership. Since the form of corporate ownership remains intact, albeit in ways which would be unrecognizable in the declining years of the last century, then this alone is a compelling indictment of the fate of anti-trust legislation. But is it fair to judge the record in this way? After all, is not anti-trust legislation at least a minor success? Does it not affect prices, corporate designs and overbearing conglomerates at least a little? Perhaps it does, but it must be remembered that the essence of anti-trust legislation concerned the way in which the corporate form of ownership threatened the very basis of American democracy and entrepreneurial endeavour. As Schwartz has made clear, competition is ". . . desirable on principle . . . like political liberty and because political liberty is jeopardised if economic power drifts into relatively few hands" (United States Department of Justice, 1955, p. 2). Similarly, the anti-monopoly movement depended upon a very clear, and quite general, indictment of the form of corporate ownership. Accordingly, to argue that anti-trust legislation is but another lever for the adjustment of prices or the optimization of output, is to misrepresent the nature of anti-trust legislation and to diminish the extent of its failure. Even if anti-trust legislation does affect prices and so on, and there is evidence to suggest that it might, this would pale into insignificance beside its original aims. It is in this sense that it can be judged as a failure.

When all is said and done it may be possible to construct a type of legal regulation which does not depend upon the logic of subjective rights and the concept of private property, but this sort of regulation would still be limited by its formal role as an independent agency of review. To the extent that the form of regulation is not separated out, it would be necessary to ask in what sense can we talk of a distinctly legal regulation. For example, the possibility of viable regulation would seem to depend upon the very dissolution of the idea of law as an agency of review. Instead, it has been argued that the only way to alter the relations of ownership is through a process of re-defining the parameters of control, title and possession. Needless to say, this is more difficult than it sounds, but it is only by altering the strategies of decision-making, the forms of calculus and the status of the relations of title, possession and control that the relations of ownership can be regulated in any meaningful sense of the word. This is the painful lesson of nearly a century of anti-trust legislation and perhaps the inevitable fate of any form of legal regulation of economic affairs.

Bibliography

Aaronovitch, S. and Sawyer, M. (1975). *Big Business*. Macmillan, London.
Aglietta, M. (1979). *A Theory of Capitalist Regulation: The U.S. Experience*. NLB, London.
Althusser, L. (1969). *For Marx*. Allen Lane/Penguin, Harmondsworth.
Althusser, L. (1971). *Lenin and Philosophy and other Essays*. NLB, London.
Althusser, L. (1976). *Essays in Self Criticism*. NLB, London.
Althusser, L. (1972). *Politics and History*. NLB, London.
Althusser, L. and Balibar, E. (1970). *Reading Capital*. NLB, London.
Andrle, V. (1976). *Managerial Power in the Soviet Union*. Saxon House, Farnborough.
Appleman-Williams, W. (1961). *Contours of American History*. World Publishing, New York.
Arnold, T. W. (1937). *The Folklore of Capitalism*. Yale University Press, New Haven.
Arthur, C. (1976/77). Towards a materialist theory of law. *In Critique* 7, pp. 1-46.
Aubert, V. (1952). White collar crime and social structure, *American Journal of Sociology* **58**.
Balibar, E. (1977). *On the Dictatorship of the Proletariat*. NLB, London.
Baran, P. and Sweezy, P. (1966). *Monopoly Capital*. Penguin, Harmondsworth.
Barber, R. J. (1970). *The American Corporation*. MacGibbon & Kee, London.
Berg, M., ed. (1979). *Technology and Toil in Nineteenth Century Britain*. CSE, London.
Berki, S., ed. (1966). *Anti-trust Policy*. D.C. Heath & Co., Boston.
Berle, A. and Means, G. (1967). *The Modern Corporation and Private Property*. Harcourt Brace Jovanovich, New York.
Berliner, J. (1957). *Factory and Manager in the U.S.S.R.* Harvard University Press, Cambridge, Massachusetts.
Berman, H. J. (1950). *Justice in Russia*. Harvard University Press, Cambridge, Massachusetts.
Bettleheim, C. (1976). *Economic Calculation and Forms of Property*. Routledge and Kegan Paul, London.
Bettleheim, C. (1978). *The Transition to Socialist Economy*. Harvester, Brighton.
Bhaskar, R. (1979). *The Possibility of Naturalism*. Harvester, Brighton.
Bickel, A. M. (1967). *The Unpublished Opinions of Mr. Justice Brandeis*. University of Chicago Press, Chicago.
Bowie, R. R. (1955). *Government Regulation of Business, Cases from the National Reporter System*. The Foundation Press Inc., New York.
Braithwaite, J. (1979). Transnational corporations and corruption. *International Journal of the Sociology of Law* **7**.

Braverman, H. (1974). *Labor and Monopoly Capital.* Monthly Review Press, New York.
Cain, M. and Hunt, A., eds (1979). *Marx and Engels on Law.* Academic Press, London and New York.
Carlen, P. and Collison, M., ed. (1980). *Radical Issues in Criminology.* Martin Robertson, Oxford.
Carson, W. (1980). White collar crime and the institutionalization of ambiguity. *In White Collar Crime: Theory and Research* (G. Geis and E. Stotland, eds). Sage, California.
Clabault, J. M. and Burton, J. F. Jr. (1966). *Sherman Act Indictments 1955-1965.* Federal Legal Publications Inc., New York.
Clark, D. (1978). Marxism, justice and the justice model. *In Contemporary Crises 2,* pp. 27-62.
Clark, J. D. (1931). *The Federal Trust Policy.* The John Hopkins Press, Baltimore.
Clement, W. (1975). *The Canadian Corporate Elite.* McClelland, Toronto.
Cohen, G. A. (1978). *Karl Marx's Theory of History.* Clarendon Press, Oxford.
Colletti, L. (1972). *From Rousseau to Lenin.* NLB, London.
Colletti, L. (1973). *Marxism and Hegel.* NLB, London.
Cressey, D. R. (1969). *Theft of the Nation: The Structure and Operations of Organised Crime in America.* Harper & Row, New York.
Cutler, A. (1975). The concept of ground rent and capitalism in agriculture. *Critique of Anthropology* **4/5**, 72-89.
Cutler, A., Hindess, B., Hirst, P. and Hussain, A. (1977/78). *Marx's Capital and Capitalism Today,* Vols I and II. Routledge and Kegan Paul, London.
De Vroey, M. (1975). The separation of ownership and control in large corporations. *Review of Radical Political Economics* **7/2**.
Domhoff, G. W. (1967). *Who Rules America?.* Prentice-Hall, New Jersey.
Domhoff, G. W. (1971). *The Higher Circles: The Governing Class in America.* Vintage Books, New York.
Dudden, A. P. (1950). *Anti-monopolism 1865-1890.* Ph.D. thesis, University of Michigan.
Eisenberg, M. (1969). The legal roles of shareholder and management in modern corporate decision making. *California Law Review* **57/1**.
Elias, N. (1970). *What is Sociology?.* Hutchinson, London.
Fine, B., Kinsey, R., Lea, J., Picciotto, S. and Young, J., eds (1979). *Capitalism and the Rule of Law.* Hutchinson, London.
Fitch, R. and Oppenheimer, M. (1970), Who rules the corporation?, Pts. I, II, III in *Socialist Revolution,* **4, 5, 6**.
Friedmann, W. (1972). *Law in a changing society.* Penguin, Harmondsworth.
Galbraith, J. K. (1967). *The New Industrial State.* Hamish Hamilton, London.
Garner, R. A. (1977). *Social Movements in America* (second edition). Rand McNally, Chicago.
Geis, G. and Meier, R., eds (1977). *White Collar Crime.* Macmillan, New York.
Geis, G. and Stotland, E., eds (1980). *White Collar Crime: Theory and Research.* Sage, California.
Giddens, A. (1973). *The Class Structure of Advanced Societies.* Hutchinson, London.
Giddens, A. (1979). *Central Problems in Social Theory.* Macmillan, London.
Godelier, M. (1978). Infrastructure, societies and history. *New Left Review* **112**, 84-96.
Gramsci, A. (1971). *Prison Notebooks.* Lawrence & Wishart, London.
Granick, D. (1955). *Management of the Industrial Firm in the U.S.S.R.* Columbia University Press, New York.
Guest, A. G. (1961). *Oxford Essays in Jurisprudence.* Clarendon Press, Oxford.
Gurvitch, G. (1947). *Sociology of Law.* Routledge and Kegan Paul, London.
Hadden, T. (1977). *Company Law and Capitalism.* Weidenfeld and Nicolson, London.

Hall, S. (1980). The legacy of Nicos Poulantzas. *New Left Review* **119**, 60-69.
Hannah, L. (1976). *The Rise of the Corporate Economy.* Methuen, London.
Hayek, F. W. (1949). *Individualism and Economic Order.* Routledge and Kegan Paul, London.
Hazard, J. (1951). *Soviet Legal Philosophy* (translated by H. W. Babb). Harvard University Press, Cambridge, Massachusetts.
Hazard, J. N. and Shapiro, I. (1962). *The Soviet Legal System.* Parker School Studies in foreign and comparative law, Columbia University. Oceana, New York.
Hegel, G. (1973). *Philosophy of Right.* (translated by T. M. Knox). Oxford University Press, Oxford.
Hilton, R., ed. (1976). *The Transition from Feudalism to Capitalism.* NLB, London.
Hindess, B., ed. (1977). *Sociological Theories of the Economy.* Macmillan, London.
Hindess, B. (1978). Classes and politics in Marxist theory. *In Power and the State.* (G. Littlejohn *et al.*, eds). Croom Helm, London.
Hindess, B. and Hirst, P. (1975). *Pre-capitalist Modes of Production.* Routledge and Kegan Paul, London.
Hindess, B. and Hirst, P. (1977). *Mode of Production and Social Formation.* Macmillan, London.
Hirst, P. (1975). *Durkheim, Bernard and Epistemology.* Routledge and Kegan Paul, London.
Hirst, P. (1976). *Social Evolution and Sociological Categories.* George Allen & Unwin, London.
Hirst, P. (1977). Economic classes and politics. *In Class and Class Structure* (A. Hunt, ed.). Lawrence & Wishart, London.
Hirst, P. (1979). *On Law and Ideology.* Macmillan, London.
Hofstadter, R. (1949). *The American Political Tradition and the Men Who Made It.* A. A. Knopf, New York.
Hofstadter, R. (1955). *The Age of Reform.* Vintage, New York.
Hofstadter, R. (1967). *The Paranoid Style in American Politics.* Vintage, New York.
Holland, S. (1975). *The Socialist Challenge.* Quartet, London.
Holloway, J. and Picciotto, S. (1978). *State and Capital.* Edward Arnold, London.
Honoré, A. M. (1961). *Ownership. In Oxford Essays in Jurisprudence* (A. G. Guest, ed.). Clarendon Press, Oxford.
Hunt, A., ed. (1977). *Class and Class Structure.* Lawrence & Wishart, London.
Hurst, J. W. (1970). *The Legitimacy of the Business Corporation in the Law of the United States, 1780-1970.* University of Virginia, Charlottesville.
Igor Ansoff, H. (1968). *Corporate Strategy.* Penguin, Harmondsworth.
Jeffreys-Jones, R. (1978). *Violence and Reform in American History.* New Viewpoints, New York.
Jevons, N. S. (1970). *The Theory of Political Economy* (R. D. Collison Black, ed.). Penguin, Harmondsworth.
Kahn, A. E. (1953). A legal and economic appraisal of the 'new' Sherman and Clayton Acts. *Yale Law Journal* **63(3)**.
Kamenka, E. and Neale, R. S. (1975). *Feudalism, Capitalism and Beyond.* Edward Arnold, London.
Kamenka, E., Brown, R. and Tay, A. E. (1978). *Law and Society.* Edward Arnold, London.
Kaysen, C. (1951). Collusion under the Sherman Act. *Quarterly Journal of Economics*, 65.
Kaysen, C. and Turner, D. F. (1959). *Anti-trust Policy.* Harvard University Press, Cambridge.
Kelsen, H. (1945). *General Theory of Law and State.* Harvard University Press, Cambridge, Massachusetts.

Kelsen, H. (1955). *The Communist Theory of Law.* Stevens & Son, London.
Kelsen, H. (1967). *Pure Theory of Law.* U.O.C.P., Berkeley.
Knauth, O. W. (1914). *The Policy of the United States Towards Industrial Monopoly.* Columbia University Press, New York.
Kolko, G. (1963). *The Triumph of Conservatism.* Macmillan, New York.
Kolko, G. (1965). *Railroads and Regulation, 1877-1916.* Princeton University Press, Princeton.
Kronstein, H., Miller, J. T. and Schwartz, I. E. (1958). *Modern American Anti-trust Law.* Oceana, New York.
Larner, R. (1970). *Management Control and the Large Corporation.* Dunelm, New York.
Lasch, C. (1973). *The Agony of the American Left.* Penguin, Harmondsworth.
Lefebvre, H. (1976). *The Survival of Capitalism.* Allison & Busby, London.
Lenin, V. I. (1971). *Selected Works.* Progress Publishers, Moscow.
Lewis, B. (1948). Discussion. *American Economic Review,* **38**.
Littlejohn, G., Smart, B., Wakeford, J. and Yuval-Davis, N. (1978). *Power and the State.* Croom Helm, London.
Lukacs, G. (1971). *History and Class Consciousness.* Merlin, London.
Macpherson, C. B. (1975). Capitalism and the changing concept of property. *In Feudalism, Capitalism and Beyond* (E. Kamenka and R. S. Neale, eds). Edward Arnold, London.
Macpherson, C. B., ed. (1978). *Property.* Basil Blackwell, Oxford.
Mannheim, K. (1952). *Essays on the Sociology of Knowledge* (P. Kecskemeti, ed.). Routledge and Kegan Paul, London.
Marglin, S. (1974). What do bosses do? *Review of Radical Political Economics* **6**, 33-60.
Martin, D. D. (1959). *Mergers and the Clayton Act.* University of California Press, Berkeley.
Marx, K. (1955). *The Poverty of Philosophy.* Progress Publishers, Moscow.
Marx, K. (1973). *Grundrisse.* Penguin, Harmondsworth.
Marx, K. (1974). *Economic and Philosophic Manuscripts of 1844.* Progress Publishers, Moscow.
Marx, K. (1975). *Early Writings.* Penguin, Harmondsworth.
Marx, K. (1977). *Das Kapital,* Vols I, II, III. Lawrence & Wishart, London.
Mason, E. S. (1957). *Economic Concentration and the Monopoly Problem.* Harvard University Press, Cambridge.
Meszaros, I. (1970). *Marx's Theory of Alienation.* Merlin, London.
Miliband, R. (1973). *The State in Capitalist Society.* Quartet, London.
Miliband, R. (1975). Bettleheim and the Soviet experience. *New Left Review* **91**, 57-66.
Miller, G. H. (1971). *Railroads and the Granger Laws.* University of Wisconsin Press, Madison.
Miller, J. P., ed. (1962). *Competition, Cartels and their Regulation.* Elsevier/North Holland, Amsterdam.
Mowry, G. (1951). *The Californian Progressives.* California University Press, Berkeley.
Nader, R., ed. (1973). *The Consumer and Corporate Accountability.* Harcourt Brace Jovanovich, New York.
Nader, R., Green, M. and Seligman, J. (1976). *Taming the Giant Corporation.* W. W. Norton & Co., New York.
Neale, A. D. (1966). *The Anti-trust Laws of the U.S.A.* Cambridge University Press, Cambridge.
Newman, D. (1958). White collar crime: an overview and analysis. *In White Collar Crime* (G. Geis and R. Meier, eds). Macmillan, New York.

Nozick, R. (1974). *Anarchy, State, and Utopia.* Basil Blackwell, Oxford.
O'Connor, J. (1973). *The Fiscal Crisis of the State.* St. Martins Press, New York.
Olin Wright, E. (1978). *Class, Crisis and the State.* NLB, London.
Ollman, B. (1977). *Marx's Vision of Communism* in Critique 8.
Parmelee, R. and Goldsmith, R. (1940). The distribution of ownership in the 200 largest non financial corporations *T.N.E.C.* **29**, Washington Government Printing Office.
Parsons, T. and Smelser, N. (1956). *Economy and Society.* Routledge and Kegan Paul, London.
Pashukanis, E. B. (1951). Law and Marxism. *In Soviet Legal Theory* (H. W. Babb and J. Hazaard, eds). Harvard University Press.
Pashukanis, E. B. (1978). *Law and Marxism.* Ink links, London.
Patterson, O. (1979). On slavery and slave formations. *New Left Review* **117**, 31-67.
Pearce, F. (1973). Crime, corporations and the American social order. *In Politics and Deviance* (I. Taylor and L. Taylor, eds). Penguin, Harmondsworth.
Pearce, F. (1976). *Crimes of the Powerful.* Pluto Press, London.
Pepinsky, H. E. (1976). *Crime and Conflict.* Martin Robertson, London.
Perlo, V. (1957). *The Empire of High Finance.* International Publishers, New York.
Petro, S. (1962). *Fortune* (Nov.).
Poggi, G. (1978). *The Development of the Modern State.* Hutchinson, London.
Popper, K. (1968). *The Logic of Scientific Discovery* (second edition). London.
Posner, R. A. (1977). *Economic Analysis of Law.* Little, Brown & Co., Boston.
Poulantzas, N. (1973). *Political Power and Social Classes.* NLB, London.
Poulantzas, N. (1975). *Classes in Contemporary Capitalism.* NLB, London.
Poulantzas, N. (1978). *State, Power, Socialism.* NLB, London.
Quinney, R. (1963). Occupational structure and criminal behaviour. *Social Problems* **11**.
Rancière, J. (1971). The concept of 'critique' and the 'critique' of political economy. *Theoretical Practice* **1**.
Rashid, B. J. (1960). What is right with anti-trust. *Anti-trust bulletin* **5**.
Reagan, M. D. (1963). *The Managed Economy.* Oxford University Press, New York.
Renner, K. (1949). *The Institutions of Private Law and their Social Function.* Routledge and Kegan Paul, London.
Ross, E. A. (1907). *Sin and Society.* Houghton Mifflin, Boston.
Rostow, E. (1959). *Planning for Freedom.* Yale University Press, New Haven.
Savage, S. (1977). Talcott, Parsons and the structural-functionalist theory of economy. *In Sociological Theories of the Economy* (B. Hindess, ed.). London.
Scott, J. (1979). *Corporations, Classes and Capitalism.* Hutchinson, London.
Smith, A. (1884). *The Wealth of Nations.* T. Nelson & Sons, London.
Sohn-Rethel, A. (1978). *Intellectual and Manual Labour.* Macmillan, London.
Stone, C. (1975). *Where the Law Ends.* Harper and Row, New York.
Stow Persons (1963). *Social Darwinism: Selected Essays.* Prentice Hall, New Jersey.
Sumner, W. G. (1963). Democracy and plutocracy. *In Social Darwinism: Selected Essays* (Stow Persons, ed.). Prentice Hall, New Jersey.
Sutherland, E. H. (1949). *White Collar Crime.* Dryden, New York.
Sweezy, P., ed. (1949). *Karl Marx and the Close of his System (Bohm-Bawerk and Hilferding).* Merlin, London.
Sweezy, P. and Magdoff, H. (1972). *The Dynamics of U.S. Capitalism.* Monthly Review, New York.
Taft, D. (1956). *Criminology.* Macmillan, New York.
Tappan, P. (1947). Who is the criminal? *American Sociological Review* **12**.
Tarbell, I. (1966). *The History of the Standard Oil Company.* Harper and Row, New York.

Tay, A. E. S. (1978). Law, and citizen and the state. *In Law and Society* (Kamenka, E. *et al.*, eds). Edward Arnold, London.
Taylor, I. *et al.* (1973). *The New Criminology.* Routledge and Kegan Paul, London.
Thompson, E. P. (1978). *The Poverty of Theory.* Merlin, London.
Thorelli, H. B. (1954). *The Federal Anti-trust Policy.* John Hopkins Press, Baltimore.
Tribe, K. (1978). *Land, Labour and Economic Discourse.* Routledge and Kegan Paul, London.
Turner, D. (1963). Principles of American anti-trust law. *International and Comparative Law Quarterly* **6**.
United States Department of Justice (1955) *Attorney General's National Committee to Study the Anti-trust Laws.* Government Publications, Washington.
Unger, R. M. (1976). *Law in Modern Society.* Free Press, New York.
Veblen, T. (1923). *Absentee Ownership.* B. W. Huebsch, Inc., New York.
Waldman, D. E. (1978). *Anti-trust Action and Market Structure.* Lexington, Massachusetts.
Walton, P. and Gamble, A. (1972). *From Alienation to Surplus Value.* Sheed & Ward, London.
Weber, M. (1968). *Economy and Society* Vols I and II. Bedminster Press, New York.
Weibe, R. (1967). *The Search for Order.* New York.
Weinstein, J. (1968). *The Corporate Ideal in the Liberal State.* Beacon Press, Boston.
Winkler, J. (1976). Corporatism. *European Journal of Sociology* **17**, 1.
Winner, L. (1977). *Autonomous Technology.* M.I.T. Press, Cambridge.
Wright Mills, C. (1956). *The Power Elite.* O.U.P., New York.
Wright, E. O. (1978). *Class, Crisis and the State.* New Left Books, London.
Wright, E. O. (1979). The value controversy and social research. *New Left Review* **116**, 53-82.

Index

T

W